Accommodation Management and Tourism

Accommodation Management and Tourism

Gurminder Preet Singh

RANDOM PUBLICATIONS
NEW DELHI (INDIA)

Accommodation Management and Tourism

ISBN 978-93-5111-874-9

Published in 2016 in India by

Reprint : 2021

RANDOM PUBLICATIONS

4376-A/4B, Gali Murari Lal, Ansari Road
New Delhi-110 002
Phone : +9111-43580356, 011-23289044, 011-43142548
e-mail: sales@randompublications.com,
info@randompublications.com, randomexports@gmail.com

Type Setting by : Friends Media, Delhi-110089
Printed at : Mehra Printers, Delhi-110 092

Preface

Accommodation management is regarded as one of the two core activities that lend the hospitality industry its distinctiveness as a sector, the other being food and beverage management. Facilities (or sometimes 'facility') management is an emergent discipline comprising a set of generic skills applicable to the management of the widest possible range of accommodation types, including such diverse facilities as offices, factories and retail outlets as well as various kinds of residential accommodation. The term facilities management is useful in reminding us that even though the majority of businesses within the hospitality industry utilize some form of accommodation, the notion of accommodation management is typically associated with the hotel and related sectors, where some form of semi-private space is effectively rented from a vendor, by a guest/customer for a defined period. A cardinal part of hospitality industry, hotel management and tourism have wide employment opportunities. Moreover, with globalization gaining acceptance with more and more countries, the hotel management industry is truly becoming global. Considered as one of the most glamorous careers, hotel management requires professionals who can hold their nerve even in the most challenging situations.

– Author

Contents

1

Accommodation in the Tourism Industry and its Features

INTRODUCTION

In the modern times, the way people spend their vacations has undergone a great change. People like to spend good times with family and friend while at the same time exploring various tourist places across the globe. As a result the tourism industry across the globe has seen an unprecedented growth which in turn has also resulted in tremendous growth in accommodation facilities. Comfortable hotels and accommodation facilities play a very important role in popularizing any tourist destination. If a person, who is far away from home, gets to enjoy the same facilities and comforts as he enjoys at his home, then he is bound to become attached to the place. On the other hand if the tourist ends up at a place where the hotels and accommodation facilities are not satisfactory, it is quite likely that he might never return to that place. Perhaps that is why, accommodation facilities being made available at different tourists spots, have shifted focus on providing maximum comfort to tourists at reasonable rates. It is also vital to provide comfortable accommodation to people from diverse economical backgrounds. While five star hotels can cater to the needs of affluent visitors, small and medium range hotels and lodging houses are available for use by a middle class traveler. There is no doubt that tourism is an important source of employment for non-metropolitan communities, especially those that are economically underdeveloped. Furthermore, tourism could lead directly to unsightly sprawl in rural areas by creating a demand for development involving different sectors within the tourism industry. One of such sector is accommodation.

Accommodation has been a travel requirement since the first trading; missionary and pilgrimage routes were established in Asia and Europe in pre-Christian times. The basis for such accommodation was generally non-paying as travelers were provided with a roof over their heads and sustenance as part of a religious obligation or in the hope that similar hospitality might be offered to the host in the future. The first reference to commercial accommodation provision in Europe dates back to the thirteenth century. This concurs with the traditional perception that associates tourism with hotels. Traditionally, hotels played a central role in the development of tourism industry. Similarly, tourism accommodation in general can be used as a tool for tourism development. In contrary to the traditional perception, this article establishes that tourism is one of the most dynamic industries that change with time. Nowadays tourism is associated with service industry that embraces business principles like competitiveness, sustainability and many others that will hopefully come up in the proposed generic strategy.

At the same token, several scholars regard accommodation as a basic, functional business within the tourism industry. Most tourists experience the extreme luxury and opulence of tourism when accommodation is of a high standard. Such accommodation can either be informal or private or it may be provided within governments or independently. If one considers the traditional view of a hotel as an establishment that provides accommodation, food and beverage services to short- stay guests on a paying basis, the level of luxury would depend on personal choice and expectations. Hotels constitute proportion as a sub-sector of tourism accommodation business. Most of the existing studies only focused on hotels, ignoring the fact that there is a diverse array and numerous classifications of accommodation facilities related to the tourism industry.

CLASSIFICATION

They are two major classifications of accommodation, and this has been offered on the type of property and amenities which they offer. Accommodation types may differ in terms of their style of operation, size, services and the product which they offer. They are the serviced accommodation and non-serviced accommodation. Serviced accommodation are purely business oriented and are primarily built to provide lodging. They also provide all the expected services which the tourist/visitors have paid for. In addition, on the provision of such accommodation, the visitor has to pay for all the services at once for the stipulated time and must not be requires to pay additional money while there. Services accommodation includes the following; hotel accommodation, motels, Guest houses and Inns, and Bed and Breakfast. Hotel accommodations can be classified into starts depending on their facilities and amenities. It ranges from five star hotels, four star, three star, two star and one star hotel.

Non-serviced accommodation these are otherwise called partial tourist accommodation. Although it provides accommodation to tourists, it is primarily established for non-commercial purposes. Among them are

- *Free accommodation:* this type of accommodation is available to tourist at no cost and usually from friends, relations or family members.

- *Second home:* this is an accommodation owned by a tourist in form of apartment, house and villas in a destination, which serves as his second home while away from home.
- *Rented home:* this form of accommodation is available to tourist on temporary basis. It is the temporary renting of private houses as a whole by tourists while on tours in such destinations. Theses forms of accommodation allow the tourists to provide him/her with self catering.
- *Rented rooms:* the tourist this case rents a room in a family house where the owners are also living. This is the type of accommodation that is mainly used by educational tourists because it is cheap and affordable.

Other forms of non-serviced accommodation include caravans, tents, hostels, dormitories, brothels, and churches

HISTORY OF THE HOTEL INDUSTRY

Until about the middle of the nineteenth century, a bulk of the journeys was undertaken was for business and vocational reasons by road and within the boundaries of countries. The volume of travel was relatively small and was confined to a fraction of the rich segment of the population in any country. India is known as a friendly place for guests. "Atithi Devo Bhava" or "Guest is God" has been the slogan since time immemorial. There were no hotels in the ancient times and needs of travellers for food and accommodation were taken care by householders. Kings built Dharamshalas, constructed roads, planted trees and arranged for drinking water. Muslim rulers built Sarais.

In USA Inns took the name of taverns. As civilization and industrialization took place, establishment of accommodation took place. British were the first one to contribute to this sector. 'Victory hotel' and 'Albion hotel' were perhaps the first to acquire the name 'Hotel in India'. The first western style hotel was opened by Pallongee Pestonjee in 1840 with the name 'British Hotel' in Mumbai.

The twentieth century was a turning point in the history of the hotel industry in India. Big business owners and corporate owners entered the accommodation sector. In 1902, Indian Hotel Company was incorporated and in 1904, J. N. Tata opened the Taj Hotel in Mumbai. Thereafter a number of other hotels were opened such as Ajanta, New Woodland, Grand Hotel, Associated Hotel of India Ltd., East India Hotels Ltd., Oberoi Hotels, and Wild Flower Hall and so on.

After independence many private and public sector entrepreneurs entered into the accommodation business such as Air India, Indian Tourism Development Corporation, Indian Tobacco Company Limited, and Clarks Group of Hotels and so on.

DEFINITION OF A HOTEL

A hotel provides accommodation, meals and refreshment for irregular periods of time for those who may reserve their accommodation either in advance or on the premises. Hotel is defined in several ways: "A place which supplies board and lodging" or "A place for the entertainment of the travellers". A hotel is an institution or a building in which lodging, meals and other services are provided for travellers. A hotel also provides amenities like Fridge and television and facilities like room services, laundry services, valet, shops, auto rentals, airline ticketing, reservation, banking and postal services. "A hotel is a world within a world with its peculiar movements and fashions". A hotel is a fixed immobile installation. Its products and services cannot move to tourists. It is an open and unique system where the tourist moves in, consumes the product and returns with an intangible product.

REGULATORY FRAMEWORK OF HOTEL INDUSTRY

At the international level, the International Hotel Association (IHA) was founded in London in 1946. It has its headquarters in Paris now. It brings under its network thousands of international hotels and individual hoteliers from all over the world. It deals with various aspects of hotel management and links them together. It tries to unite the hotel associations of all countries and provides opportunities to discuss and solve their problems. It also trains young workers at IHA hotels. It publishes the International Hotel Guide and International Hotel Review every year. At the national level, the Federation of Hotel and Restaurant Association of India (FHRAI) regulates the hotel industry in India. It was founded in 1954. The Federation caters to various needs of the industry. It establishes link with Government and provides relief in day to day working of hotels. It also carries out surveys and research studies for the Hotel industry.

TYPES OF ACCOMMODATION

According to physical features the accommodation industry can be broadly divided into three types:

- *Traditional/ Hotel Accommodation:* Traditional accommodation includes hotels and motels. They can further be subdivided into various types.
- *Supplementary Accommodation:* This includes premises, which offer accommodation but not necessarily hotel services. In the Indian context it includes bungalows, government rest houses, and youth hostels and so on.
- *New accommodation Concepts:* These are new concepts of accommodation, which have come into being. It has the combination of both the types discussed earlier. They include Condominiums, Time-sharing, Pensions, Paradors, Camping grounds, Villas, Eurotel and Apart hotels.

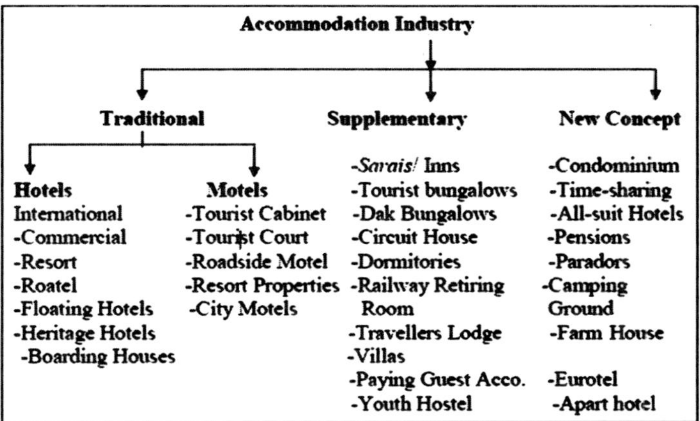

TRADITIONAL ACCOMMODATION

- *International Hotel:* International hotels are the modern western style hotels in almost all metropolitan and other big cities as well as principal tourist centers. These hotels are luxury hotels and are classified on the basis of internationally accepted system of classification. The hotels are placed in star categories. There are five such categories ranging from 5 stars to one star depending upon the facilities and services provided. Hotels belonging to international chains are owned by public companies and controlled by a Board of Directors.
- *Commercial Hotels:* The commercial hotels cater primarily to the individual travellers as compared to international hotel where the focus is on the group travel. Most of the commercial hotels receive the travellers who are there on business. They are situated in important commercial and industrial centers or in big towns or cities. Private owners run these hotels and their success depends on their efficiency and kind of services provided.
- *Resorts:* Resort hotels cater to the need of holidaymaker, and those tourists who travel for health or change of climate. Resort hotels are located near the sea, mountains and other areas of natural beauty. Rest, relaxation and entertainment are the key factors around which resorts are built. The type of services and amenities located in resort properties include recreation facilities such as a swimming pool, golf course, tennis courts, skiing, boating, surf riding and other various indoor sports. Other important amenities include coffee shops, restaurants, conference rooms, lounge, shopping arcade and entertainment. Resort can be classified on the basis of climate and topography such as summer, winter, and hill, Health Resorts, Forest Resorts and Beach Resorts.

- *Roatel:* Roatel is an air-conditioned coach. It provides sleeping accommodation, food and transport all in one. The sleeping coach has rooms with beds in three tiers besides a cupboard for clothes. It provides each passenger with bedding, reading light, a shelf for articles, personal mirror. A kitchen with sink, cupboards, and refrigerators get attached to this coach.
- *Floating Hotels:* This hotel facility is provided on the surface of water on sea, river or lake. It has excellently finished drawing room, sitting, dining and sleeping rooms with wall-to-wall carpeting. The houseboats of Kashmir are examples of Floating Hotels. They are classified into various categories viz. Deluxe, A, B, C and D and are rated accordingly. These are made of Cedar wood. The designed terrace can serve as an open-air cocktail terrace or a place for viewing the morning sunrise. All modern amenities like, a well-equipped kitchen, telephone, TV, video etc are to be found in the houseboat.
- *Heritage Hotels:* A new classification standard of heritage hotel has been introduced to cover hotels in palaces, havelies, castles, forts and residences built prior to 1950. In India, this type of hotel is extremely popular with foreign tourists. The hotel should have at least fifteen rooms. The traditional structure reflects the ambience and lifestyle of kings and Nawabs of bygone era. This scheme was introduced to save these properties from decaying due to disuse. This way they have been made financially viable as they belong to the approved sector and get proper care besides adding to the capacity of accommodation sector. These hotels have adequate sporting facilities, continental and traditional cuisine, other facilities like parking facilities, cloakrooms having modern facilities and lobby or lounge having furniture of high standard. There should be a reception, cash and information counter attended by trained and experienced personnel, well maintained dining and bar room and the staff must understand English.
- *Motels:* They are the same as tourist hotels except that they are geared to accommodate the motor traveling public. According to Webster "Motel is a building or institution providing lodging, meals and services to the public." It offers its services for sale, individually or in various combinations. Motel is an abbreviation of the phrase 'Antomata Motel'. It is a type of accommodation inexpensive for its category and easy to manage. This is the accommodation usually found by the side of highways. Reception is greatly simplified. The provision of a close circuit television permits contact between guest and front office-staff. Money operations, the checking of passport and registration are fully mechanized. Services are efficient with the

degree of personal attention. It gets its image the way in which it portrays itself.

- *Tourist Cabinets or Camps:* It consists of frame cottages. The cottages are rented at low rates. They range in size from 5 to 12 units. They provide bed and shelter.
- *Tourist Court:* It offers facilities for private bath, car shelters and some times cooking facilities. These are situated at the roadside, generally on the highway on the outskirts of town or in resort areas. Many of them now have a restaurant, swimming pool and air-conditioned facilities.
- *Roadside Motels or Highway Motels:* These are situated outside the towns in the countryside along with the main highways and preferably in an important road junction.
- *Resort Properties:* Florida, California, Miami, Arizona have a wide variety of such accommodations. This type of Motel enables many more travellers to reach the resort area by motorcar.
- *City Motel and Motor Motels:* These motels are built within the limits of the city. The limitation of suitable land area and the increased value makes it more difficult to provide parking space. They have a basement, ground floor, first floor and adjoining area for parking facilities. In these motels one can find all the facilities plus convenient parking.

SUPPLEMENTARY ACCOMMODATION

All establishments under this heading are designed to offer accommodation and meals in return for cash payment per day spent on the basis of services provided.

- *Sarais or Inns:* Kings built the Sarais on both sides of the roads in India where arrangements are made for food and shelter for the convenience of pilgrims, merchants and state officials.
- *Tourist Bungalows:* These bungalows are situated at tourist centers for the benefit of tourists and are maintained moderately. These establishments cater to the middle class tourists and budget travellers and also the youth of the country and those coming from overseas. These bungalows provide the nucleus of the tourism infrastructure for the domestic tourists and facilities suitable to meet the requirements of the average Indian tourist and the budget travellers.
- *Dak Bungalows:* These are set up primarily for officials travelling on government duty. These are small rest houses, having limited number of rooms and situated in places important from the point view of government's working. They are moderately furnished and are offered at a very low cost.

- *Circuit House:* Compared to tourist bungalows, these houses are superior as regard to the facilities offered. These are meant for senior government officials. The accommodation in these houses is provided to the bonafide tourists possessing 'tourist card'. There are big halls with several individual beds. Each bed is provided with a rack and a pigeonhole, which can be locked. Guests can use them for their personal belongings and valuables. The bathrooms and toilets are common. Their charges are nominal and there are more suitable for the student's groups. They do not provide food.
- *Railway Retiring Rooms:* These are owned by railway and are situated within the railway station. Accommodation is provided to bonafide railway passengers holding confirmed and current tickets. The rates charged by these establishments are fixed and reasonable. They are moderately furnished rooms with attached bath and toilets.
- *Traveller's Lodge:* These are modest hotels situated in remote places of tourist interest. The rooms in these lodges are moderately furnished but they are cozy and air-conditioned. These are self-sufficient establishments as it is not possible for the guests to go to the far-off town or city for the purchase of the things of daily requirement. They provide a dining hall with fixed or slightly fixed menu and daily necessities of life like oil, comb, towel, tea and coffee.
- *Boarding House:* These are the establishments, which provide accommodation usually with meals at definite period of time, week or month. Their facilities are restricted for use by resident guests. It is a small enterprise intended for clients staying for a certain duration. As a rule accommodation in these units has to be arranged in advance. These are also called guesthouses.
- *Paying Guest Accommodation:* It is a British concept. The paying guest accommodation system has become popular in India also. Many foreign tourists love it because it gives them an opportunity to interact with Indian families. The benefit of this system is that it is quick to respond to seasonal demands. It is very popular in Rajasthan and Goa.
- *Youth Hostels:* The concept was introduced in 1900. A youth hostel is defined as a building, which offers clean, simple, inexpensive shelter to young people experiencing their own country or the world, travelling independently or in groups on holiday or for educational purposes. It is a place where young people of different social background and nationalities can meet and come to know each other. The comfort in modest, the stay is limited and price is low. Youth hostels are created and controlled by non-commercial organization whose aim is the development of youth tourism. On the international

scale, the hostel movement has gained momentum all over the world. The youth hostels are so located as to offer complete package tour of a country covering monuments, places of historical and cultural importance. These are equipped to accommodate young men and woman, tourists who travel on foot or bicycle or other means of locomotives and who, at very little cost, are provided with a place to sleep, eat or even to make their own meal and then clean up.

- *Forest Lodges:* The rest houses at sanctuaries, which fill in the shortage of accommodation at such places, are called Forest Lodges. The state concerned makes land available free of cost, provides water and electricity connections and also undertake supporting construction for staff quarters, garbage and dormitory for drivers. Their location is finalized with the concerned ministry and State Forest Department. ITDC is entrusted with the responsibility for the management of all the forest lodges. These lodges are very popular among nature tourists who love wildlife as they provide a clear view of the forests to the residents from the guest rooms. Examples of forest lodges are Kaziranga Wild Life Sanctuary in Assam, Bharatpur Sanctuary in Rajasthan and others
- *Hospices:* These are the type of accommodation used by persons who travel mainly for religion. The owner of the establishment offers accommodation to pilgrims who could find a place to sleep, a fire to keep them warm and something to eat.

NEW ACCOMMODATION CONCEPTS

Most of these are based on American and European concepts. They are neither totally traditional nor supplementary accommodation.

- *Condominiums:* They are a recent innovation. It involves joint ownership of a complex. These are hotels with apartments. The condominium units are sold to undivided owners, who give it on contract basis to Management Company to operate the hotel and rent the space to visiting tourists. The management company receives fees for the services. At the end of the year, they share the profit or loss with the owners of the condominiums. Family tourists prefer this type of accommodation as they provide enough space and facility to cook and they are also economical.
- *Time Sharing:* Time-sharing is a specialized condominium ownership. This concept came from the Europe. This system started when people experienced difficulties in getting reservations at a resort of their choice at their preferred time. The people started prepaying. If the tourist wants to spend 2 weeks in a particular place for next 10 years, he can get this guaranteed accommodation by paying much less than

the usual charges. This time-sharing can also be exchanged by selling this to their friends if in a particular year they don't want to do so. In India Dalmia Resorts, Sterling Resorts and others are offering this facility.

- *All-Suite Hotels:* This is the newest concept in hotel keeping. These hotels have suites, which have the same charges as any deluxe room in a hotel. This concept has brought units within the range of junior executives. They are provided only the basic services. Private caterers provide restaurant services and not the management of the hotel. These services are provided in India by Sheraton, Hilton, Hyatt and Radisson and others.
- *Pensions:* These are found in Europe and USA. These are accommodations with facilities owned and run by a family usually living in the same building. Pensions are known as residential hotels. These were developed in the USA when people discovered that permanent living in hotels has many advantages. These are mostly available in cities. They play an important role in accommodating tourists specially those with a limited budget.
- *Paradors:* This is Spanish concept. These are castles, convents and monasteries converted into hotels by the government. Paradors are similar to Palaces in Rajasthan.
- *Camping Grounds/Tourist Camps:* These are usually located within the cities in the open spaces. They provide facilities for parking, tent pitching, water, electricity, toilet etc. These are equipped to receive mobile form of accommodation used by tourists who sleep in the tents and enjoy the natural environment. Campers have to pay an admission fees. In the sixties when overland traffic from Europe to India via the Asian Highway was considerable, Government of India had set up camping sites in major cities. Now domestic tourists use these.
- *Farm Houses:* These are very popular in U.K and India. Tourists who are interested in healthy food and natural outdoor life prefer these. Big farmers build farmhouses on the land used for cultivation and package it to tourists for extra income. In Denmark, it has been quite successful in packaging farm holidays through travel agents for international market.
- *Villas/ Chalet:* These are single-family houses for sale or rent to tourists or holidaymakers.
- *Eurotel:* This type of accommodation is much common with apartment houses and its characteristic feature is that the co-owners can use another apartment in another places and another building through exchange system agreed upon in advance.
- *Apart hotel:* This concept was first developed in Spain. These buildings

are hotels because hotel services are provided and yet they are not hotels because the accommodation consists of an apartment, which may be sold if desired. The purchaser of the apartment gets the full services of a hotel during the periods these are not self occupied, can add their apartments to the pool of hotel accommodation and thus derive income from the hotel.

CATEGORISATION OF HOTELS IN INDIA

Accommodation is the most important component of tourism. Tourists need certain regulations and standardization of the services they get for a price. Categorization separates accommodation into different classes. There has to be a standard method of classifying them into different categories. Different countries have different systems of classification. Different stars ranging from 1 star to 5 stars deluxe signify different categories. Categorizing one hotel into a particular group is not easy because of its diversity. Government of India, Department of Tourism is following the widely accepted categorization. A committee is constituted by the Department of Tourism, which has seven members. Government of India appoints chairman, there are members each from Federation of Hotels and Restaurant Association of India (FHRAI), Travel Agents Association of India (TAAI), Indian Association of Tour Operations (IATO), Director of Tourism of that State, Principal of Institute of Hotel Management of that state and the Director of India Tourist Office is also a member. The Hotels apply for classification with fees. The committee gives advance notice before inspecting these hotels. If they fit into the criteria, they are given the stars. This remains valid for next three years. The following are the facilities checked by the committee members:

- 1 star: The establishment applying for one star should have:
  - Minimum 10 rooms.
  - Restaurant is not necessary.
  - One Bathroom for two rooms.
- 2 star:
  - Minimum 10 rooms.
  - Every room should have an attached bathroom.
  - Restaurant not necessary.
  - There should be a place to take food.
- 3 star:
  - Minimum 20 rooms.
  - All the public areas should have air conditioning.
  - At least 50 percent rooms should be air-conditioned.
  - A few shops selling necessities for tourists (Stationery, Flowers etc.)
  - Restaurants should be conditional?

- 4 star:
  - Minimum 25 rooms.
  - All rooms should be air-conditioned.
  - The public areas should be air-conditioned.
  - There should be more than one restaurant.
  - Shopping Arcade with a florist and drycleaner.
- 5 star:
  - Minimum 25 rooms.
  - All rooms should be air-conditioned.
  - Wall to wall carpeting.
  - Entire public area should be air-conditioned.
  - There should be at least two specialty restaurants.
  - Shopping arcade, florist and drycleaner.
  - Swimming pool of dimension 10*3 meter.
  - Facility to use telephones.

Further, many hotels don't apply for classification even when they are providing facilities similar as these classified hotels provide. They can be called unclassified hotels.

HOTEL ROOM TYPES, LOCATION AND RATES

In the travel industry, it is very important for Tour Operators or planners to select the right type of accommodation for his client or tourist. The type of room, location and room rates are the prime factors, which are considered while planning a tour.

TYPE OF ROOM

Hotels provide different types of rooms at different rates, which are as follows:

- Deluxe Room- With extra facilities.
- Suite- Separate rooms for living and sleeping.
- Standard Room: Located in less convenient sections.
- Economy/ Budget room- Smaller than other rooms.

BEDDING TYPES

- King Bed- Size of Bed is 86^{II} x 80^{II}
- Queen Bed- Size 60^{II} x 75^{II}
- Standard Bed-54^{II} x 75^{II}
- Twin Bed- 39^{II} x 75^{II}

ROOM RATES

Room rates are usually based on the location of room such as pool side, beach front, market front, ocean view, hill view and so on. Taxes also vary according to the state. Within the same hotel, price charged may vary depending on the season. Mostly in the peak season the hotels charge high rates and in the lean season they charge low rates. Following are the different room rates:

- Flat Rate: Flat rate is a discounted rate offered to a group at certain times of the year.
- Rack Rate- Standard rate charged by hotel based on type of room and bedding.
- Group Rate- Discounted rate based on the pre-set number of rooms.
- Package Rate- Rate for complete package such as New Year's Eve package.
- Wholesale Rate- Given to tour operators who buy the rooms in bulk.
- Special Rate- Promotional rate offered to corporate clients, government employees, repeats customers and so on.
- Family Rate- Free accommodation to the children with parents.
- Run of the House Rate- Special rate to be offered for the best room available at the time of check-in.

RESERVATION OF ACCOMMODATION

In hotel management, reservation is a very important function. This is also known as selling accommodations. These hotels rely on their representatives, reservation offices in different locations, travel agents, airlines, cruise companies and tour operators. Tour operators make the reservation on the basis of information about number of people in a particular tour, number of rooms required, type of room desired, client preference, number of children, arrival date, departure date and other requirements. Accommodation should be according to the itinerary planning. It is hotel management's responsibility to honour confirmed reservations made by the tour planner. Many tour companies are using Computer Reservation System (CRS) for the reservation. It produces the list of hotels in a specified city with room types and rates available in each hotel for the specified period. The rules and conditions applicable can also be obtained through the Computer. Sheraton Group of Hotels first used this in 1956. Today, all the hotels have their own CRS. Another new development is the use of Internet. Tour operators can see what the accommodations looks like on screen. Thereafter, the tour operator has to make payments on behalf of his clients. The client doesn't have to pay directly to hotel management. He simply shows the hotel voucher. The tour companies are entitled for commission on reservation, which may vary from city to city, and type of hotel property.

HOTEL ORGANISATION

Hotels of today have come of age. They are major establishments. They are looked after by professional managers and trained staff. Smallest details have to be worked out for the satisfaction of clients. This has led the hotel industry to organize them in an efficient way. There are various departments in a modern hotel. These are following:

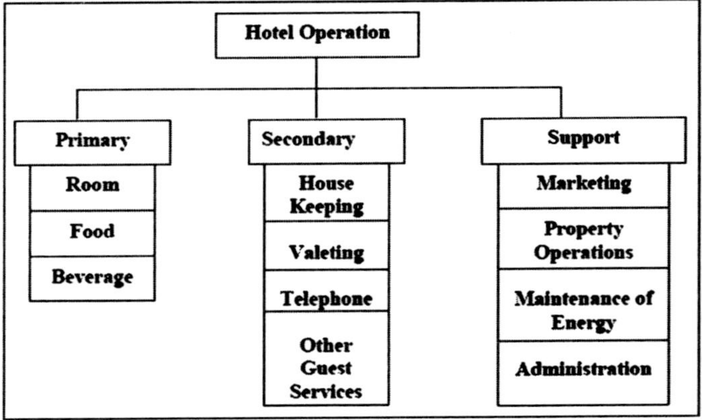

ROOMS

Rooms provide an accommodation function. These include services of front desk, reception, uniformed services- bellboys who handle luggage, parking and house keeping. Rooms department also looks after Accounting and control of Administration department.

FOOD AND BEVERAGE

This department is the prime factor in the success of any hotel. Dinner for conventions, meetings and marriages and other functions are the responsibility of this department. This department also manages bars.

HOUSE-KEEPING

This department looks after the servicing of guest roomscleaning of bedrooms, staircases, public areas, floral arrangements and so on. In some hotels laundry is part of this department while in others it is a separate department.

HOTEL MARKETING

Hotel room is a perishable commodity, which should be kept in mind while marketing a hotel product. He must consider following:

- Research and analysis.
- Establish USP (Unique selling proposition)
- Determine objectives and strategies.
- Advertise.
- Continuous market research and monitoring the progress.

Effective public relations are required with the local press. Satisfaction of consumer needs is the key factor in the success of hotel. The whole approach needs to be consumer oriented rather than market oriented.

IMPACT OF HOTEL INDUSTRY

Henry Ford of Modern hotels says, "The guest is always right" This statement signifies the challenge being faced by hotel professionals to provide services that meet the demands of the guests. This means providing goods and services to travellers where travel and tourism is a part of big business. The importance of tourism and hotel industry cannot be underestimated. According to W.T.O. (World Tourism Organization), tourism is the world's largest industry, ahead of automobiles and petroleum products. There are more than 20 million rooms worldwide in the accommodation sector.

This is likely to increase by 4% annually. There are 100 budget hotel projects, which will add 10,000 hotel rooms in the organized sector. This would attract investment of Rs.10000 cores and generate direct employment to 30,000 people and indirect employment to nine times this number, in related activities. It has been rightly stated, "No Hotel, No Tourism". The expansion of tourism will bring about the development of hotel industry. Of the foreign exchange earned to the tune of Rs. 30,000 crores, 50% belongs to the hotel industry.

The Bhagwati Committee said it would offer nine times employment to the number of persons directly employed in the hotels. The hotel industry has direct impact on regional and rural development. Cottage industry is directly benefited from this by promoting handloom, carpet, handicrafts and so on. Hotel industry also has an impact on the socio-cultural environment. The tourists get attracted to the art, festivals, folk dances and culture of the host region.

This helps generate revenue for the hotel industry as well as the region where tourists take special interest in the art and culture. Inn keeping and hotel keeping are two important parts of the evolutionary process, which followed the development of passenger transportation. The inns were located along the roadside and at the traffic terminal. Similarly Railways created a demand for accommodation at terminals. Shipping ports and Air transport too have an influence on the location of accommodation facilities. As the railways in the nineteenth century found it necessary to build hotels to supplement its main business, so did the airlines of twentieth and twenty-first centuries. Major hotel chains are subsidiaries of airlines. For example KLM owns Hilton International, Air France owns Meridian Hotels and Air India owns Centaur Hotels. At present there are six Groups or Chains of Hotels in India, namely:

- The Ashok Hotel Chain run by Indian Tourism Development Corporation (ITDC)
- The Welcome Group – Indian Tobacco Company (ITC)
- Taj Group of Hotels – Indian Hotel Company Ltd.
- Oberoi Group of Hotels –The East India Company Ltd.
- Centaur Group – Hotel Corporation of India (Air India)
- Clark Group

Since the liberalization of the economy in the 1990s, Hotel industry has also grown fast. It is now in the position to build quality hotels. Rules for foreign collaboration have also been liberalized. Foreign investors can invest up to 51% of the equity in foreign exchange. Number of approved hotels in classified categories has increased. These are not the only accommodation that is being offered. Unclassified hotels, which are members of Federation of Hotels and Restaurants Association of India (FHRAI), too have added to the number of hotels. FHRAI too has minimum standards for its membership entitlement. As India is hosting 2010 Commonwealth Games, the country is gearing up for the demand for accommodation, which will increase manifold. Government too has to play an important role in policy development to promote this vital sector.

THE ROLE OF ACCOMMODATION IN TOURISM DVELOPMENT

Tourist accommodation performs an important function within both the context of rural and urban tourism. It provides the opportunity for visitors to stay for a length of time to enjoy the locality and its attractions, while their spending contributes to the local economy. Accommodation forms a base for the tourist's exploration of the urban and non-urban environments. The tendency for establishments to locate in urban areas preclude peripheral opportunities from expansion thus intensifying their need to find a relevant *modus operandi* rather than relying on what happens in the metropolitan areas and within established urban tourism initiatives.

Generally, accommodation do not attract tourist on its own right, rather they provide support services that are the core element of tourism industry. It can thus be argued that accommodation does not generate the tourist's motivation for travelling. The motivation to travel is usually led by the desire to experience a wider tourism product at a particular resort or locality with accommodation as one of the crucial tourism product. Accommodation as a tourism product has to reflect the vital components of any business product. For sustainability, a product has to be well positioned or located. The location needs to be accessible in terms of transport, information technology, and infrastructure.

Location often determines the appeal and accessibility of properties. Typically the distance decay principle applies to decision making when considering accommodation locations. However, accommodation is an integral part of the over all tourism infrastructure as without it tourists will not visit the location. There are situations where its provision has dominated development plans. Moreover, it also assists in attracting wider investment in the tourism product at the locality. Some scholars agrees that accommodation could feature as an element in wider economic development strategies but it needs to play a primary and varied role as a successful tourism product too. It is difficult to generalize about the proportion of total tourist expenditure that is allocated to accommodation because this varies greatly according to the market, accommodation type and nature of product purchased. A generally accepted estimate is that a third of the total trip expenditure is allocated to this sector. This figure decreases in the case of fully inclusive packages.

In addition, accommodation acts as a catalyst for a range of additional sales opportunities within the complex tourism and hospitality business. Casino hotels have discounted accommodation in anticipation of generating considerable profit from customers at the gaming tables, while golfing hotels may seek to generate good profits from green fees rather than room revenues. Indeed, accommodation pricing in general is a complex and sometimes controversial area in tourism industry.

CONCLUSION

Accommodation is the largest and arguably the most important sub-sector of the tourism industry. It is large and highly diverse. Together with the transport industry, accommodation industry caters for international tourists, regional tourists and national tourists as well as locally based tourists. In a way, it meets the needs of virtually all tourism market groups. The rapid change within this sector of tourism does not only bring fierce competition, but it also brings about new products and new services standards. It is the new product, with new service standards that becomes the focal point of this article. Challenges posed by technological development within the accommodation sector of the industry will still be addressed from different perspective.

2

Control of Hotel Industry

STAFFING

Staffing, which is one of a hotel's most important management functions, is an ongoing challenge because of the high rate of employee and manager turnover. Full-service hotels can experience annual turnover rates in excess of 100 per cent in certain employee classifications. Some managers consider an annual employee turnover rate of 33 per cent low. At this rate, the entire hotel must be completely restaffed every three years. The higher the turnover rate, the larger the number of employees who must be replaced. For example, if a hotel with 450 employees has a 75 per cent annual turnover rate, it will be completely restaffed every 16 months.

Staffing is the responsibility of the human resources department, which is considered in more detail in chapter 5. In an attempt to reduce employee turnover, hotel and lodging businesses are giving increasing attention to job design, seeking to enhance those job characteristics that give the employee the greatest satisfaction and motivation.

Good job design must take into account the needs of employees as well as the demands of the job. Well-thought-out job design begins when management conducts a job analysis—that is, a thorough evaluation of the specific tasks performed for a particular job and the time required to perform them. Job analysis is an ongoing process, as many jobs change with improvements in technology and pressure to improve product quality. The job analysis is the basis for the job description and job specification.

A job description includes the job title, pay, a brief statement of duties and procedures, working conditions, and hours. The job specification is an outline of the qualifications necessary for a particular job. In response to the limits of specialization, organizations can redesign jobs to improve coordination, productivity, and product quality while responding to an employee's needs for learning, challenge, variety, increased responsibility, and achievement.

Such job redesign often involves job rotation, the systematic movement of employees from one job to another; job enlargement, an increase in the number of tasks an employee will do in the job; job enrichment, the attempt to give the employee more control over job-related activities; and flextime, a flexible work schedule that permits employee input in establishing work schedules. In team-driven job redesign, a concept similar to job rotation, employees can transfer back and forth among teams that provide different services or products. Hotels recruit employees from a variety of sources.

Newspapers and employee referrals are used to recruit nonskilled hourly employees. Supervisory and management employees generally are recruited through colleges and universities, promotions from within, professional associations, and management recruiters. Hotels that take more time in making their selections are more successful in retaining employees. Discussions of employee training and development often concentrate on training techniques without giving a full explanation of what a hotel is trying to accomplish. As training and development impart job skills and educate employees, supervisors, and managers, they also improve current and future employee performance, which affects the bottom line. Effective training includes problem solving, problem analysis, quality measurement and feedback, and team building.

Performance evaluation, also called performance appraisal, is the systematic review of the strengths and weaknesses of an employee's performance. The major difficulty in a performance appraisal is quantifying those strengths and weaknesses. The performance of some jobs is easy to quantify, while for others it is more difficult. An important part of the appraisal process is a well-established job description, so that the employee and the supervisor have similar expectations.

Compensation includes the monetary and nonmonetary rewards that managers, supervisors, and employees receive for performing their jobs. In order to set compensation levels, the human resources department must periodically conduct job evaluations, which determine the value of the job to the hotel. Knowledge of the value of the job to the organization and of wage rates for each job classification allows the hotel to establish a fair compensation policy.

ATTRIBUTES AND QUALITIES OF HOUSEKEEPING STAFF

Most essential especially for floor and public area supervisors, room attendants and housemen who are in guest contact, such staff would be normally uniformed. Hence each staff member must ensure that his/her uniform crisp, clean and well pressed. Lady staff must wear light make-up and restrict their jewellery to the minimum such as wedding bands and ear tops. Hair must be tied in a burn or worn short. Shoes worn must be low heeled and sturdy as housekeeping staff work long hours on their feet.

Grooming and Personal Hygiene:

- Gentlemen should shave every day.
- Trim moustaches daily.
- Trim nails twice a week-once On Wednesday and on Sunday
- There should be no hair covering any part of the ear, collar. Staff look smarter when hair doesn't cover the forehead. Staffs are advised to trim their hair once every three weeks.
- Shirt cuffs and collars Il1ust always be clean.
- Bath everyday. Use soap and Shampoo to prevent skin infections and body odour due to unclean hail'.
- Cloths should be pressed every day and have a freshly laundered look.
- Brush the teeth at least twice every day, gargle after smoking or eating to prevent bad breath.
- Wash the hands as often as necessary especially after any other activity where hands may get unclean.

HONESTY

This is a very essential attribute for housekeeping staff, especially Room Attendants, who have access to all guest rooms. Guest belongings, sometimes invaluable are often found lying around in the room. The temptations to thieve are great.

It is only the personal quality of discipline and integrity that checks these temptations:

- *Eye for Detail*: It is one of the greatest qualities that house keeping staff must have. It is with this quality that the finer aspects of housekeeping are taken care of and it is what determines a good service from an average one. This quality enables housekeeping staff to take into consideration the minutest details.
- *Co-Cooperativeness*: Housekeeping staff needs to be co-operating with other departments to achieve more efficiency.
- *Briefing and Scheduling of Staff*: Briefing is that process at the beginning of a work shift which is provided by management to facilitate a two-way communication between management and staff. It is the one time during a shift that all housekeeping staff are together to share information and feelings before they disperse to their work areas.
  - *Briefing Schedule*:

  a. Personal hygiene and grooming.

  b. Any new policies and procedures introduced by managcl1enL must be made out and explained to the staff.

  c. At n briefing the duties or each staff member and the areas of

accountability are explained. This would mean that staffs are assigned a floor and allotted their number of rooms. The staffs likewise, are told which floors or public areas they are assigned to for cleaning. They are also told which supervisor would be in charge.

d. Briefing is a time which can be used as a training opportunity. Simple tasks may be demonstrated so that they can be practiced under supervision at their work place.

RULES ON GUEST FLOORS

Prior to commencing work, all house keeping staff must follow some floor rules that lend an air of efficiency and least inconvenience to guests.

- Speech amongst the floor staff must be restricted to a minimum. In case communication is necessary, this must be done in low tones even when guests are not in sight.
- Unnecessary movements like running or jumping must be avoided.
- The passageways must be kept free of equipments, trays or trolleys.
- Room attendants must greet all guests just as to The Time of the day.
- Staff must be helpful and readily give required information.
- Remember the guest is always right. Arguing with a guest is prohibited.
- The door of the room in which the attendant is cleaning should always be kept wide open.
- If the guest returns when the room is being cleaned the room attendant may ask the guest if they can continue or come later.
- Always follow the procedure of entering a room even if the room is seemingly vacant.

CLEANING A ROOM

Prior to reporting on a 1loor the room attendant already knows the status of a room in her given lot of rooms. The room attendant can prioritize room to be attended to first on the basis of immediate needs. Before entering the room knock at the door firmly with the index finger knuckle announcing clearly" Housekeeping". When there is no answer, repeat the knock after ten seconds announcing yourself as before. If there is still no answer open the door and knock announcing inside the room "Housekeeping". When there is no reply and one is relatively sure that there is no one in, open the door wide and keep it that way till the entire cleaning cycle in the room is complete.

ROOM CLEANING PROCEDURE

- Switch off the room air-conditioner. Draw all curtains and open the windows for airing the room.

- Check the maintenance requirements and report to the department head.
- Turn the mattress side-to-side on succeeding days followed by end-to-end turning. Smooth out mattress to air it.
- Clean the bath room.
- Clean the ceiling and air-conditioning vents for cobwebs.
- Collect all loose papers or magazines and stack them neatly on the desk.
- Clean all the surfaces in single circular motions with a dry cloth. Use a hand dust pan to collect any unwanted matter on the surface without lifting dust in the air Ensure that all surfaces are spotlessly clean. Pay special attention to nooks and corners especially those points that may not obviously be visible to the guests eye.
- Use a stiff upholstery brush or vacuum cleaner on upholstered furniture arms, backs and seats.
- Clean lamp shades with a clean dry duster.
- Disinfect telephone mouthpiece with Dettol. Wipe balance of the telephone with a damp cloth, check phone for the dial tone.
- Clean mirror with a dry cloth.
- Dust closet, shelves, hangers and rods. Brush the closet floor.
- Dust both sides of all room doors, baseboards, window sills, inside and out, bottom
- And centre sashes or windows, close windows.
- Wash the floors.
- Arrange furniture if necessary
- Switch on the air-conditioning.
- Have a last look at the room referring to the checklist for completion of work.

CLEANING A BATHROOM

- Cleaning activity starts from the ceiling downwards to the floor.
- Floors are cleaned from the wall farthest to the door to the exit.
- Open all exhaust vents.
- Collect all trash in bathroom waste basket and deposit in trash hamper of the maids-cart.
- Clean the ceiling and air-conditioning vents for cobwebs.
- Wipe off light bulbs and shades with dry cloth. Check that all bulbs are working.
- Wipe down tile walls using a sponge or damp cloth. Follow with a dry cloth ensuring that tiles are free of water marks.
- Clean mirror first with dry cloth then with glass cloth and finally with dry cloth.

- Wipe dry the shower curtain with a sponge.
- Scrub to dry the area next to the wash basin.
- Scrub the toilet bowl and bidet using the special brush or mop and the prescribed sanitizer. The inner rim should be cleaned. Ensure it is dry and spotless inside. Clean the WC from the outside with a sponge till it is sparkling find dry. Clean the lid and toilet seat of the toilet bowl dry and close them.
- Scrub the floor with the prescribed mop and ensure it is dry
- Finally close the windows shut all lights and close the bathroom doors.

DIRTY DOZEN

- Top of the door edges and ceiling.
- Air-conditioning ducts and diffuser grills. Under bathroom counters.
- Behind the WC bowl-the s-trap.
- In the toilet roll niche
- Faucet nozzle filter
- Top of the picture frames
- Area above racks
- Toilet vents
- Rear surface of doors
- Interior surface of drawers
- Beneath the table

ROOM MAINTENANCE PROCEDURE

As hose keeping has contact with all rooms and public areas practically in every shift, it is they who detect report and ensure the completion of all maintenance work. This requires close co-ordination with the engineering department.

WEEKLY CLEANING PROCEDURE

In addition to daily cleaning routine, a room attendant normally has some cleaning chores that are of a time-consuming nature. Such items may sometimes be beyond the physical capacity and need the assistance of a skill worker.

Such tasks are:

- Polishing of brassware
- Scrubbing of bathroom tiles
- Cleaning of window panes
- Scrubbing of balconies and terraces
- Vacuuming of under heavy furniture.

PUBLIC AREA CLEANING

A house maid is assigned to do this task and is responsible for the cleanliness of ceilings, walls and floors, carpeted floors should be vacuum cleaned daily, tile floors to be brushed clean and then wet mopped. They should also remove stains. Floor tile edges, corners, baseboards and the immediate wall area above are to be inspected to ensure that there are no water marks. Wooden railings and-skirtings has to clean with dry clothes.

All corridor lighting fixtures are to be cleaned as often as required. It is also the responsibility of a houseman to clean fire extinguishers and fire extinguisher recesses including glass door and metal paneling. Metal railing and paneling to be polished weekly using min cream so that the shine remains. The house keeping department is responsible for the cleanliness of the interior of elevator cars.

A thorough cleaning of walls, ceilings, and floors should be carried out at least once daily. The volume of traffic may require more frequent cleaning of elevator floors. The Door houseman is assigned the task of cleaning the stairways on a daily or more frequent schedule depending up on traffic requirements. Floor terraces, balconies, shopping arcade and offices are also to be cleaned.

***While cleaning the offices should be scheduled at times when the offices are not in service*:**

- Carpet cleaning can be done by electrical method *e.g.* vacuum cleaner
- *Manual method ex*: carpet brush.
- Cleaning of ceramic tiles marble can sweep, wash, use electric scrubber with prescribed liquid cleaning agents and solutions. It is as a daily cleaning procedure.
- Cleaning Methods
- Cleaning basically involves the removal of dust and other foreign matter from surfaces. The choice of a cleaning method depends on various factors. They are.
  - The nature of soiling.
  - The nature of surface soiled.
  - The properties of cleaning agents suitable for the surface.
  - The best way to clean without disposing dust to other areas.
  - The method should restore the surface to its original colour.

GENERAL PRINCIPLES THAT CAN BE APPLIED TO ALL CLEANING

- All loose dust and litter should be removed before dealing with any stubborn stains/dirt.
- Use lighter cleaning methods first before attempting stronger methods
- Before any implement or cloths are used, they should be made clean and dry.
- Abrasives should be used as a last resort as they can damage the surface.
- Use all agents that is least offensive in smell if alternatives are available.

- When cleaning a surface, be cautions of marring the surrounding area *e. g.* finger prints on wall, grazing other article etc.
- Be sure that during the process of cleaning areas do not become accident prone *e.g.* wet, slippery floor etc.

CLEANING AGENTS

One of the basic methods used is cleaning with water. The role of water is to hold the dirt and remove it away as in rinsing. This is done with the aid of detergents. Multipurpose liquid Cleaning agents are available that can either diluted in water or used directly with a dry cloth. For glasses liquid glass cleaning agents are used.

CLEANING EQUIPMENTS

- Mechanical equipments.
  - Electric vacuum cleaner with full range of nozzles and attachments for all types of surfaces.
  - Electric polishers and scrubbers
  - Shampoo machines.
- Containers
- Brushes
  - Toilet Brush
  - Sink Brush Scrubbing Brush
  - Carpet hand brush
  - Soft hand brush
- Brooms: Yard Brooms
- Mops
- Bath room wipers
- Cleaning cloths

JOB DESCRIPTION OF HOUSEKEEPING STAFF

MAIN HOSPITAL

Duties and Responsibilities:

- 'A' for each type of linen to be maintained.
- All Ledgers are to be put up for Joint Directors signature through housekeeping Manager on a quarterly basis.
- Maintain a sepearate Indent for the cleaning agents used in Laundry and the Indent should be signed by the housekeeping Manager.
- Daily use of cleaning agents are to be recorded and the records to be put up for housekeeping managers signature monthly.
- Linen and curtains are to be checked for wear and tear quarterly.
- Torn or faded linen is to be segregated and to be shown to joint director quarterly. If any item is found unserviceable the same should be written off the ledger getting after the approval of Jt.Director.

- Torn or faded linen is to be used for cleaning purposes.
- Periodical Maintenance of washing Machine, Ironing Machine, Iron Box, Sewing Machine, and floor scrubbing Machine to be carried out and the record to be maintained.
- Floor scrubbing Machine is to be taken by other housekeeper only with the permission of the linen housekeeper.
- Washing charges for various linen are to be fixed and approval. For any change in the charges, prior approval to be taken from secretary.
- Tailoring rates for various items of stitched materials are to be maintained. For any revision in charges prior approval to be taken from secretary.
- Planning and scheduling the standard procedure for cleaning all types of linen to be displayed in laundry and to be followed strictly.
- Time schedule to be prepared for collection of clean/soiled linen and to be followed strictly.
- Ensure proper discipline among Housekeepers, Sweepers, Dhobi, and Tailor working in linen department. Make sure that they wear name badges.
- Floor scrubbing machines are to be chain locked when not in use.
- Training classes are to be taken for junior housekeepers when required.
- Train and Guide the trainees housekeeper posted in linen department.
- Sell all waste materials and deposit the sale proceeds to secretary.
- Supervision and checking the cleanliness of the surrounding area of main hospital.
- Responsible for the cleanliness of sweepers uniform.
- Any other job given by the housekeeping manager or the senior management staff from time to time.

DESIGNATION–FLOOR EXECUTIVE: HOUSEKEEPING (OUT PATIENT DEPARTMENTS AND BASEMENT AREA)

- Supervision and checking the cleanliness of out patient departments and Basement area.
- Maintenance of sweepers attendance Register, wage sheets, deployment, control and details for continuous duties.
- Control over all keys of all departments in OPDS.
- Preparing inventories for furniture and keeping records for their maintenance.
- Indenting cleaning agents and equipments and ensure their proper use and keeping records.
- To develop proper use of cleaning procedures.
- Reporting and checking of all maintenance work.

- Supervision of quality maintenance and infection control.
- Ensure proper discipline of Housekeepers and sweepers working in out patient department and make sure that they wear name badge.
- Planning and scheduling the standard procedures in writing for the proper care of all types of floors, walls, windows, furniture, bathrooms, Lavatories and other equipments to be prepared and follows trictly.
- Maintenance of House Keeping department room and attending to phone calls promptly.
- Make sure the tyre cart is secured and locked after working hours.
- Disposal of refuse is to be monitored.
- Training and taking classes for juniors
- Experimenting new techniques and equipments for cleaning.
- Maintenance details of continuous duties of housekeepers.
- Maintenance responsible for the sweepers uniform collected after working hours from the sweepers.
- Responsible for the cleaning schedule of freshwater tank, filters, coolers and septic Tanks and the cleaning and due dates are to be displayed in the boards as well as in the Register. The register shall be put up for Housekeeping managers signature every month.
- Maintain the Leave list of all sweepers working in main hospital, free hospital, Laico and other supporting areas and day off Roster of sweepers working in OPDs.
- Maintaining the checklist of furniture, electrical plumbing, carpentry and mason work in the OPDs.
- Any other job given by the housekeeping manager or the senior management staff from time to time.

DESIGNATION–WARD EXECUTIVE: HOUSEKEEPING (1ST AND 2ND FLOOR OF MAIN HOSPITAL.)

- Supervision and checking the cleanliness of 1st and 2nd floor.
- Control of all keys of 1st and 2nd Floor
- Preparing inventories for 1st and 2nd floor furniture and keeping records for their maintenance.
- Indenting cleaning agents and equipments and ensure their proper use and keeping necessary records.
- Supervision for quality maintenance and infection control.
- Ensure proper discipline of housekeepers and sweepers in 1st and 2nd floor and make sure the wear name badges.
- Planning and scheduling the standard procedures in writing for the proper care of all types of floors, walls, windows, furniture, bathrooms, lavatories and other equipments to be placed and to be followed strictly.

- Attending to patients complaints
- Development and standardization of newer and improved method of cleaning for better results at lower costs.
- Take adequate precautions for controlling cross infections.
- To assist in quality health care and patient care programme.
- Ensure up keep and maintenance of hospital property.
- Training and taking classes for juniors
- Maintain day off roaster of sweepers in 1st and 2nd floor.
- Responsible for the sweepers uniform collected after working hours from the sweepers of 1st and 2nd floor.
- Any other job that may be assigned by the housekeeping Manager or the senior management staff from time to time.

DESIGNATION–WARD EXECUTIVE: HOUSEKEEPING (3RD AND 4TH FLOOR MAIN HOSPITAL)

- Supervision and checking the cleanliness of 3rd and 4th floor.
- Control of all keys of 3rd and 4th floor.
- Preparing inventories for 3rd and 4th floor furniture and keeping records for their maintenance.
- Indenting cleaning agents and equipments and ensure their proper use and keeping records.
- Supervision for quality maintenance and infection control.
- Ensure proper discipline of Housekeepers and sweepers in 3rd and 4th floor and make sure they wear name badges.
- Planning and scheduling the standard procedures in writing for the proper care of all types of floors walls, windows, furniture, bathrooms lavatories and other equipments to be placed and to be followed strictly.
- Attending to patient's complaints.
- Development and standardization of newer and improved method of cleaning for better results at lower costs.
- Take adequate precautions in controlling cross infections.
- To assist in quality health care and patient care programme
- Ensure upkeep and maintenance of hospital property
- Training and taking classes for juniors.
- Maintain day off roster for sweepers in 3rd and 4th floor.
- Responsible for the sweepers uniform collected after working hours from the sweepers of 3rd and 4th floor.
- Maintaining the checklist of furniture, Electrical, plumbing, Carpenting and Mason works in 3rd and 4th floor.
- Any other job that may be assigned by the housekeeping manager or the senior management staff from time to time.

DESIGNATION–SENIOR TRAINEES: HOUSEKEEPING (COMPASSION 503, SINCERITY 143, GRACE 140)

- Work under the supervision of executive Linen housekeeper.
- Planning and scheduling the standard procedures for cleaning in writing and follow strictly.
- Indenting cleaning agents, equipments and ensure the proper use and maintain their records.
- Preparing inventories for furniture and keeping records for their maintenance.
- Attend all theory and practical classes as per the programme.

JOB SPECIFICATIONS OF HOUSEKEEPING STAFF

Job specifications should be written as job descriptions are prepared. Job specifications are simple statements of what the various incumbents to positions will be expected to do.

JOB SPECIFICATION—EXAMPLE

The incumbent will work as a member of a housekeeping team, cleaning and servicing for occupancy of approximately 18 hotel guestrooms each day. Work will generally include the tasks of bed making, vacuuming, dusting, and bathroom cleaning. Incumbent will also be expected to maintain equipment provided for work and load housekeeper's cart before the end of each day's operation. Housekeepers must be willing to work their share of weekends and be dependable in coming to work each day scheduled.

EMPLOYEE REQUISITION

Once job specifications have been developed for every position, employee requisitions are prepared for first hirings. Note the designation as to whether the requisition is for a new or a replacement position and the number of employees required for a specific requisition number. The human resources department will advertise, take applications, and screen to fill each requisition by number until all positions are filled. For example, the first requisition for GRAs may be for 20 GRAs. The human resources department will continue to advertise for, take applications, and screen employees for the housekeeping department and will provide candidates for interview by department managers until 20 GRAs are hired. Should any be hired and require replacing, a new employee requisition will be required.

STAFFING HOUSEKEEPING POSITIONS

There are several activities involved in staffing a housekeeping operation. Executive housekeepers must select and interview employees, participate in an orientation programme, train newly hired employees, and develop employees for future growth. Each of these activities will now be discussed.

Selecting Employees

Sources of Employees

Each area of the United States has its own demographic situations that affect the availability of suitable employees for involvement in housekeeping or environmental service operations. For example, in one area, an exceptionally high response rate from people seeking food service work may occur and a low response rate from people seeking housekeeping positions may occur. In another area, the reverse may be true, and people interested in housekeeping work may far outnumber those interested in food service. Surveys among hotels or hospitals in your area will indicate the best source for various classifications of employees. Advertising campaigns that will reach these employees are the best method of locating suitable people. Major classified ads associated with mass hirings will specify the need for food service personnel, front desk clerks, food servers, housekeeping personnel, and maintenance people. Such ads may yield surprising results. If the volume of response for housekeeping personnel is insufficient to provide a suitable hiring base, the following sources may be investigated:

- Local employment agencies
- Flyers posted on community bulletin boards
- Local church organizations
- Neighbourhood canvass for friends of recently hired employees
- Direct radio appeals to local homemakers
- Organizations for underprivileged ethnic minorities, and mentally disabled people

If these sources do not produce the volume of applicants necessary to develop a staff, it may become necessary to search for employees in distant areas and to provide regular transportation for them to and from work. If aliens are hired, the department manager must take great care to ensure that they are legal residents of this country and that their green cards are valid. More than one hotel department manager has had an entire staff swept away by the Department of Immigration after hiring people who were illegal aliens. Such unfortunate action has required the immediate assistance of all available employees to fill in.

Processing Applicants

Whether you are involved in a mass hiring or in the recruiting of a single employee, a systematic and courteous procedure for processing applicants is essential. For example, in the opening of the Los Angeles Airport Marriott, 11,000 applicants were processed to fill approximately 850 positions in a period of about two weeks. The magnitude of such an operation required a near assembly-line technique, but a personable and positive experience for the applicants still had to be maintained. The efficient handling of lines of employees, courteous attendance, personal concern for employee desires, and reference to suitable departments for those unfamiliar with what the hotel or hospital has to offer all become earmarks for how the company will treat its employees. The key to proper handling of applicants is the use of a control system whereby employees are conducted through the steps of application, prescreening, and if qualified, reference to a department for interview.

The opportunity for employees to express their desires for a specific type of employment. Even though an employee may desire involvement in one classification of work, he or she may be hired for employment in a different department. Also, employees might not be aware of the possibilities available in a particular department at the time of application or may be unable to locate in desired departments at the time of mass hiring. Employees who perform well should therefore be given the opportunity to transfer to other departments when the opportunities arise. The laws regulated by federal and state Fair Employment Practices Agencies no person may be denied the opportunity to submit application for employment for a position of his or her choosing. Not only is the law strict on this point, but companies in any way benefiting from interstate commerce may not discriminate in the hiring of people based on race, colour, national origin, or religious preference. Although specific hours and days of the week may be specified, it is a generally accepted fact that hotels and hospitals must maintain personnel operations that provide the opportunity for people to submit applications without prejudice.

Prescreening Applicants

The prescreening interview is a staff function normally provided to all hotel or hospital departments by the human resources section of the organization. Prescreening is a preliminary interview process in which unqualified applicants—those applicants who do not meet the criteria for a job as specified in the job specification–special qualifications—are selected out. For example, an applicant for a secretarial job that requires the incumbent to take shorthand and be able to type 60 words a minute may be screened out if the applicant is not able to pass a relevant typing and shorthand test. The results of prescreening are usually coded for internal use and are indicated on the Applicant Processing Record.

If a candidate is screened out by the personnel section, he or she should be told the reason immediately and thanked for applying for employment. Applicants who are not screened out should either be referred to a specific department for interview or, if all immediate positions are filled, have their applications placed in a department pending file for future reference. All applicants should be told that hiring decisions will be made by individual department managers based on the best qualifications from among those interviewed.

A suggested agenda for a prescreening interview is as follows:

- The initial contact should be cordial and helpful. Many employees are lost at this stage because of inefficient systems established for handling applicants.
- During the prescreening interview, try to determine what the employee is seeking, whether such a position is available, or, if not, when such a position might become available.
- Review the work history as stated on the application to determine whether the applicant meets the obvious physical and mental qualifications, as well as important human qualifications such as emotional stability, personality, honesty, integrity, and reliability.
- Do not waste time if the applicant is obviously not qualified or if no immediate position is available. When potential vacancies or a backlog of applicants exists, inform the candidate. Be efficient in stating this to the applicant. Always make sure that the applicant gives you a phone number in order that he or she may be called at some future date. Because most applicants seeking employment are actively seeking immediate work, applications more than 30 days old are usually worthless.
- If at all possible, an immediate interview by the department manager should be held after screening. If this is not possible, a definite appointment should be made for the candidate's interview as soon as possible.

THE INTERVIEW

An interview should be conducted by a manager of the department to which the applicant has been referred. In ongoing operations, it is often wise to also allow the supervisor for whom the new employee will work to visit with the candidate in order that the supervisor may gain a feel for how it would be to work together. The supervisor's view should be considered, since a harmonious relationship at the working level is important. Although the acceptance of an employee remains a prerogative of management, it would be unwise to accept an employee into a position when the supervisor has reservations about the applicant. Certain personal characteristics should be explored when interviewing an employee. Some of these characteristics are native skills, stability, reliability, experience, attitude towards employment, personality, physical traits, stamina, age, sex, education, previous training, initiative, alertness, appearance, and personal cleanliness. Although employers may not discriminate against race, sex, age, religion, and nationality, overall considerations may involve the capability to lift heavy objects, enter men's or women's restrooms, and so on.

In a housekeeping department, people should be employed who find enjoyment in housework at home. Remember that character and personality cannot be completely judged from a person's appearance. Also, it should be expected that a person's appearance will never be better than when that person is applying for a job. Letters of recommendation and references should be carefully considered. Seldom will a letter of recommendation be adverse, whereas a telephone call might be most revealing.

If it were necessary to select the most important step in the selection process, interviewing would be it. Interviewing is the step that separates those who will be employed from those who will not. Poor interviewing techniques can make the process more difficult and may produce a result that can be both frustrating and damaging for both parties. In addition, inadequate interviewing will result in gaining incorrect information, being confused about what has been said, suppression of information, and, in some circumstances, complete withdrawal from the process by the candidate. The following is a well-accepted list of the steps for a successful interview process.

- Be prepared. Have a checklist of significant questions ready to ask the candidate. Such questions may be prepared from the body of the job description. This preparation will allow the interviewer to assume the initiative in the interview.
- Find a proper place to conduct the interview. The applicant should be made to feel comfortable. The interview should be conducted in a quiet, relaxing atmosphere where there is privacy that will bring about a confidential conversation.
- Practice. People who conduct interviews should practice interviewing skills periodically. Several managers may get together and discuss interviewing techniques that are to be used.
- Be tactful and courteous. Put the applicant at ease, but also control the discussion and lead to important questions.
- Be knowledgeable. Be thoroughly familiar with the position for which the applicant is interviewing in order that all of the applicant's questions may be answered. Also, have a significant background knowledge in order that general information about the company may be given.
- Listen. Encourage the applicant to talk. This may be done by asking questions that are not likely to be answered by a yes or no. If people are comfortable and are asked questions about themselves, they will usually speak freely and give information that specific questions will not always bring out. Applicants will usually talk if there is a feeling that they are not being misunderstood.
- Observe. Much can be learned about an applicant just by observing reactions to questions, attitudes about work, and, specifically, attitudes about providing service to others. Observation is a vital step in the interviewing process.

Interview Pitfills

Perhaps of equal importance to the interviewing technique are the following pitfalls, which should be avoided while interviewing.

- Having a feeling that the employee will be just right based on a few outstanding characteristics rather than on the sum of all characteristics noted.
- Being influenced by neatness, grooming, expensive clothes, and an extroverted personality—none of which has much to do with housekeeping competency.
- Over generalizing, whereby interviewers assume too much from a single remark.
- Hiring the "boomer," that is, the person who always wants to work in a new property; unfortunately, this type of person changes jobs whenever a new property opens.
- Projecting your own background and social status into the job requirement. Which school the applicant attended or whether the applicant has the "proper look" is beside the point. It is job performance that is going to count.
- Confusing strengths with weaknesses, and vice versa. What is construed by one person to be over aggressiveness might be interpreted by another as confidence, ambition, and potential for leadership, the last two traits being in chronic short supply in most housekeeping departments. These are the very characteristics that make it possible for management to promote from within and develop new supervisors and managers.
- Being impressed by a smooth talker—or the reverse: assuming that silence reflects strength and wisdom. The interviewer should concentrate on what the applicant is saying rather than on how it is being said, then decide whether his or her personality will fit into the organization.
- Being tempted by overqualified applicants. People with experience and education that far exceed the job requirements may be unable for some reason to get jobs commensurate with their backgrounds. Even if such applicants are not concealing skeletons in the closet, they still tend to become frustrated and dissatisfied with jobs far below their level of abilities.

The application of the techniques and avoidance of the pitfalls will be valuable tools in the selection of competent personnel for the housekeeping and environmental service departments. For many years, the approach of many managers was to write a job description and then fill it by attempting to find the perfect person. This approach may overlook many qualified people, such as disadvantaged people or slow learners.

Job descriptions may be analysed in two ways when filling positions:

- What is actually required to do the work, and
- What is desirable.

Is the ability to read or write really necessary for the job? Is the ability to learn quickly really necessary? A person who does not read or write or who is a slow learner can be trained and can make an excellent employee. True, it may take additional time, but the reward will be a loyal employee as well as less turnover. It has been proven many times that those who are disadvantaged or slightly retarded, once trained, will perform consistently well for longer periods. There are agencies who seek out companies that will try to hire such people.

Results of the Interview

If the results of an interview are negative and rejection is indicated, the candidate should be informed as soon as possible. A pleasant statement, such as "Others interviewed appear to be more qualified," is usually sufficient. This information can be handled in a straightforward and courteous manner and in such a way that the candidate will appreciate the time that has been taken during the interview. When the results of the interview are positive, a statement indicating a favourable impression is most encouraging. However, no commitment should be made until a reference check has been conducted.

Reference Checks

In many cases, reference checks are made only to verify that what has been said in the application and interview is in fact true. Many times applicants are reluctant to explain in detail why previous employment situations have come to an end. It is more important to hear the actual truth about a prior termination from the applicant than it is to hear that they simply have been terminated.

Reference checks, in order of desirability, are as follows:

- Personal (face-to-face) meetings with previous employers are the least available but provide the most accurate information when they can be arranged.
- Telephone discussions are the next best and most often used approach. For all positions, an in-depth conversation by telephone between the potential new manager and the prior manager is most desirable; otherwise a simple verification of data is sufficient to ensure honesty.
- The least desirable reference is the written recommendation, because managers are extremely reluctant to state a frank and honest opinion that may later be used against them in court.

Applicants who are rated successful at an interview should be told that a check of their references will be conducted, and, pending favourable responses, they will be contacted by the personnel department within two days. Applicants who are currently employed normally ask that their current employer not be contacted for a reference check. This request should be honoured at all times. Applicants who are currently working usually want to give proper notice to their current employers. If the applicant chooses not to give notice, chances are no notice will be given at the time he or she leaves your hotel. In some cases, the applicant gives notice and, upon doing so, is "cut loose" immediately. If such is the case, the applicant should be told to contact the department manager immediately in order that the employee may be put to work as soon as possible.

Interview Skills versus Turnover

There is no perfect interviewer, interviewee, or resultant hiring or rejection decision in regard to an applicant. We can only hope to improve our interviewing skills in order that the greatest degree of success in employee retention can be obtained. The executive housekeeper should expect that 25 per cent of initial hires into a housekeeping department will not be employed for more than three months. Some new housekeeping departments have as much as a 75 per cent turnover rate in the first three months of operation. However, regardless of the outcome of the interview, the processing record should be properly endorsed and returned to the personnel department for processing.

ORIENTATION

A carefully planned, concerned, and informational orientation programme is significant to the first impressions that a new employee will have about the hospital or hotel in general and the housekeeping department in particular. Too often, a new employee is told where the work area and restroom are, given a cursory explanation of the job, then put to work. It is not uncommon to find managers putting employees to work who have not even been processed into the organization, an unfortunate situation that is usually discovered on payday when there is no paycheck for the new employee.

Such blatant disregard for the concerns of the employee can only lead to a poor perception of the company. A planned orientation programme will eliminate this type of activity and will bring the employee into the company with personal concern and with a greater possibility for a successful relationship. A good orientation programme is usually made up of four phases: employee acquisition, receipt of an employee's handbook, tour of the facility, and an orientation meeting.

Employee Acquisition

Once a person is accepted for employment, the applicant is told to report for work at a given time and place, and that place should be the personnel department. Pre-employment procedures can take as much as one-half day, and department managers eager to start new employees to work should allow time for a proper employee acquisition into the organization. At this time it should be ensured that the application is complete and any additional information pertaining to employment history that may be necessary to obtain the necessary work permits and credentials is on hand. Usually the security department records the entry of a new employee into the staff and provides instructions regarding use of employee entrances, removing parcels from the premises, and employee parking areas.

Application for work permits, and drug testing, will be scheduled where applicable. All documents required by the hotel's health and welfare insurer should be completed, and instructions should be given about immediately reporting accidents, no matter how slight, to supervisors. The federal government requires that every employer submit a W-4 for each employee on the payroll. The employee must complete this document and give it to the company. Mandatory deductions from pay should be explained, as should other deductions that may be required or desired. At this time, some form of personal action document is usually initiated for the new employee and is placed in the employee's permanent record. The permanent information that will be carried on file. The PAF is serially numbered, is created from data stored on magnetic discs, and is maintained in the employee's personnel file.

When a change has to be made, such as job title, marital status, or rate of pay, the PAF is retrieved from the employee's record, changes are made under the item to be changed, and the corrected PAF is used to change the data in the computer storage. Once new information is stored, a new PAF is created and placed in the employee's record to await the next need for processing. A long-time employee might have many PAFs stored in the personnel file. When either regular or special performance appraisals are given, the last PAF will be used to record the appraisal.

These forms are usually found on the reverse side of the PAF. Since performance appraisals may signify a raise in pay, the appropriate pay increase information would be indicated on the front side of the PAF. All recordings on PAFs, whether on one side or both, require the submission of data, storage of information, and creation of a new PAF to be stored in the employee's record. The PAF and performance appraisal system should be thoroughly explained to the new employee, along with assignment of a payroll number. The employer should also explain how and when the staff is paid and when the first paycheck may be expected.

The Employee Handbook

The new employee should be provided with a copy of the hotel or hospital employee's handbook and should be told to read it thoroughly. Since the new housekeeping employee is not working just for the housekeeping department but is to become integrated as a member of the entire staff, reading this handbook is extremely important to ensure that proper instructions in the rules and regulations of the hotel are presented. The handbook should be developed in such a way as to inspire the new employee to become a fully participating member of the organization. Note the tone of the welcoming letter and the manner in which the rules and regulations are presented.

Familiarization Tour of the Facilities

Upon completion of the acquisition phase, a facility tour should be conducted for one or all new employees. For new facilities, access to the property should be gained within about one week before opening, and many new employees can be taken on a tour simultaneously. It is possible for employees to work in the hotel housekeeping department for years and never to have visited the showroom, dining rooms, ballrooms, or even the executive office areas. A tour of the complete facility melds employees into the total organization, and a complete informative tour should never be neglected. For ongoing operations, after acquisition, the new employee may be turned over to a department supervisor, who becomes the tour director. An appreciation of the total involvement of each employee is strengthened when a facilities tour is complete and thorough. If necessary, the property tour might be postponed until after the orientation meeting; however, the orientation activity of staffing is not complete until a property tour is conducted.

Orientation Meeting

The orientation meeting should not be conducted until the employee has had an opportunity to become at least partially familiar with the surroundings. After approximately two weeks, the employee will have many questions about experiences, the new job, training, and the rules and regulations listed in the Property and Department Handbooks. Employee orientation meetings that are scheduled too soon fail to answer many questions that will develop within the first two weeks of employment. The meeting should be held in a comfortable setting, with refreshments provided. It is usually conducted by the director of human resources and is attended by as many of the facility managers as possible. Most certainly, the general manager or hospital administration members of the executive committee, the security director, and the new employees' department heads should attend. Each of these managers should have an opportunity to welcome the new employees and give them a chance to associate names with faces.

All managers and new employees should wear name tags. In orientation meetings, a brief history of the company and company goals should be presented. A planned orientation meeting should not be concluded without someone stressing the importance of each position. Every position must have a purpose behind it and is therefore important to the overall functioning of the facility. An excellent statement of this philosophy was once offered by a general manager who said, "The person mopping a floor in the kitchen at 3:00 A.M. is just as valuable to this operation as I am—we just do different things." The orientation meeting should be scheduled to allow for many questions. And there should be someone in attendance who can answer all of them. Although the new employee will be gaining confidence and security in the position as training ends and work is actually performed, informal orientation may continue for quite some time. The formal orientation, however, ends with the orientation meeting. Finally, it should be remembered that good orientation procedures lead to worker satisfaction and help quiet the anxieties and fears that a new employee may have. When a good orientation is neglected, the seeds of dissatisfaction are planted.

TRAINING

General

The efficiency and economy with which any department will operate will depend on the ability of each member of the organization to do his or her job. Such ability will depend in part on past experiences, but more commonly it can be credited to the type and quality of training offered. Employees, regardless of past experiences, always need some degree of training before starting a new job. Small institutions may try to avoid training by hiring people who are already trained in the general functions with which they will be involved. However, most institutions recognize the need for training that is specifically oriented towards the new experience, and will have a documented training programme.

Some employers of housekeeping personnel find it easier to train completely unskilled and untrained personnel. In such cases, bad or undesirable practices do not have to be trained out of an employee. Previous experience and education should, however, be analysed and considered in the training of each new employee in order that efficiencies in training can be recognized. If an understanding of department standards and policies can be demonstrated by a new employee, that portion of training may be shortened or modified. However, skill and ability must be demonstrated before training can be altered. Finally, training is the best method to communicate the company's way of doing things, without which the new employee may do work contrary to company policy.

First Training

First training of a new employee actually starts with a continuation of department orientation. When a new employee is turned over to the housekeeping or environmental services department, orientation usually continues by familiarizing the employee with department rules and regulations. Many housekeeping departments have their own department employee handbooks. For an example, which contains the housekeeping department rules and regulations for Bally's Casino Resort in Las Vegas, Nevada. Compare this handbook with that of the generic handbook. Although these handbooks are for completely different types of organizations, the substance of their publications is essentially the same; both are designed to familiarize each new employee with his or her surroundings. Handbooks should be written in such a way as to inspire employees to become team members, committed to company objectives.

A Systematic Approach to Training

Training may be defined as those activities that are designed to help an employee begin performing tasks for which he or she is hired or to help the employee improve performance in a job already assigned. The purpose of training is to enable an employee to begin an assigned job or to improve upon techniques already in use. In hotel or hospital housekeeping operations, there are three basic areas in which training activity should take place: skills, attitudes, and knowledge.

Skills Training

A sample list of skills in which a basic housekeeping employee must be trained follows:

- *Bed making*: Specific techniques; company policy
- *Vacuuming*: Techniques; use and care of equipment
- *Dusting*: Techniques; use of products
- *Window and mirror cleaning*: Techniques and products
- *Setup awareness*: Room setups; what a properly serviced room should look like
- *Bathroom cleaning*: Tub and toilet sanitation; appearance; methods of cleaning and results desired
- *Daily routine*: An orderly procedure for the conduct of the day's work; daily communications
- *Caring for and using equipment*: Housekeeper cart; loading
- *Industrial safety*: Product use; guest safety; fire and other emergencies

The best reference for the skills that require training is the job description for which the person is being trained.

Attitude Guidance

Employees need guidance in their attitudes about the work that must be done. They need to be guided in their thinking about rooms that may present a unique problem in cleaning.

Attitudes among section housekeepers need to be such that, occasionally, when rooms require extra effort to be brought back to standard, it is viewed as being a part of rendering service to the guest who paid to enjoy the room.

Carol Mondesir,1 director of housekeeping, Sheraton Centre, Toronto, states that:

- A hotel is meant to be enjoyed and, occasionally, the rooms are left quite messed up. However, as long as they're not vandalized, it's part of the territory. The whole idea of being in the hospitality business is to make the guest's stay as pleasant as possible. The rooms are there to be enjoyed.

Positive relationships with various agencies and people also need to be developed.

The following is a list of areas in which attitude guidance is important:

- The guest/patient
- The department manager and immediate supervisor
- A guestroom that is in a state of great disarray
- The hotel and company
- The uniform
- Appearance
- Personal hygiene

Meeting Standards

The most important task of the trainer is to prepare new employees to meet standards. With this aim in mind, sequence of performance in cleaning a guestroom is most important in order that efficiency in accomplishing day-to-day tasks may be developed. In addition, the best method of accomplishing a task should be presented to the new trainee. Once the task has been learned, the next thing is to meet standards, which may not necessarily mean doing the job the way the person has been trained. Setting standards of performance is discussed in Chapter under "Operational Controls."

Knowledge Training

Areas of knowledge in which the employee needs to be trained are as follows:

- Thorough knowledge of the hotel layout; employee must be able to give directions and to tell the guest about the hotel, restaurants, and other facilities
- Knowledge of employee rights and benefits
- Understanding of grievance procedure
- Knowing top managers by sight and by name

Ongoing Training

There is a need to conduct ongoing training for all employees, regardless of how long they have been members of the department.

There are two instances when additional training is needed:

- The purchase of new equipment, and
- Change in or unusual employee behaviour while on the job.

When new equipment is purchased, employees need to know how the new equipment differs from present equipment, what new skills or knowledge are required to operate the equipment, who will need this knowledge, and when. New equipment may also require new attitudes about work habits. Employee behaviour while on the job that is seen as an indicator for additional training may be divided into two categories: Events that the manager witnesses and events that the manager is told about by the employees. Events that the manager witnesses that indicate a need for training are frequent employee absence, considerable spoilage of products, carelessness, a hig

Events that the manager might be told about that indicate a need for training are that something doesn't work right something is dangerous to work with, something is making work harder. Although training is vital for any organization to function at top efficiency, it is expensive. The money and man-hours expended must therefore be worth the investment. There must be a balance between the dollars spent training employees and the benefits of productivity and high-efficiency performance. A simple method of determining the need for training is to measure performance of workers: Find out what is going on at present on the job, and match this performance with what should be happening. The difference, if any, describes how much training is needed.

In conducting performance analysis, the following question should be asked: Could the employee do the job or task if his or her life depended on the result? If the employee could not do the job even if his or her life depended on the outcome, there is a deficiency of knowledge. If the employee could have done the job if his or her life depended on the outcome, but did not, there is a deficiency of execution. Some of the causes of deficiencies of execution include task interference, lack of feedback and the balance of consequences.

If either deficiency of knowledge or deficiency of execution exists, training must be conducted. The approach or the method of training may differ, however. Deficiencies of knowledge can be corrected by training the employee to do the job, then observing and correcting as necessary until the task is proficiently performed. Deficiency of execution is usually corrected by searching for the underlying cause of lack of performance, not by teaching the actual task.

Training Methods

There are numerous methods or ways to conduct training. Each method has its own advantages and disadvantages, which must be weighed in the light of benefits to be gained. Some methods are more expensive than others but are also more effective in terms of time required for comprehension and proficiency that must be developed. Several useful methods of training housekeeping personnel are listed and discussed.

On-the-job Training

Using on-the-job training, a technique in which "learning by doing" is the advantage, the instructor demonstrates the procedure and then watches the students perform it. With this technique, one instructor can handle several students. In housekeeping operations, the instructor is usually a GRA who is doing the instructing in the rooms that have been assigned for cleaning that day. The OJT method is not operationally productive until the student is proficient enough in the training tasks to absorb part of the operational load.

Simulation Training

With simulation training, a model room is set up and used to train several employees. Whereas OJT requires progress towards daily production of ready rooms, simulation requires that the model room not be rented. In addition, the trainer is not productive in cleaning ready rooms. The advantages of simulation training are that it allows the training process to be stopped, discussed, and repeated if necessary. Simulation is an excellent method, provided the trainer's time is paid for out of training funds, and clean room production is not necessary during the workday.

Coach-Pupil Method

The coach-pupil method is similar to OJT except that each instructor has only one student. This method is desired, provided that there are enough qualified instructors to have several training units in progress at the same time.

Lectures

The lecture method reaches the largest number of students per instructor. Practically all training programmes use this type of instruction for certain segments. Unfortunately, the lecture method can be the dullest training technique, and therefore requires instructors who are gifted in presentation capabilities. In addition, space for lectures may be difficult to obtain and may require special facilities.

Conferences

The conference method of instruction is often referred to as workshop training. This technique involves a group of students who formulate ideas, do problem solving, and report on projects. The conference or workshop technique is excellent for supervisory training.

Demonstrations

When new products or equipment are being introduced, demonstrations are excellent. Many demonstrations may be conducted by vendors and purveyors as a part of the sale of equipment and products. Difficulties may arise when language barriers exist. It is also important that no more information be presented than can be absorbed in a reasonable period of time; otherwise misunderstandings may arise.

Training Aids

Many hotels use training aids in a conference room, or post messages on an employee bulletin board. Aside from the usual training aids such as chalkboards, bulletin boards, charts, graphs, and diagrams, photographs can supply clear and accurate references for how rooms should be set up, maids' carts loaded, and routines accomplished. Most housekeeping operations have films on guest contact and courtesy that may also be used in training. Motion pictures speak directly to many people who may not understand proper procedures from reading about them. Many training techniques may be combined to develop a well-rounded training plan.

Development

It is possible to have two students sitting side by side in a classroom, with one being trained and the other being developed. Recall that the definition of training is preparing a person to do a job for which he or she is hired or to improve upon performance of a current job. Development is preparing a person for advancement or to assume greater responsibility. The techniques are the same, but the end result is quite different.

Whereas training begins after orientation of an employee who is hired to do a specific job, upon introduction of new equipment, or upon observation and communication with employees indicating a need for training, development begins with the identification of a specific employee who has shown potential for advancement. Training for promotion or to improve potential is in fact development and must always include a much neglected type of training—supervisory training.

Many forms of developmental training may be given on the property; other forms might include sending candidates to schools and seminars. Developmental training is associated primarily with supervisors and managerial development and may encompass many types of experiences. The various developmental tasks that the trainee must perform over a period of 12 months. Development of individuals within the organization looks to future potential and promotion of employees. Specifically, those employees who demonstrate leadership potential should be developed through supervisory training for advancement to positions of greater responsibility.

Unfortunately, many outstanding workers have their performance rewarded by promotion but are given no development training. The excellent section housekeeper who is advanced to the position of senior housekeeper without the benefit of supervisory training is quickly seen to be unhappy and frustrated and may possibly become a loss to the department. It is therefore most essential that individual potential be developed in an orderly and systematic manner, or else this potential may never be recognized. Even though there will be times that the trainee may be given specific responsibilities to oversee operations, clean guestrooms, or service public areas, advantage should not be taken of the trainee or the situation to the detriment of the development function.

Development of new growth in the trainee becomes difficult when the training instructor or coordinator is not only developing a new manager but is also being held responsible for the production of some aspect of housekeeping operations.

RECORDS AND REPORTS

Whether you are conducting a training or a development programme, suitable records of training progress should be maintained both by the training supervisor and the student. Periodic evaluations of the student's progress should be conducted, and successful completion of the programme should be recognized. Public recognition of achievement will inspire the newly trained or developed employee to achieve standards of performance and to strive for advancement. Once an employee is trained or developed and his or her satisfactory performance has been recognized and recorded, the person should perform satisfactorily to standards. Future performance may be based on beginning performance after training. If an employee's performance begins to fall short of standards and expectations, there has to be a reason other than lack of skills. The reason for unsatisfactory performance must then be sought out and addressed. This type of follow-up is not possible unless suitable records of training and development are maintained and used for comparison.

EVALUATION AND PERFORMANCE APPRAISAL

Although evaluation and performance appraisal for employees will occur as work progresses, it is not uncommon to find the design of systems for appraisal as part of organization and staffing functions. This is true because first appraisal and evaluation occurs during training, which is an activity of staffing. Once trainees begin to have their performance appraised, the methods used will continue throughout employment. As a part of training, new employees should be told how, when, and by whom their performances will be evaluated, and should be advised that questions regarding their performance will be regularly answered.

Probationary Period

Initial employment should be probationary in nature, allowing the new employee to improve efficiency to where the designated number of rooms cleaned per day can be achieved in a probationary period. Should a large number of employees be unable to achieve the standard within that time, the standard should be investigated. Should only one or two employees be unable to meet the standard of rooms cleaned per day, an evaluation of the employee in training should either reveal the reason why or indicate the employee as unsuitable for further retention. An employee who, after suitable training, cannot meet a reasonable performance standard should not be allowed to continue employment. Similarly, an employee who has met required performance standards in the specified probationary period should be continued into regular employment status and thus achieve a reasonable degree of security in employment.

Evaluation

Evaluation of personnel is an attempt to measure selected traits, characteristics, and productivity. Unfortunately, evaluations are generally objective in nature, and raters are seldom trained in the art of subjective evaluation. Initiative, self-control, and leadership ability do not lend themselves to measurement; therefore such characteristics are estimated. How well they are estimated depends to a great extent on the person doing the estimating. Two raters using the same form and rating the same person will probably arrive at different conclusions.

Certain policies on the use of evaluations should be established so that they are understood by both the person doing the evaluating and the person being evaluated. These policies must be established and disseminated by management. In order to establish such policies, the following questions, among others, must be answered and communicated to all those involved in the evaluation: What will evaluations be used for? Will evaluations influence promotions, become a part of the employee's record, be used as periodic checks, or be used for counseling and guidance? What qualities are going to be evaluated? Who is going to be evaluated? Who will do the evaluating? Reliable evaluations require careful planning and take considerable time, skill, and work.

An evaluation must be understood by the employee. Evaluation should be used at the end of a probationary period, and the employee must understand at the beginning of the period that he or she will be observed and evaluated. Each item, as well as what impact the evaluation will have on future employment, should be explained to the employee. People undergoing periodic evaluations, such as at the end of one year's employment, should also know why evaluations are being conducted and what may result from the evaluation. In both situations, the evaluation should be used for counseling and guidance so that performance may be improved upon or corrected if necessary.

Certainly, strong points should be pointed out. An employee should be made aware of good as well as not-so-good evaluations. Evaluations should be made for a purpose and not for the sake of an exercise. They should ultimately be used as management tools. Evaluations should be developed to fit the policies of the particular institution using it and the particular position being evaluated. The same evaluation may not be suitable for every position.

OUTSOURCING

In certain locales, such as isolated resorts, hotels are tempted to use contract labour because the local market does not support the necessary number of workers, particularly in housekeeping. Advocates of outsourcing are quick to point out the advantages of the practice. Scarce workers are provided to the property, and there is no need to provide expensive employee benefits. The entire staffing function is assumed by the contractor. There are no worries regarding recruiting, selecting, hiring, orienting, or even training the employees. Merely issue them uniforms and send them off to clean rooms. Some employers may even be willing to relax their responsibilities regarding employment law such as immigration and naturalization requirements. Management should never forget that once a contracted employee dons a company uniform, the guest believes that person is an employee of the hotel. The guest also believes the hotel has made every reasonable effort to screen that person in the hiring process to ensure that he or she is of good moral character, who has the best interest of the guest at heart.

Unfortunately, there have been several incidents in which the outsourced employees did not quite have the best interest of the guest in their hearts. There have been more than a few cases in which outsourced workers were wanted felons who inflicted considerable bodily harm on guests during the performance of their duties. A number of these incidents have resulted in lawsuits, with awards against the hotel in the millions of dollars. This author does not recommend outsourcing in housekeeping, and cautions operators who ignore this advice to keep their guard up and continue to meet their legal and ethical responsibilities regarding employees and employment law.

HOUSE KEEPING CONTROL DESK

The housekeeping control desk is the central hub of the housekeeping department. This is the area in the department where all information is received and from where messages are conveyed to housekeeping and other staff present in various parts of the hotel. Thus, the control desk may be considered the nerve centre for to–and–fro communication in the housekeeping department. one of the main functions of the control desk is ensuring smooth coordination between housekeeping and other departments such as maintenance, front office, food and beverages, security, sales and marketing and so on. The location of control desk is normally adjacent to the Executive Housekeeper's office. This desk is manned 24-hours otherwise the lifeline of housekeeping communication would stop.

ROLE OF CONTROL DESK

- The role of the housekeeping control desk is to facilitate communication to various parts of hotel. this role can be exercised in many forms which are as follows;

- The control desk receives messages from in house guests over the telephone apart from maintaining the intra and inter–departmental channels of communication. Hotel room directories provide the control desk extension number to the guests which they can use if they require housekeeping services.
- The control desk attendant receives all the message of the guests such as a request for extra blankets, baby-sitter services, which she transmit to the concerned floor supervisor for further action.
- Front office also alerts the desk attendant about the expected and existing crews in the house. So that the rooms can be make ready for the new arriving crew after the departure of existing crew in a very short period of time.
- In most of the hotels, this is the area where housekeeping employees; report for work; collect keys and signing for them; persue the log book get their briefing and at the end of their shift, report back to.
- Its is the control room attendants who receives departure room numbers from the front office and transmits them to the appropriate floor supervisor.
- The floor supervisor informs the desk attendant once rooms are cleaned and ready for sale and this is updated in the computer so that front office can easily obtain the information o f the status of room.
- The main physical feature visible in most control desk is the key cabinet. On the wall, where all floor masters keys and store keys are kept under lock and key themselves.
- Another common feature here is a large notice board displaying notices like
  - Room numbers of the groups in the house
  - Room numbers of crews in the house
  - Night cleaning schedule
  - VIPs in the house
  - Weekly cleaning schedules
  - Daily roster of supervisors and staff
  - Any other significant information relating to in-house guest or the hotel staff.
- One of the most important roles of the control desk is maintaining various important records, registers, forms and formats so that they are available and easily accessible for reference to managers and supervisors.

COORDINATION WITH FRONT OFFICE

The control desk acts as the nerve centre for coordination with the other departments in the hotel. the control desk attendants receives the night report, the arrivals and departures list, VIP list, and the list of crews and groups in the house from the front office. Based on these documents, the housekeeping department schedules the workers for cleaning, maintenance and servicing of guestrooms and related areas.

- To ensure efficient rooming of guests, both housekeeping and front office must inform each other of changes in a room's status. Knowing whether a room is occupied, vacant, on change, out of order (OOO), under repair, or similar for proper room management
- There should be coordination to clean front office public areas
- There must be coordination between housekeeping and front office department to share information on occupancy levels which helps to forecast occupancy for the year and makes it easier to draw up a budget, establish par stock levels and estimate required staff strength.
- There should be coordination know about the daily room report and housekeeping discrepancy report.
- It also helps to gear renovations and spring cleaning to low occupancy periods there by preventing loss of revenue.
- The housekeeping and front office department also coordinate with each other for other important information which require special attention like
- 7. *Night report*: this report, prepared each night by front desk attendant, indicates the rooms occupied that night and ones that are to become check-outs the following day. Based on this report, the executive or assistant housekeeper schedules employees for servicing these rooms. Once the rooms have been cleaned and made ready, the floor supervisor calls the control desk or the front desk directly, releasing the room for sale.
- *VIPs in house*: this information is essential so that the staff can take a little extra care and keener precautions in cleaning and supervising VIP rooms.housekeeping can take extra care in cleaning the VIP rooms by equipping the rooms with additional amenities as per the policy of the management. These amenities can be; bathrobe; bath slippers; extra soaps; hangers; and glass tumblers.
- *Groups in the house*: the group rooming list must be provided before the group's arrival to the housekeeping as groups tends to move together in terms of arrival, departure, sightseeing tours and meals. Their rooms need to be readied together in view of strict time parameters. Group rooming lists enable the hk department to organize their work and have the group's room ready on time.
- *Crews in the house*: Sometimes the arrival of a crew and the departure

of another crew from the same airline may overlap. In such circumstances, it is important for the allotted rooms to be cleaned within a short period of time. Thus for this there should be a effective coordination between front office and housekeeping.

- *Flowers*: sometimes the management extends its compliments to a guest with a special gesture of a flower arrangement in the room as recognition of the importance of a person. This requirement of flower arrangements for certain guests is conveyed to housekeeping by the front office on a daily basis.
- Apart from the communications the front office needs to depend on housekeeping for the provision of clean uniforms to its staff.

COORDINATION WITH ENGINEERING DEPARTMENT

The housekeeping control desk have to coordinate with the engineering department for maintenance request that the room attendants registers while servicing the guest room or in the floor.

- The housekeeping department depends on maintenance to keep things in order.
- While carrying out their scheduled work, housekeeping employees may find some deficiencies in the hotel facilities, such as faulty electrical plugs, dripping faucets, leaking pipes or malfunctioning air-conditioning units etc.
- A need for urgent repairs is reported to maintenance over telephone and these requests are usually taken into action immediately.
- There are various heads under which maintenance work is done they are:
- *Electrical work*: Air conditioning and heating; fused bulbs, lights and lamps that are not functioning; defective plugs and plug points; short circuits; and faulty geysers, refrigerators, and minibar fall under this category.
- *Boiler work*: This is necessary to maintain a supply of hot water to guestroom.
- *Mechanical work*: This entails repair or replacement of any faulty equipment, such as vacuum cleaners, ice-cube machines, and so on.
- *Plumbing work*: This deals with faulty faucets (taps), showers, drainage systems, water closets, and so on.

All maintenance requirements needed on floors are entered in the maintenance register kept in the control desk. The control desk attendant notes down the room number, the maintenance work required and the name of the GRA or the supervisor who called attention to the problem. The desk attendant prepares a maintenance slip in duplicate. She retains the second copy in her book and forwards the first copy to the engineering department. The engineering department then prepares a 'work order slip' and sends the concerned technician directly to the floor.

When the job is completed, a copy of tradesperson's completed 'work order ' is sent to the executive housekeeper for acknowledgement of work completed satisfactorily. If this copy is not sent to the executive housekeeper within an appropriate amount of time, housekeeping issues another 'work order', which signals maintenance to provide a status report on the request repair.

FILES AND RECORDS OF THE DESK

Many important forms, formats, records, and registers are maintained at the control desk.

MAINTENANCE REGISTER

This register is used for recording all the maintenance work required in rooms. Based on the information contained in the register, the control desk attendant fills out the work order form to be sent to the maintenance department.

Table. Maintenance Register

Maintenance register Date:						
Room Number	Time Complaint Lodged	Nature of Complaints	Lodged By	Received by	Time of Completion	Signature

Table. Maintenance Slip

Maintenance slip Room Number Date: Time:
Nature of Complaint
Control Desk Supervisor Signature———————————————

WORK ORDER FORMS

The work order forms are used by the control desk to initiate scheduled maintenance in guestrooms and public areas. A sample work order form is illustrated below:

Table. Work Order Slip

Work Order Room Number			Date.................................		Time.........................		
Carpenter	Mechanic	Plumber	Electrician	A/C – Heating technician	AV/Audio technician	IT	Other
Nature of Complaint Name of Technician assigned...............................							
Date of Completion				Time of Completion..................			
Housekeeping Supervisor Signature..........................				Technician's Signature...............			

KEY CONTROL REGISTER

This is one of the most important registers maintained at the housekeeping control desk. It is a part of the key-security system to be followed by the housekeeping department. Each employee who is handed over a key, any key, from key cabinet is supposed to sign for it in a key control sheet in this register. The format of a key control sheet is illustrated below:

Table. Format of a Sheet in the Key Control Register

Key Control Sheet Date:							
Key code	Name of staff	Signature	Time out	Issued by	Time in	Signature	Received

LOG BOOK

Another important register kept for reference at the housekeeping control desk is the log book. The log book is used to record all messages that staff from an earlier shift want to convey to the employees on the next shift. All supervisors reporting for work should use the log book for any important messages left for them by the staff of the previous shift. The format of the log book is illustrated below:

Table. Format of a Page in the Housekeeping Log Book.

Housekeeping Log Book Shift.................... Time....................... Date..................
Log entries - - - -
Name and signature of the desk attendant ....

ROOM CHECKLISTS FILE

A floor supervisor checks each room prepared by the room attendant, before the room is handed to front office for sale. She uses the room checklist to guide her to examine as per the standards set by the management during her inspection. She ticks the items found okay and makes comments on things which are not upto the standards. The deficiencies have to be rectified by the room attendants immediately. The checklist reflects the performance of the room attendant as well as the supervisor. it is handy to refer to it in the event of a guest complaint. All room checklists are deposited by the floor supervisors at the control desk and filed for a month.

Table. Room Checklist.

Room Checklist		
Floor..........Room No............Room Attendants Name................Floor Supervisor's Name..........		
Room Items	**Tick Ok**	**Comments**
Wardrobe Hanger		
Laundry Lists		
Laundry Bags		
Shoe shine card		
Wardrobe under –liners		
Spare Pillows		
Bed		
Side table		
Lamp bulb working		
Bible / Koran / Gita		
Pad and Pen		
Telephone Directories		
Date.................................. .... Signature of Floor Supervisor..................................		

GUEST MESSAGE REGISTER

The housekeeping control desk also acts as a point of contact for in-house guests who require any housekeeping related services. The housekeeping control desk is responsible for taking these guest messages and passing them onto the concerned staff. The message could be about the provision of certain guest loan items or a request to a second service additional blankets, fresh towels, maintenance requirements etc.A guest messages register is maintained for this purpose at the control desk. The format is illustrated below:

Table. Guest Message Register

Guest Message Register **Date :**								
Room no	**Time of request**	**Nature of request**	**Received by**	**Signature**	**Action taken**	**Time**	**Service completed**	**Time**

BABY SITTER REGISTER

Babysitting is provided as a service by most hotels' housekeeping departments for guests who have small children. The guests requiring the service contact the housekeeping control desk and the desk attendant enters the request in the babysitting register.

Table. Baby Sitting Registers

Baby Sitting Register								
Date	Room No	Name of Guest	Time from	Time to	Received by	Person Assigned	Sitter's signature and time-in	Sitter's signature and time out

LEAVE APPLICATION FROM

Leave application forms are stocked at the control desk so that they are easily accessible to employees who wish to take leave. The format of a leave application form is illustrated below:

Table. Leave Application Form

leave application form	
Employee Name...............................	Date of Joining..............................
Department....................................	Weekly Off.....................................
Designation and Grade......................	Date of Application......................
Sir / Madam, I, ...wish to avail, casual / sick / earned / leave of ....days, from the date...............................to............................	
Purpose...	
Signature of employee... Signature of HOD: Approved /Refused.. Signature of Personnel Manager..	

MEMO BOOK

This contains records of all the pending maintenance work for which the housekeeping department initiated work orders. This information is made in copies so as to alert the concerned housekeeping supervisor that work is incomplete. The format of sheet in the meme book is as illustrated below.

Table. Memo Book

Memo book						
Work Order No	Date	Description of maintenance work	Location/Room No	Reported By	Job completed by	Signature of supervisor.

LOST AND FOUND SLIP/LOST AND FOUND REGISTER

'Lost and Found' is a term used in hotel terms for those articles left by guests or misplaced by guests in a hotel. Such articles can range from jewellery, costly electronic goods, and travel documents to simple garments. The hotel is obliged to protect such items and return them to the guests. Whenever such items are found by the room attendant or any staff of housekeeping they have to directly report to housekeeping control desk where lost and found is filled. The format of lost and found slip is illustrated below

Table. Lost and Found Slip

Lost and Found
Valuable/Non valuable
No

Finder's Name................................ Date....................
Location /Room no........................... Time...............
Description of article ....
....
....
Name of the guest...................................
Address...
Signature of depositor Signature of receiver

A. Received by owner
Name................................
Address............................ Telephone No:..............
Date.................................. Signature.......................

B. Dispatched by Post, Postal receipt No.............
Name ....
Address........................... Telephone No..............
Date................................ Signature.......................

C. Retrived by finder
Name...................................... Signature..........................
Cloak No.................................. Gate pass No....................

Property handed over by
Name................................ Designation.......................
Signature............................ Date.............................

Table. Lost and Found Register

No.
Lost and Found Record

Date / time	Received be Owner			Received by Finder			Dispatched by	
	Name	Address	Signature	Name	Signature	Gate Pass No.	Name.	

ACCIDENT BOOK

This records all the accidents of any sort that employees or guest have met with at the hotel. The format is illustrated below,

Table. Accident Book

S.No	Date of Accident	Name of staff/ guest	Nature of Accident	Action Taken	Supervisor in charge

Other Files and Registers that are maintained by the housekeeping control desk are

ROOM OCCUPANCY REPORT FILE

All room occupancy reports are filed for the future reference. The room occupancy reports are important to Executive Housekeeper to determine the level of workload anticipated so as to provide the necessary staff to meet the efficiency each day.

DUTY ROASTER FILE

The duty roaster is filed for information, if required by any one in the department.

ROOM INSPECTION CHECKLIST FILE

All room inspection checklists are filed in the room inspection checklists file kept at the control desk. These reports may be referred to in case there are guest complaints on cleaning.

The Executive housekeeper will be able to find the supervisor in charge inspecting the particular guestroom in this file and confirm whether he/she checked the particular surface in question.

STORE INDENT BOOK

The stores indent book is kept at the control desk so that the supervisors may indent for housekeeping supplies that are required by GRA's.the supervisors fill up the indent sheet in the book and the desk supervisor forwards it. It stores after approval for the issue of supplies. The format of store indent sheet in the store indent book is illustrated below

stores indent book Date........................			
S No	Indented Items	Quantity Indented	Quantity Issued with Remarks
Made By.................................... Approved By.............................. Storekeeper....................................			

OPERATION OF PRICING: DECISIONS AND STRATEGIES

The pricing process is a central mechanism of a private enterprise or market system. Price adjustments facilitate the logical allocation of resources; both buyers and sellers use them to clear markets of gluts and to stimulate production when supply is short. A competitive price system features such adjustments to achieve maximum economic efficiency. From an industry's perspective, pricing can extend or limit markets; from a company's perspective, it can increase or reduce its share of the market.

Price is the ingredient of the marketing mix that has been subjected to the most intensive analysis-particularly by economists. But as an aspect of the mix, it cannot be divorced from other ingredients. It must incorporate and reflect them. Optimal prices cannot be established, and pricing remains an art with a host of factors to be evaluated for which there are no precise measures and weights. Although theoretical models exist for establishing optimal prices, in practice, theory does not enable managers to determine the correct price. Marketing management is guided by personal assessments of market conditions, costs, and competitive situations. The actual price established is usually the result of executive value judgments.

PRICING FACTORS

Marketing managers may not share the economists' concern with price as the primary marketing factor. In a survey of 200 businesses, it was found that "business management did not agree with the economic views of the importance of pricing-one-half of the respondents did not select pricing as one of the five most important policy areas in their firm's marketing success." Consumers do not respond to price alone; they respond to value.

A lower price does not necessarily mean expanded sales. Moreover, marketing activities influence price. For example, governmental agencies have investigated advertising as a cause of higher prices. What is price? It is the amount paid to purchase something, or a monetary summation of the conditions that give value to a product or service. How important is the pricing decision? In microeconomic theory it has received great attention; in marketing, the significance of price varies among industries, competitive situations, and products. Pricing is significant where the market impact, profit results, or both, of price variations is great, and where firms have considerable discretion over the prices charged. In many instances pricing decisions are severely constrained and are sometimes relatively unimportant.

Large purchasers of industrial goods, for instance, may specify prices at which they will buy, determine product specifications, and send specifications to suppliers for competitive bids. For other products price may not be a relevant factor. In some technical areas where products require much research and development and involve much uncertainty, a cost-plus scheme may be used. In other situations, sellers may be almost completely free to set prices, while in still others, they may only be able to decide whether or not to sell at a price. Where industries are dominated by relatively few large firms, price is not usually the critical competitive variable. Each firm recognizes that price reductions will be met by the other large firms and the profits of all will suffer. Greater attention may then be given to non price factors. In an economy of scarcity, price is accorded more attention than any other marketing factor. In an economy of abundance, non price factors assume increasing marketing importance and products are differentiated on other bases than price. Style, colour, symbols, and brands become more significant and higher rather than lower prices may actually increase sales. For abundance brings widespread discretionary income, and price becomes a less significant component of the marketing mix than the economic literature might lead one to believe. Non price competition and price confusion, rather than price clarity, now seem to be the rule.

Buyers are concerned not only with price, in their purchases, but also with service, status, and image. Low price alone does not result in a transaction. Consumers are not mechanical price calculators and price reactors, as so much theory leads one to believe. They do not know all the prices, for in reality, discounts, trade-ins, special deals, and premiums cloud the actual price. Prices are limited by direct and indirect competition, costs, and consumer reaction. Several disciplines help in improving pricing decisions. Economic theory affords guidelines and concepts of demand and elasticity. Accounting furnishes considerations of costs, break-even, and rate of return on investment.

Marketing adds to this a consideration and understanding of market behaviour particularly the role of consumers and intermediaries. Pricing is a sensitive and complex decision area affecting sales, costs, and profits for both industrial and consumer goods. For consumers, price reductions and increases have symbolic meanings. A customer may associate a price reduction with a reduction in quality, the anticipation of new models, or even lower prices or poor market acceptance.

Higher prices may indicate better quality, a good image, and good value. Customer perceptions of price are important. Whereas pricing is usually perceived as a short-run action, its implications can be long-run, even to the point of shaping industry structures. Markets that may be viewed as systems of information on cost and demand determine the appropriateness of prices. They contain signals that businessmen must decode. But market information is ambiguous, fragmentary, and imperfect; it contains much uncertainty and is interpreted differently by various executives. To those who can read the signals properly, increased profits are the results. But invariably, pricing decisions are wrong and must be altered, as is evidenced by changing list prices. Thus, pricing is a process of adjustment in which incomplete data are used for important decisions. As new information is gathered, the offering can be adjusted in two ways: alteration of the price, or alteration of the product to meet the price.

THE PRICING DECISIONS

No single pricing programme is suitable for all firms, since the complexity of pricing situations varies by product, cost, demand, and industry structure, and prices must relate to objectives, information, knowledge of alternative policies, and strategies and adjustments. The business executive is faced with the problem of establishing the best price under assumed cost-and-demand conditions. The lack of information, the dynamics of the market, and the problems of measuring both costs and demand make it a difficult task. Yet, estimates must be made of what management expects demand, cost, and competition to be under various conditions. Then it can develop pricing programmes that affect survival, profits, growth, volume, market share, R & D, and image.

A distinction is often made between price determination and price administration. The activities and focus of each are different. Price determination refers to the processes and activities employed to arrive at a price for a product. It includes consideration of relative prices of products within the same line, and differences in price for similar products of differing grades and qualities. Price administration refers to the activities involved in fitting basic prices to particular sales situations. For example, prices may be administered to bring them into line with such factors as geographic locale, functions performed by customers, position of distribution channel members, or special sales situations. Included in price administration is the determination of discount structures. Thus, price determination refers to the establishment of a "base price" that is adjusted through price administration to reflect varying sales and competitive situations.

Six concepts and considerations useful in establishing prices are as follows:

- Pricing decisions should adopt a systems perspective. Executives must consider the whole marketing system-manufacturers, wholesalers, retailers, and consumers-and the impact at each stage.
- Prices must be related to market segments. The kind and strength of customer attitudes and the purchase desires of various market segments affect the prices that can be charged, and customer acceptance of prices by a sufficient market sector is essential.
- The determination of the best price is usually impossible, and executives must often settle for satisfactory prices in view of profit and market-share objectives.
- Price is not to be considered merely as the result of costs; it is also a method of stimulating sales.
- Since they have both economic and political dimensions, pricing

policies are more likely to be governed by tradition than by innovation. They are concerned not only with competition, elasticity of demand, marginal and average costs, industry structure, substitutability of products, and product and market characteristics, but also with numerous governmental constraints.

- Pricing policies must be reviewed and changed as basic conditions shift. This means that good pricing practices are research based.

What are the major pricing decisions to be made? They include determination of:

- Prices for each product or service.
- Discount structures.
- Price relationships among products.
- Price maintenance level.

These decisions should be based on information from market research, sales analysis, distribution cost accounting, standard costs, surveys, experiments, sales forecasts, simulations, and statistical techniques. The information required concerns competitive prices, cost data, demand estimates, product profitability, salesmen and customer reactions, and middlemen needs. But information about future demand schedules, future competitive reactions, and future costs is incomplete at best. Thus prices must be based on guesses and assumptions, yet they should be determined logically.

USEFUL CONSTRUCTS AND GUIDES

Although each pricing decision is unique, some constructs and concepts are useful in analysing pricing situations. The models of market structure, concepts of costs, demand concepts and the company philosophy of followership or leadership, are very helpful. With full knowledge of them, a "right price" can be established. But decision makers are confronted with incomplete or outdated information. The reasoning process they employ considers answers to two kinds of questions. First is "what if" or conditional reasoning. They assess possible courses of action, and the probable consequences of each. For example, if I change prices to A, what is the probability that competitors will meet the change, will not meet it, or will meet it partially, and what will be the consequences of each competitive reaction?

Second, there is a consideration of the relationship of price changes to changes in the other aspects of the marketing programme, advertising, distribution channels, product packaging, and personal selling. Prices may also be established through research. Various prices may be tested in limited areas and the "best" price selected. Research of customers' opinions and reactions to products is often sought as a basis for price. Sometimes products are tailored to meet predetermined price points, and product quality is changed so that prices can be maintained and product-line requirements and distributors' price points met. Although price is not merely the result of costs, price-cost factors are accorded major consideration. Moreover, since price affects volume, volume affects costs, and costs affect prices, the pricing decision is a circular one. Also, a variety of cost concepts may be applied. Prices can be based on total costs, average, or variable costs. The last basis leads to a marginal approach to costs. The major contribution of economic reasoning to the consideration of costs is the idea of marginal cost. Businessmen tend to rely more on an average cost approach to pricing than on a marginal approach.

Average costs, which are rarely pertinent to an optimal decision, satisfy the desire to "cover our costs and make a profit." In reality, this reliance on average costs can lead to a decision that can actually reduce sales, increase costs, and reduce profits. However, some executives advocate that sunk costs should be ignored. They are not affected by current decisions-nothing can be done about them. Yet it is also recognized that over the long run, they must be covered. A consideration of the impact of sales volume on costs provides a useful train of thought. For instance, price theory suggests a U shape for average costs-they decline to a point with increasing volume, reach their minimum, and then increase as volume increases.

This seems to make sense, since the concept introduces the notion of economies of scale and the impact of capacity on costs, indicating that volume beyond a certain point may increase costs. In addition to cost factors, pricing decisions in basic industries are greatly influenced by governmental considerations. Some industries such as steel are treated like public utilities and, sensitive to governmental reaction, must justify price increases. Although no laws exist that require governmental approval of price increases in these industries, such increases are judged as to their being warranted. A variety of pricing practices are of particular concern to certain industries.

For example, bidding is significant in defence marketing, hedging in commodity marketing, markdown in fashion merchandise, dumping in international marketing, price deals in food marketing, and loss leaders and discounting in retailing. In formulating marketing strategy, we have dealt with only the broader relationships of pricing to selected elements in the marketing mix. Price decisions in specific situations require both experience and practical knowledge. Theory alone will not suffice. In fact, where pricing is of critical concern, pricing specialists become necessary.

PRICING INFLUENCES

Since prices have great impact on both revenue and competitive reactions, pricing policies are usually determined at a high executive level. The pricing task involves not only a maze of variables but also conflicting situations. Conflicts exist among manufacturers and distributors, retailers and wholesalers, and consumers and retailers. For example, intermediate and ultimate customers weigh the prices they pay, competitors are influenced and react, suppliers watch margins carefully, financial institutions consider the impact on stock, and the government assesses competitive implications. Among the present and future external factors that influence pricing policy are number and concentration of competitors, the degree of competition, profitability, ease of entry, product heterogeneity, size, legal aspects, channels of distribution, elasticity of demand, total industry demand, kind and size of buyers, and spatial forces.

But basically these are handled through consideration of anticipated cost-revenue relationships. For in the long run, prices are constrained at their upper bound by market reaction and competition and at their lower bound by costs full or incremental. The latter are most significant in the immediate term, whereas total costs reflect a long-run situation. Prices may also be the result of competitive conditions such as total collusion or "cutthroat" competition. Either is unlikely for any protracted period of time, however-the former for legal reasons and the latter for economic considerations. Although precise cost information cannot be obtained, it is even more difficult to gain information about consumer reactions to prices. The latter is obtained from surveys, experiments, and observation. For example, consider the cost-price relationships of an automobile with its thousands of parts. What are the actual materials and labour costs of each? What is the overhead burden and how should it be spread? How are joint costs to be allocated? How many autos can be sold at each price? What are the price interrelationships among items of a product line? These are difficult problems to face.

But such costs, particularly increased costs, are price factors and the cost-price spiral is widely recognized. Also, as prices increase, sales may decline, which often results in increasing costs, since fixed costs are spread over fewer units. In reality, cost accounting of the marginal variety, which is advocated as a basis for pricing, is not often used. Both the ambiguity of costs and the difficulty of deriving the data make this impractical. In practice, the relationship of actual costs to prices may be rather loose, and in fact the prices of finished goods and raw materials or components can move in different directions. Prices should be based on both costs and market influences. In essence, maximum prices are governed by market factors and minimum prices by costs, and as they change, so should prices. The tendency exists, however, to maintain prices once they have been established. It should be noted that it is not the actual price or price change that is so significant, but rather the customer's perception and interpretation of these changes.

PROBLEMS IN SETTING PRICES

What are the major problems in establishing prices? First, costs cannot be determined precisely. Second, management must deal with expectations-expected demand, expected costs, and the maximization of expected profits.

This is particularly true of new products. Although cost estimates are more reliable than demand estimates, both are subject to wide error. They are based on the patterns of past data, which may deviate widely in the future, especially demand data, which incorporate a host of unpredictable market forces. Pricing must also be viewed from the perspective of a company's total product line, since products have complementary and competitive demands, joint and common costs, and by-products. Sometimes the demand for product A influences the demand for product B. This relationship is termed the cross elasticity of demand, with a negative cross elasticity referring to products that are complementary, a positive cross elasticity to substitutable products, and a zero cross elasticity to unrelated products. For example, an increase in the demand for pizza will increase the consumption of certain cheeses, while a large increase in the use of a company's brand R detergent may decrease the use of its brand S detergent.

Since market situations confronting products within a line differ, sellers have varying degrees of discretion in setting prices for particular items in a line, and should consider products both as separate entities and as members of a product set. Cost-plus pricing or uniform markups ignore individual product acceptance, market demands, and competitive conditions. In reacting to competitors' price changes, a company can sit tight, meet the change, or modify its own price or other elements of its marketing mix. Where customers consider not only price, but also availability, delivery, quality, service, and reliability, sensitivity to price diminishes.

When products are not homogeneous, companies have wider latitude in pricing situations. But when products are homogeneous and a price is cut, competitors may have to meet the reduction. Companies have the choice of following a price rise or not. Executives should study the reasons for price changes, their temporary and permanent effects, the impact on profits and. market share, likely industry response, and the alternatives available, before making decisions. Both purchasing situations and the decentralization of authority affect pricing policies. Prices may vary by the quantity purchased, and the purchaser's geographic area, trade position, and the functions he performs, as well as by the method and timing of purchases. In large, decentralized companies featuring profit-centre accounting, intra company pricing and transfer pricing, can influence product prices and raise significant conflicting problems. In some industries price changes in basic commodities occur frequently. Can computer programmes be developed to spell out the decision maker's thought processes in reacting to price changes? After studying a pricing executive in action over a period of time, one researcher developed a flow-chart programme that quite accurately predicted price reactions.

The programme included such information as personal biases and organizational influences in price reactions as well as market shares, anticipation of competitors' reactions, and intentions of the district office. The computer programme provided a simulation of the price-reaction process. Pricing policies are sometimes charged with emotion. Monopoly prices, price determination, and administered pricing are among the terms evoking emotional reaction. Also, the practice of price-cutting is often viewed with disdain or as an unethical practice by others in an industry, even to the point of indicating shoddy merchandise and service. Typically, new products have a monopoly position for a period a degenerative monopoly position.

Eventually competitors will develop competing and even improved products. The pricing executive must decide whether to charge relatively high or low initial prices, and the marketing consequences and related strategies are quite different in each situation. Obviously, regardless of economic models, it is difficult to establish an optimum price because demand and costs change over time.

The attention usually settles on current profit maximization rather than on the long-run maximization; the whole life cycle of a product and the total product line, rather than a single item, must be considered in pricing; and price must be considered from the perspective of the total marketing mix. Where products are relatively homogeneous; several large firms constitute a significant part of the market; and buyers are well informed, then estimates of buyer reaction become a significant aspect of the pricing picture. So do competitive reactions that may be ferreted out by the use of marketing intelligence. Studies of what competitors have done in the past, coupled with detailed analyses of the current competitive situation, may furnish guides on what they are likely to do. This reasoning process, utilizing subjective probability estimates, can provide decision makers with good guides for contemplated price changes. A specific illustration is seen in the following example: Since early 1955, the Everclear Plastics Company had been producing a resin called Kromel, basically designed for certain industrial markets.

In addition to Everclear, three other firms were producing Kromel resin. Prices among all four suppliers were identical; and product quality and service among producers were comparable. Everclear's current share of Kromel industry sales amounted to 40%. Four industrial end uses comprised the principal marketing area for the Kromel industry. These market segments will be labeled A, B, C, and D. Three of the four segments were functionally dependent in segment A in the sense that Kromel's ultimate market position and rate of approach to this level in each of these three segments was predicated on the resin's making substantial inroads in segment A. The Kromel industry's only competition in these four segments consisted of another resin called Verlon, which was produced by six other firms. Shares of the total Verlon-Kromel market currently stood at 70% Verlon industry, and 30% Kromel industry.

Since its introduction in 1955, the superior functional characteristics per dollar cost of Kromel had enabled this newer product to displace fairly large poundages of Verlon in market segments B, C, and D. On the other hand, the functional superiority per dollar cost of Kromel had not been sufficiently high to interest segment A consumers. While past price decreases in Kromel had been made, the cumulative effect of these reductions had still been insufficient to accomplish Kromel sales penetration in segment A. In the early fall of 1960, it appeared to Everclear's management that future weakness in Kromel price might be in the offing. The anticipated capacity increases on the part of the firm's Kromel competitors suggested that in the next year or two potential industry supply of this resin might significantly exceed demand, if no substantial market participation for a Kromel industry were established in segment A. In addition, it appeared likely that potential Kromel competitors might enter the business, thus adding to the threat of oversupply in litter years.

Segment A, of course, constituted the key factor. If substantial inroads could be made in this segment, it appeared likely that Kromel industrial sales growth in the other segments not only could be speeded up, but that ultimate market share levels for this resin could be markedly increased from those anticipated in the absence of segment A penetration. To Everclear's sales management, a price reduction in Kromel still appeared to represent a feasible means to achieve this objective, and perhaps it could still be profitable to Everclear. However, a large degree of uncertainty surrounded both the overall attractiveness of this alternative, and under this alternative the amount of the price reduction which would enable Kromel to penetrate market segment A.

PROBLEM STRUCTURING AND DEVELOPMENT OF THE MODEL

Formulation of the problem required a certain amount of artistry and compromise towards achieving a reasonably adequate description of the problem. But it was also necessary to keep the structure simple enough so that the nature of each input would be comprehensible to the personnel responsible for supplying data for the study.

Problem components had to be formulated, such as:

- Length and planning period;
- Number and nature of courses of action;
- Payroll functions; and
- States of nature covering future growth of the Verlon-Kromel market, interindustry and inter-Kromel industry effects of a Kromel price change, implications on Everclear's share of the total Kromel industry, and Everclear's production costs.

Initial discussions with sales management indicated that a planning period of five years should be considered in the study. While the selection of five years was somewhat arbitrary, sales personnel believed that some repercussions of a current price reduction might well extend over seven years into the future. A search for possible courses of action indicated that four pricing alternatives covered the range of actions under consideration:

- Maintenance of status quo on Kromel price, which was $1.00/1b.
- A price reduction to $.93/1b. within the next three months.
- A price reduction to $.85 1b. within the next three months.
- A price reduction to $.80/1b. within the next three months.

Inasmuch as each price action would be expected to produce a different time pattern in the flow of revenues and costs, and since no added investment in production facilities was contemplated, it was agreed that cumulative, compounded net profits over the 5-year planning period would constitute a relevant payoff function. In the absence of any unanimity as to the "correct" opportunity cost of capital, it was decided to use two interest rates of 6 and 10% annually in order to test the sensitivity of outcomes to the cost of capital variable.

Another consideration came to light during initial problem discussions. Total market growth over the next five years in each market segment constituted a "state of nature" which could impinge on the Everclear's profit position.

It was agreed to consider three separate forecasts of total market growth, a "most probable, optimistic, and pessimistic" forecast. From these assumptions a base case was then formulated. This main case would first consider the pricing problem under the most probable forecast of total Verlon-Kromel year-by-year sales potential in each segment, using an opportunity cost of capital of 6% annually. The two other total market forecasts and the other cost of capital were then to be treated as sub-cases, in order to test the sensitivity of the base case outcomes to variations in these particular states of nature. However, inter-and intra-industry alternative states of nature literally abounded in the Kromel resin problem.

Sales management at Everclear had to consider such factors as:

- The possibility that Kromel resin could effect penetration of market segment A if no price decrease were made.
- If a price decrease were made, the extent of Verlon retaliation to be anticipated.
- Given a particular type of Verlon price retaliation, its possible impact on Kromel's penetration of segment A.
- If segment A were penetrated, the possible market share which the Kromel industry could gain in segment A.
- If segment A were penetrated, the possible side effects of this event on speeding up Kromel's participation in market segments B, C, and D.

- If segment A were not penetrated, the impact which the price reduction could still have oil speeding up Kromel's participation in segments B, C, and D.
- If segment A were not penetrated, the possibility that existing Kromel competitors would initiate price reductions a year hence.
- The possible impact of a current Kromel price reduction on the decisions of existing or potential Kromel producers to increase capacity or enter the industry.

While courses of action, length of planning period, and the payoff measure for the base case had been fairly quickly agreed upon, the large number of inter- and intra-Kromel industry states of nature deemed relevant to the problem would require rather lengthy discussion with Everclear's sales personnel. Introductory sessions were held with Everclear's sales management, in order to develop a set of states of nature large enough to represent an adequate description of the real problem, yet small enough to be comprehended by the participating sales personnel. Next, separate interview sessions were held with two groups of Everclear's sales personnel; subjective probabilities regarding the occurrence of alternative states of nature under each course of action were developed in these sessions. A final session was held with all contributing personnel in attendance; each projection and/or subjective probability was gone over in detail, and a final set of ground rules for the study was agreed upon. A description of these ground rules appears.

NONPRICE COMPETITION

Given acceptable levels of prices, non price factors can become most important. Yet, adequate economic theories of non price competition are lacking. In marketing, great attention is given to such non price aspects as product-differentiation, branding, imagery, packaging, service, buyer behaviour, and styling. The most important factor in modern competition is not price, but product research and development, just as to a survey of more than 200 successful firms. Then come sales research and planning, management of sales personnel, advertising and sales promotion, product service, and finally, pricing. These non price factors, which are ignored in economic theory, must be considered in establishing pricing policies.

ELASTICITIES

In addition to understanding the nature of demand, the measurement of various aspects of demand is basic to good pricing strategy. In particular, the measurement of price elasticities and buyer price expectations are significant. Elasticities vary with the substitutability and characteristics of products. The concepts of price or demand elasticity refers to the sensitivity of buyers to price changes. When small variations in price bring about relatively large variations in buyer reaction, the price elasticity is high. The situation is reversed for low elasticity.

Since various customers react differently to price changes, knowledge of demand elasticities helps to set prices. But the major problem is that detailed data are not available. Yet, several techniques can be used to approximate elasticities, including market tests, statistical techniques of historical or cross-sectional analysis, and surveys. Management need not determine precise elasticities; rather it needs reliable estimates and guides as to the break-even levels and likely profitability of price changes. There are two basic ways of measuring elasticities-cross-cut analysis and historical data. Cross-cut analysis pertains to a point in time. Examples are interviewing buyers, using panels, simulating price situations, and conducting pricing experiments. Often, companies conduct experiments by increasing or decreasing prices in test cities and analyse the impact on sales, market share, and profits. The problems of statistical interpretation are many, however. Historical data are analysed by time series analyses that portray the association between prices and sales over time; this method is widely used in estimating elasticities. Regression and correlation analysis are its major tools, and the analysis ignores factors other than price that affect demand.

PRICING STRATEGIES AND TECHNIQUES

Pricing strategies depend on a point in time. Are markets rising or falling? What are competitors' reactions? What is happening to costs? Strategies can be adopted that tend to discourage or invite competitors, that relate to the payout in research and development, or that generate images of qualities or bargains.

Companies can decide to have high, low, or competitive prices. They can be price followers or leaders and can use several bases for price variations: geographical price discrimination, discounts and allowances, channel and service discounts, guarantees against price declines, and firm prices over time. Regardless, pricing strategies must be reviewed and realistically overhauled, for they tend to become "baked in" and to reflect traditional approaches, especially in retailing.

Prices are often set mechanistically by following formulas or rules. This procedure, although easy to follow, does not lead to "good pricing." Yet the most common technique of pricing is a mechanistic one-cost plus pricing, the addition of a margin to a cost base. Prices are often built up from an estimate of average cost and are not necessarily related to market opportunity.

Total unit costs are determined and a percentage markup is added that ignores cost-price sales relationships and market factors. In reality, however, pricing is not so rigidly determined, and market factors force modification of prices specified by formula. Often, variations of this average-cost method are used in which different markups are added to various products, based on what each product can bear in the marketplace. New-product pricing presents different problems from those of pricing mature products. New products place the manufacturer more or less in a monopoly position, but one that will erode. They also create situations in which price reactions are largely guesswork. Two general pricing strategies are used here-skimming or penetration pricing. The former refers to "skimming the cream" from a number of market segments in succession by means of a relatively high price, thus recouping investments quickly. It encourages new competitors to enter the market because of attractive margins. The philosophy is one of segmenting markets by time, getting a premium price from those segments that will pay it, and then gradually reducing prices. Thus, the core markets are cultivated first, and then attention is directed to the fringes.

Penetration pricing refers to the establishment of price levels low enough to penetrate markets deeply, and to discourage potential competitors from entry. Although prices are set relatively low, expanding markets arc recognized. Pursuit of this policy slows down the recouping of investments and expenses. Which policy to use depends on the total marketing plan and an assessment of cost-revenue market factors. A skimming policy is effective where demand is relatively inelastic.

It pays with new products, where smaller volumes can be produced economically and a high price does not attract heavy competition. Penetration pricing is suited to markets that are price sensitive. Its value is greatest in situations where production or distribution costs, or both, decrease with volume and low prices discourage competition. In addition to penetration and skimming, pricing objectives may be stated in terms of realizing a satisfactory rate of return on investment, such as 18 per cent. Or they may be expressed in terms of satisfactory profit objectives or sales volume goals at any rate of return. Pricing strategies must be perceived in terms of the whole product line rather than in terms of each individual product.

For instance, some products are priced to engender prestige for the rest of the line rather than to gain their own sale, as is the case with fine china and silverware. Other prices are set to permit "trading up," to establish images, or to meet price lines and price points.

GOVERNMENT INFLUENCES ON PRICING

Price differentials are competitive weapons. To implement them, markets must be segmented and the bases for differentials established. The former requires consideration of demand elasticities; the latter has legal dimensions. Government involvement in pricing decisions takes a number of legal forms. Others include governmental pressure to prevent price rises, or even to roll them back in basic industries such as steel. Governmental involvement seems to relate price increases to the impact on inflation and increased productivity. Such actions as withholding governmental orders or dumping metals from stockpiles back up such informal price control. Government has the influence to block or roll back price increases. Price differentials are subject to government scrutiny and regulation. They are established on the basis of quantity, distribution level, geo graphic area, and cash payment. Distribution discounts may be instituted on a net or list basis just as to distribution levels. Quantity discounts may be cumulative or non cumulative, and may apply to part of a line or a whole line. Basing points, f.o.b. factory, and uniform delivered pricing are examples of geographic differentials. Discounts for cash are very common. Legally, price discrimination can be defended on the bases of meeting competition in good faith, of cost savings in dealing with different customers, and of promoting and not injuring competition. It is the effect of price discrimination, and not the act itself, that determines legality. The legal aspects of price discrimination and government involvement in pricing, particularly the provisions of the Robinson-Patman Act, arc. Although these legal constraints are significant in establishing price differentials, the practical guidelines are confusing and the economic consequences are mixed, since price discrimination can actually benefit society.

Both the Federal Trade Commission and the Justice Department are interested in pricing practices, particularly in the administration of prices. In the administration of price differentials, marketing managers must be concerned with legal problems of collusion and price discrimination as well as the impact on sales, profits, and competition. Undoubtedly more government involvement in pricing practice is the wave of the future. Price is the ingredient of the marketing mix that has enjoyed the most extensive economic analysis. In deciding marketing strategies, however, it cannot be separated from the other components.

The importance of price as a marketing factor varies with kinds of products and market situations. Sometimes non price factors become more significant than price ingredients. Pricing programmes of firms, even within the same industry, vary greatly. Pricing strategies should consider both cost and demand conditions, and the dynamics of markets, thereby accounting for both internal and external variables.

Although the determination of an optimal price is usually impossible, a satisfactory one can be developed by analysis. The major pricing decisions include determining prices for each product or service, discount structures, price relationships among product lines, and price maintenance levels. Problems encountered in establishing prices relate to the inability to determine costs precisely, the difficulties of dealing with expectations, and the variations in impact of policies on different products in a company's product line. Marketing intelligence is a critical component of effective price determination.

HOSPITALITY MAINTENANCE AND ENGINEERING

ESTABLISHING THE COLLECTIVE MODEL

Interest in employment, now the preserve of many individuals, but not all, in western economies, derives from the fact that'Work dominates the lives of men and women ... the management of employees both individually and collectively remains a central feature of organisational life'. Before beginning an examination of employment relations in the HI, it is useful to outline the historical development of employment relations and their relevance as a field of study, thereby introducing the reader to some of the key terms used throughout the book.

Hyman academic interest in employment relations was prompted when the potential stability of social order was put under threat by militant behaviour among a growing number of unionized industrial manual workers, who were no longer prepared to tolerate very bad terms and conditions of employment. This challenge to social order, which began in the late nineteenth century, was met by two responses. First, the social welfare reformers, in keeping with their predecessors who had successfully campaigned for health and safety legislation earlier in the nineteenth century, urged legal intervention to improve the conditions under which work was performed and the terms under which it was undertaken. They achieved limited success, notably the introduction of minimum wages in four manufacturing industries in 1906. The second and main response, which was to characterize public policy on employment relations until 1979, was that voluntary collective bargaining provided the best means to secure order within employer-employee relations. Collective bargaining is a process whereby employers and trade unions negotiate the substantive terms and conditions of employment, such as pay and hours of work, and procedural agreements that facilitate the resolution of disputes between the parties.

Industrial relations, the term in usage at the time, focused on the institutions of collective bargaining in fixing these'rules' of employment, largely within male-dominated manufacturing environments. Collective agreements were not legally enforceable. While public services such as the health service, the railways and the coal mines came to assume importance in industrial relations following the mass nationalization programme after the Second World War, private services remained the'Cinderella' of British industrial relations. Even though the growth of private services such as retailing and hospitality opened up more employment opportunities for women, whose main work opportunities had been in domestic service in the earlier part of the century, unregulated, female service work was deemed not to be part of industrial relations.

Even so, the lack of collective bargaining arrangements prompted the Labour government to extend the scope of minimum wage legislation to embrace these sectors. Thus in 1945 the newly named wages councils, a form of'state-sponsored' collective bargaining, were able to fix remuneration and paid holidays for many'unprotected' workers in private services.

COLLECTIVE CONSENSUS AND A MORE ACTIVE STATE

Greater state intervention in employment matters was a response by both Conservative and Labour governments to the mounting economic difficulties of the 1960s, *e.g.* statutory and voluntary incomes policies. State intervention also constituted a response to the perceived failure of voluntary collective bargaining to provide an effective regulatory mechanism for social order and social welfare, notably to protect the interests of the low-paid, many of whom were women. This perceived breakdown prompted the government to appoint a Royal Commission in 1965, the Donovan Commission, to investigate the state of employer-worker relations, in order to recommend how the'system' could be reformed.

The Donovan prescription sought to maintain voluntarism, and placed the onus on employers to improve the rules of employment, and to introduce more formal procedures for the resolution of disputes. Donovan's prescription was not universal, because it could not be applied to large parts of private services comprising small, informally managed, non-union workplaces, where female and part-time employment was concentrated. A different approach based on legal intervention in employment relations began to develop, based on employment protection for individual employees. Early employment protection rights of the 1960s included the right to a written statement of terms and conditions of employment, statutory redundancy pay and equal pay. Workers lacking the protection of a trade union and with no recourse to formal workplace procedures could resolve an employment dispute, which is those in scope of the law, by going to an industrial tribunal.

The 1970s represented a significant turning point for legal intervention in employment relations. Britain joined the European Economic Community in 1972. This heralded the start of a wide-ranging programme designed to establish a floor of new rights relating to matters including unfair dismissal, maternity leave, sex and race discrimination and health and safety at work. The main beneficiaries were to be those working in private services. Events of the 1980s and early 1990s effectively killed the model of voluntary collective bargaining. In pursuit of an overriding objective to deregulate the labour market and employment, successive Conservative governments systematically dismantled institutions deemed to interfere with the free working of the labour market, notably the trade unions and wages councils. Paradoxically, in spite of the government's antipathy to the EU's social action programme and subsequent opt out of the social chapter, the EU continued to influence British employment relations in a significant way. Rulings from the European Court of Justice obliged Britain to introduce new legislation, *e.g.* the transfer of undertakings or the amendment of existing legislation relating to equal pay and sex discrimination.

The floor of employment rights was both strengthened and extended. Managers reasserted the right to manage increasingly flexible and non-standard workers under the banner of'managerialism', in workplaces that might be labelled'bleak houses'. An alternative version of management thinking stressed the benefits of'commitment' over'control'. Both approaches came to signify the two variants of HRM.'Soft' HRM emphasized fostering commitment, improving quality and developing the human resource, whereas'hard' HRM was contingent and calculating in its utilization of the human resource.

If organizations were to survive the effects of adverse economic conditions, globalization and increasing competition, the imperative was to integrate HRM within business strategy. The impact of HRM on industrial relations was widely debated. Other key issues in the wider academic debate included the extent of continuity and change in industrial relations, the sharp decline in trade union membership, the impact of deregulation and whether employment relations could be re-regulated.

NEW LABOUR: NEW HOPE?

By the mid-1990s individual relationships were catapulted firmly to the forefront of analysis of the employment relationship. Recognition of this change had been apparent from WIRS in 1990, perhaps most notably within the HI. HI managers are free to exercise a high degree of managerial prerogative in the absence of unorganized labour, termed'unbridled individualism'. The election of a Labour government for the first time in nearly 20 years in 1997 raised expectations that there would be a new agenda for employment relations, although Heery's assessment was that'it is extremely doubtful whether New Labour will issue in a new industrial relations'. New Labour's stakeholder economy is based on fairness and partnership. Fairness at work is to be achieved in two ways.

The government signed up to the EU social chapter and set about introducing a new floor of minimum employment standards, including a National Minimum Wage, and family-friendly measures. Social partnership between employers and workers is designed to foster a more consensual and cooperative relationship between employers and employees. The Low Pay Commission whose first task was to recommend the initial rate of the NMW, provides an early manifestation of social partnership comprising employer, worker and independent representatives. Although many of the Conservatives' trade union reforms remain in place, the introduction of statutory trade union recognition procedures might help reverse the steep decline in trade union membership. By the time of WERS in 1998 the system of collective representation had crumbled'to such an extent that it no longer represented the dominant model'. In reality employment relations could conform to different and diverse patterns. Private service establishments employing 25 or more employees were numerically more important than private sector manufacturing and the public sector put together. Their share of employment increased from 26 per cent in 1980 to 44 per cent in 1998, reinforcing the point that alternative ways to view and reform employment relations were long overdue, particularly in circumstances of'bleak house' or'black hole' employment. Although we find these terms wanting in respect of the HI, they highlight the relevance of the industry as a unit of analysis. Consequently we shall show how these types of workplaces throw up major problems for employment relations reform.

Agenda for the Twenty-first Century

In calling for a new industrial relations paradigm, Ackers now argues that the new problem of social order focuses on links between employment and society, and that such a link provides an explicit ethical framework for policies like social partnership. He rejects the traditional industrial relations notion of workers as unattached individuals in their out-of-work lives, and argues that industrial relations can no longer ignore issues of work-life balance and corporate social responsibility. Indeed social concerns underpin'Fairness at Work' and the'Welfare to Work' programme, and family-friendly issues are a new addition to WERS.

Hence a new definition of industrial relations as neo-pluralism: Employment relations are the study of the social institutions involved in the normative regulation of the employment relationship and business's interaction with other stakeholders in society. Thus Ackers rejects as inappropriate Kelly's industrial relations paradigm for the twenty-first century, which derives from a redefinition of Marxism based on socialism, workers' mobilization, economic militancy and strikes, and organized labour. Edwards identifies three pressing issues in contemporary employment relations:'high commitment' or'high involvement' work systems, the international context and economic performance.

The first, although interesting, is very rarely found anywhere in Britain. Its alternative of'low skills' and'low wages' strikes right at the heart of much hospitality employment. This links to economic performance, where the absence of collective bargaining is likely to have contributed to income inequality and the perpetuation of low pay in the HI, although pay may be subsidized by the state through social security and taxation. The further subsidy of low pay through tips as a defensible employment practice is a matter of conjecture. We shall also explore if particular employment relations practices can be linked to successful performance outcomes. The international context and its implications for employment relations in the HI are considered below and in subsequent chapters. A fourth pressing issue can be added. Employment relations discourse needs to recognize that prejudice and bias have been built into much of the theoretical and practical analysis, thus distorting its perspective. Gender is not the only example, but may be the most obvious. In spite of an increasing interest in what may be described as'women's issues', such as (un)equal pay and employment opportunities, family-friendly policies and sexual harassment, one major barrier to understanding employment relations is an assumption that they are gender neutral. The argument is that adding women's issues to the agenda is simply not good enough. Management, trade unions and the state are not gender neutral, and therefore we need to recognize the gendered characteristics of the employment relationship and work and integrate this into our understanding of the field of employment relations. Other'omissions' include age, ethnicity and the role of customers.

We shall explore these issues throughout the book where it is possible or relevant to do so. All these issues were placed under review in The Future of Work Programme launched by the ESRC in 1998. The Programme has supported 27 projects designed to rectify gaps in our understanding and improve the quality of information available to the policy-makers in the UK. Topics under investigation have included the future of unskilled work, business re-engineering and performance, the changing position of ethnic minorities and women in the labour market, the future for trade unions and the changing nature of the employment relationship.

EMPLOYMENT RELATIONS IN THE HOSPITALITY INDUSTRY

Three terms denote the relations between managers and workers in the employment relationship-industrial relations, employee relations and employment relations. These terms are often used interchangeably, but can also convey subtle differences of meaning. They may coincide with other fields of academic enquiry and practical activity concerned with'people management', namely personnel management and HRM. Edwards provides an insightful analysis of the employment relationship, taking as his starting point the distinction made by Fox and Flanders between market relations and managerial relations. At the root is an economic exchange between capital and labour, in which the price of labour is set as a contract of employment. In this economic exchange between the buyer and seller of labour, the parties do not share equal power resources.

In common law the employer has the right to command and the employee has a duty to obey. The commodity at the heart of the bargain is the worker's labour power. The employer will seek to maximize control over that'labour process' in order to generate a surplus as profit. The employment relationship, as an exchange and in recognition of its broader context, has also been termed the effort-reward bargain:'an economic, social and political relationship, for which employees provide manual and mental labour in return for rewards allotted by employers'. Labour only becomes useful if it can be persuaded by management to work, but this is only the beginning. Workers must demonstrate commitment, continue working to the required standards, and not deviate from those standards.

In other words workers must follow'rules', otherwise management may need to deploy corrective or punitive measures via the disciplinary procedure. Bonamy and May argue that a weakening of employment relationships since the 1970s has given rise to the emergence of employment as a service relationship. This relationship demands increased recognition of the professional qualities of the'autonomous' worker, which poses problems of incompatibility with an employment contract built upon subordination. Pay is determined by time worked, whilst idle time due to poor organization and absenteeism is reduced. This is manifested in new forms of employment contract, externalization of employment to agencies and the sub-contracting of activities. Edwards notes that, if we were starting from scratch, 'employment relations' might be the best label.

Employment relations do not rule out all variants within the employment relationship including:

- Trade unions and formal collective bargaining;
- Individually based management/workforce relations conducted informally;
- Managerialism;
- More democratic and highly participative non-union relations;
- Men, women and disadvantaged groups;
- Employees and workers, including atypical workers and the self-employed.

Further:

- Employment relations is the main term used in the WERS sourcebook;
- Industrial tribunals have been renamed employment tribunals;
- The cornerstone of New Labour's industrial relations policy is the Employment Relations Act 1999.

A necessary departure for this book, as noted earlier, is to relocate the nexus of the employment relationship to include a relatively ignored third actor in the employment relationship-the customer. The notion of the customer in the employment relationship has been increasingly incorporated into the sociology of work, but less so in employment relations. Front-line workers, such as receptionists and servers in bars and restaurants, have to serve two'masters': their superior manager and the customer. Individual workers can have a simultaneous and coterminous employment relationship with the organization and the customer. Organizations in services are best seen as inverted pyramids, with most workers in direct customer contact. Direct service workers engage directly with customers in an exchange that carries both economic and social connotations. Their ability to deliver successfully hinges upon a social relationship with indirect service workers, whose actions are also instrumental to the provision of good customer service, *e.g.* an enjoyable meal or clean bedrooms. Indirect service workers are not in regular customer contact, so customer influence may be more economic than social. Hence, customers cannot be excluded from an analysis of the employment relationship.

An earlier definition has been revised:

- Employee relations in hotels and catering are about the management of employment and work relationships between managers and workers and, sometimes, customers; it also covers contemporary employment and work practices.
- Before exploring the facets of the employment relationship, we need to outline why our attitude towards things influences the way in which we see any given situation, and how it.
- Triplets watch a local football match from adjoining seats, getting an almost identical view of the game. The result is United 5 City 1. One triplet is deliriously happy, the second feels very low, while the third is able to provide a balanced analysis of events, conceding that the result was a fair one, although two of United's goals were the result of dubious refereeing and City deserved more than a single goal.
- Why did their particular attitude affect their view of the game?

Fox proposed two frames of reference as a means by which'the problems of industrial relations can be seen realistically and laid more open to solution'. The unitary perspective is a'management ideology' built on the belief that everyone in the organization shares the same goals, and that'conflict' is pathological and derives from deviance. Trade unions are seen as an intrusion, competing with management for worker loyalty.

Fox's main argument was that the unitary perspective was a naive and unrealistic frame of reference that might'distort reality and thereby prejudice solutions'. Yet in reality many managers do perceive their organizations in unitary terms, regarding themselves as the sole source of authority. Unitarism has underpinned the'human relations school' of management, including Mayo, Likert, McGregor, Schein and Herzberg, and reasserted itself in'managerialism' and HRM. Fox suggested that the more realistic approach to managing people was to recognize that organizations are pluralistic, comprising various groups, each with their own basis of authority and sets of interests.

The'rules' of employment are not just the preserve of management. A new pay rate set by management will not necessarily be seen as fair by workers, creating an issue of potential dispute. Therefore conflict or differences between individuals and groups are inevitable. Management should recognize this inevitability, and find the ways and means to regulate such differences. An institutional approach-collective bargaining between employers and trade unions, and the development of formal procedures to deal with disputes about pay, grievances and discipline-was considered to be the most appropriate solution. However, this is flawed to the extent that it implies both parties to the bargain have equal power resources at their disposal.

Later Fox revised his thinking and added a third perspective of radicalism, prompted by a wave of'shop floor' discontent and'wildcat' strikes at workplace level. Such worker behaviour was perceived as a reaction against exploitative and oppressive employers whose sole aim was to maximize profit. Conflict was caused by the economic disparity of society as a whole, with the principal disparity between capital and labour-employers who own and manage the means of production and workers who have their capital to sell.

This view underpins the labour process approach. This approach stresses the contradiction of managerial goals, with regulation and control having to be balanced by the need to gain workers' consent. Even today Edwards argues that unitarism cannot be written off as naive and outdated any more than radicalism because of the apparent disappearance of discontent. Ackers' neo-pluralism refocuses the employment relationship beyond the workplace by connecting the old pluralist and voluntary frames of reference with new questions raised by contemporary society. The health of society is put first, encouraging industrial relations policy initiatives that are driven by social concerns, not just a business agenda. Further he argues that the employment relationship bears hidden ethical considerations of trust and responsibility in relation to human beings.

As we shall show, both managers and workers in a variety of work and employment situations in the HI do see their workplaces in unitary terms, but this does not necessarily infer the absence of conflict. Areas of potential dispute, conflict and difference do exist between managers and workers, between managers and other managers, and between workers and customers, demonstrating that workplaces are pluralistic. In cases where workers'fiddle' or'pilfer' from their employer, the nature of their behaviour is more in keeping with a radical perspective.

Thus it is possible to observe facets of unitarism, pluralism and radicalism in the same employment relationship in which management, for the most part, remains the more powerful. Even so, areas of common interest self-evidently exist otherwise all these relationships would break down. Consent provides the basis for resolving conflict and achieving cooperation. Cooperation is built on trust between individuals engendered at workplace level rather than through elaborate organizational mechanisms. Yet securing workers' consent is neither a straightforward nor certain process. Therefore, a mix of overt and covert conflict and cooperation underpins all employment relationships and, as we shall argue, workplace harmony owes more to pragmatic acceptance and accommodation among the parties in the employment relationship than to ideological belief.

THE RULES OF EMPLOYMENT AND POWER RELATIONS

We have already noted that the employment relationship is underpinned by rules, hence the continuing validity of Clegg's definition of industrial relations as'The study of the rules governing employment' which Edwards explains in more detail: This does not limit the subject to the collective relations between managements and trade unions, for a rule can derive from other sources, and there are rules governing non-union groups; nor does it restrict analysis to one sector, for it covers all paid forms of employment. A rule is a social institution involving two or more parties which may have its basis in law, a written collective agreement, an unwritten agreement, a unilateral decree or merely an understanding that has the force of custom. In non-union settings, as much as union ones, rules determine rates of pay, hours of work, job descriptions and many other aspects of employment. The subject is about the ways in which the employment relationship is regulated. To regulate means to control, to adapt or adjust continuously or to adjust by rule.

MANAGERIAL ISSUES

While rules may be the substantive rules of employment, *e.g.* pay and conditions of employment, implicit in the notion of rules affecting people is the concept of behaviour. Management's job is to control and direct workers' behaviour to perform work to the desired standards, and thereby ensure that the rules of employment are adhered to.

Four key issues arise:

1. Rules are not always absolute and may be gendered.
2. Managerial control of workers' behaviour is underpinned by a power relationship.
3. This power relationship is unequal and may be gendered.
4. Managers have a choice of means to maximize control.

The first point is that one should caution against perceiving rules in too absolute a sense. At one end of the spectrum rules embodied in the law of the land provide a good example of formal rules. Any breach may incur very severe penalties, *e.g.* health and safety. In a workplace setting rules in practice may derive from informal understandings that can in one set of circumstances be interpreted by the worker as a permissive concession or in a different set of circumstances as something to be observed at all costs. Strawberries as a worker's perquisite during the Wimbledon lawn tennis championship are a good example. Experienced workers know that taking home unwanted strawberries is'permitted' during busy periods. When fewer staff are needed, increased managerial surveillance will be deployed to dismiss staff caught in possession of company property.

Rule-learning is part of what Polanyi refers to as'tacit skills'. As argued elsewhere:

Tacit skills, such as learning to deal with customers, are learnt in and through the very act of doing, often involving trial and error and not from following a body of procedurally-designed rules. They are seen as an interpretive achievement of the user as to how the'rules' fit the task in hand. By mastery of the rules comes the power to extend them. This example embracing the customer provides a developmental point to Edwards' observation that rule-making is difficult, and that rules have to be interpreted in action for them to have any real meaning. Specifically in the labour contract this is because the worker's ability to work is only realised as useful labour in the course of carrying out that work, hence'a rule is a complex social institution'.

In service work physical appearance and'personality', or'aesthetic labour', are an implicit part of the employment contract. Only female flight attendants, not their male colleagues, are subjected to regular weigh-ins to ensure they comply to specified weight: height ratios. This demonstrates clearly how a rule may be gendered. The second point to note is that the very essence of management seeking to control workers' behaviour is underpinned by a power relationship. Power is the capacity to pursue one's own interests individually and collectively, involving the capacity to oppose the actions of others and to pursue one's own objectives, and is embedded in continuing relationships. This does not mean power has to be exercised by either party in an overt sense. The threat of power may be sufficient to maintain broadly consensual employment relationships, such that any disputes or differences are resolved amicably without recourse to either party seeking to deploy sanctions against the other. The third point assumes a power inequality in the employment relationship. Self-evidently an employer is more powerful than an individual worker. The employer's ability to terminate a worker's services is likely to be more detrimental to the worker than to the employer, in spite of employment protection legislation.

Yet the individual behaviours of workers, such as high labour turnover, may be detrimental to an employer, even though they are not concerted. When workers combine collectively, with or without the backing of a trade union, there is some tilt in the balance of power, because collective sanctions may be imposed against the employer. Ultimately the outcome of the process by which each side seeks to gain concessions will depend on the relative power of the parties. For example, a plentiful supply of suitable workers in the labour market makes existing workers more readily dispensable and replaceable on the employer's terms. The opposite would be true for workers with scarce skills who can command high wages. As Wajcman argues, gender relations are power-based and women's subordination in the workforce and workplace owes as much to trade unions as it does to managers. Spradley and Mann provide a graphic account of how the subordination of one group of female workers was brought about by another group of male workers who were the custodians of the male proprietor's trust.

The male bartenders controlled the orders, and sought to make the cocktail waitresses' job difficult by giving orders in an inconsistent and confusing way. Any mistakes became the waitresses' responsibility, even if they had been caused by the bartenders. Such was the power of the bartenders that pleasing them became more important than pleasing the customers. The fourth point is that managers have a choice of means to maximize control over workers. Friedman's'direct control' is a variant of Taylorism. Management is responsible for planning, designing and organizing the labour process, while cheap, unskilled workers perform standardized, simple repetitive tasks. Fast food is a good case in point, and also epitomizes McDonaldization, a social critique of how contemporary society and culture are being shaped by rationalist scientific management. While Taylorism sought to control the organization of work, McDonaldization is based on rationalization, replication, standardization of products and service, and quantification. In this low trust strategy worker behaviour is controlled through the use of standardized scripts in the service encounter.

In Friedman's alternative of'responsible autonomy', a high trust approach, managers delegate control to relatively privileged skilled workers who may already have elements of job control and discretion. The objective is to get workers to identify with the competitive aims of the organization so they will behave responsibly with minimum supervision. An obvious example of where such an approach might be used is in a luxury hotel, but it is also associated with empowerment and much customer-service work. As we shall argue and implied in the example of cocktail waitresses, these and other similar approaches including'hard' and'soft' HRM provide a useful framework for analysis, but are not necessarily alternatives.

The history of hotel internationalization has been characterized by American chains that secure control and integration through highly standardized procedures and manuals of operational procedures. Yet a'soft' focus on the service encounter as the driver of competitive advantage necessitates developing a culture of customised service. Mass customization illustrated by Burger King's have it your way' slogan as a challenge to McDonald's hold on the market is proposed as an alternative paradigm to McDonaldization.

WORKERS AND CUSTOMERS

Other tensions within the employment relationship impinge upon the rules of employment and power relationships. If management is about the achievement of organizational goals through people it can be argued that managers will be successful to the extent that these goals coincide with the aims and aspirations of those people, be they workers or customers. This'matching' of broadly reciprocal needs between employers and workers may be referred to as a'psychological contract', or set of contracts. It suggests managers and workers can share goals, but this is not at all straightforward. There is not a necessarily clearcut distinction between boss and worker, or a'them and us' scenario. Further we must also account for a psychological contract with customers.

Two key points are noteworthy:

1. Organizations comprise people and are, therefore, social organizations.
2. People, as social animals, may behave in unpredictable ways.

Workers

Human beings do not necessarily behave consistently or predictably, even in the same sets of circumstances. People are citizens and customers as well as employees, and these multiple identities bring different and sometimes conflicting expectations of the organization.

This makes the management of the employment relationship an uncertain process within which there is a blend of contradictory principles around the need to control and to gain the consent of workers. Workers may seek to regain control individually or collectively when they perceive that management has operated outside the rules.

At that point workers' consent has been withdrawn and management will need to find ways to restore order and regain consent. In Lucas workers' individual response to organizational rules is seen in three main ways-to conform or be deviant in employment, or to terminate their employment. These responses are similar to Marchington's'getting on','getting by' and'getting back'. These are behaviours deployed in circumstances where customer care and service quality are dependent on workers' use of their tacit skills, which contain both technical and attitudinal elements. Limiting the definition of tacit skills to employer-employee relations is too narrow. Marchington overlooked how workers exhibit their tacit skills in ways other than in respect of their relationship with the employer, notably the customer. The point that'getting back','getting by' and'getting on' are as much resistance strategies in the labour process as coping mechanisms is developed.

At workplace level personal relationships are likely to be closely connected to morale and success. Managers often'muck in' when required. In small workplaces the existence of a single leader, often the owner, may serve to inspire loyalty from the workforce, but it is not a one-way process, as workers' respect has to be earned. Is it realistic to suggest that Mina, Jo and Sadie, who wait on table in the restaurant, share all the same goals as their boss? The hotel may not be doing very well, so there may be mutual concern for the survival of the business. Yet these ladies' main goal may be to serve their customers cheerfully and effectively, while at the same time enjoying some social banter among themselves and with their customers in the process of earning a reasonable wage.

Customers

Within the triadic employment relationship a simultaneous and coterminous relationship with the organization and the customer directly impinges on how workers carry out their work, and such interactions may be rewarding or stressful. The consequent effect on workers' performance may have positive or negative implications for the rules of employment: what they can earn, their prospects of promotion or actually keeping their job. Unequivocally the worker-customer relationship affects the rules governing employment and workplace behaviour.

But so do employer-customer relationships, hence the employment relationship embodies a triadic set of power relations. This relationship embodies a socio-economic exchange, and is not simply an economic exchange around the price of labour. Fox provides a useful starting point, since he noted that organizations are social organizations and how people behave is a crucial issue in the employment relationship. Even Edwards' point that'a rule is a complex social institution' does not adequately encapsulate our position. The main justification for widening the scope of this relationship derives from the fact that the service encounter is the interaction of the producer and consumer of services, and is a more complex phenomenon where financial considerations are interwoven with social ones. In hospitality the social function of service work derives from the provision of a'home away from home'.

The service encounter entails'emotion work'-the assumption of a social-self, which effectively masks the individual's own personal dispositions to act, including the need to smile and be pleasant in an uninvolved way. We have already noted that'aesthetic' and sexual labour may also be inherent in service work. It is the'normalizing' social role of service labour that distinguishes it from other wage labour. Service work cannot be understood in terms of economic rationality alone.

Examination must be based on the supposition that service work is the intended outcome of a necessarily social process in which some social interaction occurs between one or more producers and one or more consumers. The relations between three groups of people-managers, workers and customers-embody the potential for contradiction between, on the one hand, uncertainty, unpredictability, conflict and difference and, on the other hand, consent, team effort and concerted performance. The practical benefit this book seeks to convey accrues from an understanding of the nature and scope of the rules of employment in this triadic employment relationship, and how it is regulated, primarily at workplace level.

THE EMPLOYMENT RELATIONSHIP IN A WIDER CONTEXT

This chapter concludes by considering some key external contextual influences on workplace employment relationships at two levels-internationally and, in more detail, nationally in Britain.

The International Context

The national context of British employment relations increasingly needs to be understood within a much wider international context.

Three international dimensions have particular resonance for this book:

- International competition has created more open economies that have attracted investment from foreign-owned businesses. For example the French-owned groups Accor and Envergure have respectively opened hotels within their Novotel and Campanile brands in the United Kingdom.
- On a larger scale American multinational corporations have created world brands. McDonald's, Burger King, KFC and Marriott are among those that are now household names in many countries across the world.
- Spin-offs from European integration, especially on employment law in Britain, have provided an important underpinning to the employment relationship in the HI.

Foreign investment and MNCs are clearly important factors underpinning the expansion of hospitality and tourism not only in Britain but also in developing countries. Examples ofbetter' employment practices, in so far as they may exist in the British HI, have been associated with foreign-owned businesses. Aspects of the American model of employment relations, that is non-union and market-driven, may seem to reflect some aspects of observed employment relations practice in the British HI, but the similarity has been overstated.

The United States has substantially more legal regulation than Britain, which has benefited American HI workers, while the trade unions are not entirely powerless-issues we highlight in later chapters. The European model based on social partnership designed to forge a common agenda between capital and labour is considerably more diverse and different across the member states than is often acknowledged. While we cannot expect it to reflect current developments in HI employment relations in most British workplaces, it has not necessarily produced wholesale benefits for HI workers across the EU either.

The British experience is not necessarily mirrored in other countries across the world. Differences in other countries' institutional arrangements and cultural considerations are among the factors that will affect their employment relations systems. Detailed comparison with other countries is beyond the scope of this book, but key instances of international employment relations within hospitality and tourism are cited throughout the remaining chapters.

THE BRITISH CONTEXT

Workplace employment relationships cannot be immune from wider economic, social, legal and political contextual influences. Contemporary examples, which may be influential in Britain today. The distinctions between these sets of influences are not always clear-cut as they can be interrelated.

The State

Although we have already touched upon some aspects of the state's interest in employment relations, we need to examine its role in a little more detail. The state is not a single or cohesive body, and comprises a number of institutions that have an interest in the employment relationship, whose objectives do not necessarily coincide. Parliament is the legislature, government ministers form the executive, the judiciary enforces the law, and civil servants are the administrators. The state sponsors specialist agencies in the field of employment, and has done so since the end of the nineteenth century. Three government departments impinge on employment relations within a much wider brief. The most important is the DTI, which has overall responsibility for employment relations, small firms and competitiveness. The Employment Relations directorate is responsible for developing policy and legislation affecting individual workers and trade unions, EU legislation, promoting partnership and best practice, regulation of employment tribunals and the dates of public holidays. The DTI publishes consultation documents, research papers, practical guidance on how to implement employment legislation and regulations, and codes of practice on matters such as picketing.

The Department for Education and Skills is responsible for developing the skills of young people and adults. he Department for Work and Pensions delivers support and advice in areas of work and work-related benefits, including New Deal, sickness and accidents at work, and retirement. Although publicly funded, other state agencies and bodies are independent of government because they are controlled and managed by their own executive. The main institutions discussed later in the book are ACAS, the Central Arbitration Committee and employment tribunals. The Equal Opportunities Commission, Commission for Racial Equality and Disability Rights Commission each have overall responsibility for specific types of anti-discrimination or equal opportunities legislation.

The Health and Safety Commission and Health and Safety Executive have responsibility for health, safety and welfare legislation. Their roles include the publication of codes of practice. Other bodies assist with the enforcement of minimum employment standards. The Inland Revenue's powers include obtaining information from employers, issuing enforcement notices requiring employers to pay the NMW and imposing penalties on employers not observing the NMW. Environmental Health Officers are responsible for the enforcement of health and safety standards. Many other institutions, some of which may have a political bias, offer a mixture of fact and opinion on employment relations. National bodies, which take either an employer or management view, include the Confederation of British Industry, the Institute of Directors, and the Chartered Institute of Personnel and Development. The British Hospitality Association, Restaurant Association, the British Beer and Pub Association the Hotel, Catering and International Management Association and the British Institute of Innkeeping are specific to the HI. The HtF, formerly the HI's National Training Organisation is recognized by government as the employer-led voice on all issues relating to hospitality training, education and qualifications.

The HtF also carries out research, and produces useful statistical information about the labour market. The Trades Union Congress Institute of Employment Rights and the Low Pay Network serve to defend workers' interests. The HCIMA can also be regarded as having a worker perspective since, as the professional body of hospitality managers; it serves to defend their interests as well as disseminating good management practice. Three large unions have special sections for hospitality workers: the General, Municipal and Boilermakers' Union, the Transport and General Workers Union and the Union of Shop, Distributive and Allied Workers. The National Association of Licensed House Managers was self-standing for many years, but has recently become part of the TGWU.

REFRIGERATION SYSTEMS
REFRIGERATION AND HEATING EQUIPMENT

Multifactor productivity gains averaged 1.5 per cent per year over the 1967-94 period; to comply with Federal legislation, the industry shifted from chlorofluorocarbons, an important input in the production process, to environmentally safer substitutes Multifactor productivity in the refrigeration and heating equipment industry increased at an average annual rate of 1.5 per cent over the 1967-94 period. This industry's output includes air conditioners, refrigeration equipment and systems, electric heat pumps, furnaces, refrigerated display cases, soda fountains, beer dispensers, and snowmaking machinery.

Multifactor productivity is a measure used to analyse the overall economic efficiency of an industry. It relates the growth of the industry's output to the growth rate of the combined inputs of labour, capital, and intermediate purchases. An important input for the refrigeration and heating equipment industry had been chlorofluorocarbons, a chemical compound used since the 1930s. By Federal enactment, however, CFC'S were phased out because they were linked to depletion of the ozone layer in the atmosphere. As a result, the industry has had to allocate a substantial amount of resources to the transition away from CFC'S. This article examines detailed productivity, output, and input data in the manufacture of refrigeration and heating equipment to provide measures of multifactor productivity growth over a 27-year period. Special emphasis is placed on the "productivity falloff" that began in 1973. The article also includes descriptions of recent production technology, new designs and methods of manufacturing, and market influences that could influence industry output and input.

PRODUCTIVITY

Since 1984, the Bureau of Labour Statistics has published an index of output per employee hour, or labour productivity, for the refrigeration and heating equipment industry. Labour productivity relates output to the input of labour, while multifactor productivity relates output to the combined inputs of labour, capital, and intermediate purchases. Labour productivity does not measure the exact contribution of labour, but reflects many influences that affect the use of labour, such as changing technology; economies of scale; substitution of inputs of capital and intermediate purchases for labour; managerial skills; and the level of experience and education of the work force.

While the multifactor productivity measure reflects many of these influences, it does not reflect changes in capital relative to labour and in intermediate purchases relative to labour. Labour productivity in the industry increased at an average annual rate of 1.7 per cent over the entire period studied, while in total manufacturing the rate was 2.7 per cent. Over the same period, multifactor productivity rose 1.5 per cent per year in the industry, while in the total manufacturing sector of the economy, it advanced 1.1 per cent per year. The 1.5-per cent rate of growth in multifactor productivity resulted from a 3.6-per cent average annual increase in output and a 2.1-per cent average annual gain in combined inputs.

Analysing the 1967-94 period in more detail, we find that labour productivity rose rapidly, at 5.2 per cent per year, while multifactor productivity increased 3.6 per cent per year during 1967-73. Multifactor and related productivity measures in the refrigeration and heating equipment industry, average annual rates of change, 1967-94 Each measure presented in this is computed independently. Therefore, multifactor productivity, the capital effect, and the intermediate purchase effect might not sum exactly to output per hour, due to rounding. The capital effect is the change in the ratio of capital to labour, multiplied by the share of capital costs in the total cost of output. The intermediate purchases effect is the change in the ratio of intermediate purchases to labour, multiplied by the share of intermediate purchases costs in the total cost of output.

The refrigeration and heating equipment industry did not escape the productivity falloff that affected most manufacturing industries between 1973 and 1979. Both labour productivity and multifactor productivity growth rates fell sharply from the 1967-73 period to the 1973-79 periods. Labour productivity dropped 0.3 per cent per year for the latter period, down from a 5.2-per cent per year increase for the 1967-73 period. Multifactor productivity growth fell from an annual rate of increase of 3.6 per cent to a 1.9-per cent rate for the same periods-a slowdown considerably smaller than the 5.5-percentage-point falloff that occurred in labour productivity. For the 1979-94 period, labour productivity growth recovered from the 0.3-per cent-per-year decrease during 1973-79 to post a 1.1-per cent average annual increase.

Multifactor productivity growth was subdued, rising just 0.6 per cent each year after 1979. The influence of capital on output per employee hour, referred to as the "capital effect," is measured as the change in the capital-labour ratio multiplied by the share of capital costs in total costs of output. Analogous to the capital effect is the "intermediate purchases effect" which is derived by multiplying change in the intermediate purchases-labour ratio by the share of intermediate purchases in the total cost of output Labour productivity growth equals the sum of these two effects plus multifactor productivity growth. For the entire 196794 period, the capital effect was 0.0 per cent per year, while the intermediate purchases effect averaged 0.1 per cent annually. Although the capital effect and the intermediate purchases effect were negligible for the entire period studied, they did vary in the subperiods. During 1967-73, the capital effect contributed 0.2 percentage point to the growth rate of labour productivity and the intermediate purchases effect contributed 1.3 percentage points. For the period 1973-79, the capital effect equaled-0.1 per cent on average, while the intermediate purchases effect declined 3.3 percentage points, to 2.0 per cent per year. During the 1979-94 periods, the capital effect decreased slightly to a-O.1-per cent average annual rate, while the intermediate purchases effect increased, to 0.6 per cent per year.

TECHNOLOGY CHANGE

Production techniques and, hence, rates of productivity, in this industry have been affected by new technology from a product's start to finish. With the introduction of new methods, the industry strives to reduce wasted materials, decrease rejected finished parts and products, and diminish labour requirements. Computer-aided design assists an engineer in designing a new product by taking over repetitive tasks, warning of inconsistencies in measurement, and increasing the designer's usable memory many times over by storing almost unlimited data. Computer-aided manufacture guarantees that an engineer's specifications are carried out to degrees of accuracy that were impossible before the advent of microprocessor-controlled production equipment.

Engineering firms developing new heating and cooling products have embraced CAD technology. These systems allow a shop to get more work, of a more complex nature, from fewer engineers. The systems can even be programmed by senior engineers to coach the less experienced, to ensure that all work meets design, cost, and productively standards set by the firm. Designing any new product or component usually involves several stages, at which modifications are tested within the CAD environment. This is the point at which a CAD system saves significant labour hours and material. The "brain" of these systems can modify drawings and actually test the modifications in minutes, making it unnecessary to completely redraw the component, or to manufacture one version to test a change. Most CAD systems can scrutinize a component for noise, vibration, stress, buckling, and fatigue. Computer-aided manufacturing has allowed a plant in Indiana to make finished motor vehicle air conditioners from raw castings, with almost no manual handling. The plant, which makes compressors for cars and light trucks, has 5 miles of conveyors-all monitored and controlled by six microprocessors.

Together, the conveyors take up almost 200,000 square feet of plant space. Production processes that once were performed as separate operations, and often manually, are now integrated into a "system approach." Many of the new technologies introduced into this industry are aimed at improving control of processes such as metal cutting and bending. Precise cutting of metal not only reduces waste, but also is essential "down the line," where automated equipment requires very close tolerances. A Minnesota plant uses machine vision modules to detect any flaws on metal to be used to make freezer coils.

The vision modules detect irregularities and direct controllers to reverse the flow of the material and cut off the flawed portion. This reduces labour and material requirements while producing fewer defective products. The plant also has been able to switch to a lighter gauge steel. This is because the new drives improve handling to such an extent that the material is less likely to be damaged. Environmental concerns will continue to alter the designs and methods of manufacturing in the refrigeration and heating equipment industry for some time. Meanwhile, engineers and designers have begun discussing and practicing the "design for disassembly" concept in this, and other industries as well.

The goal of this concept is to construct a product so that it can be easily disassembled into its component parts for simplified recycling. At present, the recycling of refrigeration and heating equipment is limited because of the large quantities of labour needed to take the equipment apart. This new theory of design will require yet newer technologies of the industry and of its suppliers of intermediate inputs.

OUTPUT

Changes in output in the refrigeration and heating equipment industry respond to many variables, including new residential and nonresidential construction, renovation of existing structures, automobile sales, Federal legislation regarding the environment, and the general health of the economy. For the entire 1967-94 period, output in the industry increased 3.6 per cent each year on average, compared with a 2.5-per cent average annual increase for all manufacturing. This industry is highly cyclical, with sharp swings in output: the sharpest increase occurred during 1972, when it posted a 32.5-per cent jump in output; the deepest drop took place in 1975, bringing output down 35.5 per cent from the previous year. Two industries, motor vehicles and equipment and building construction, dominate the demand for refrigeration and heating equipment.

For 23 of the 27 years between 1967 and 1994, changes in output in the industry move in the same direction as changes in output of the motor vehicles and equipment industry. The relationship between new construction and the demand for new refrigeration and heating equipment also is strong. A significant market for the industry's output is retrofit and reconstruction. This involves work on commercial buildings intended to upgrade cooling and heating equipment to meet new standards, increase the appeal of unleashed space, and reduce indoor environmental problems.

The trend for the retrofit and reconstruction market appears to be upward. Specifically, legislation at the Federal level, which began the CFC phaseout schedule, will spur the demand for retrofit and replacement. In the United States, there are more than 130 million motor vehicle air conditioners, 5 million commercial refrigeration systems, and 80 thousand air-conditioning units for commercial and institutional buildings running on CFC'S. Many of these components will have to be replaced or retrofitted. For many of the establishments in this industry, international sales represent as much as 35 per cent of total revenues.

In 1993, the value of U.S. imports of refrigeration and heating equipment increased almost 8 per cent, while the value of the exports of this industry increased 12 per cent. Exports will continue to increase due to the economic and social changes taking place in Eastern Europe and the former Soviet Union. More significant is the liberalization of trade made possible by the North American Free Trade Agreement of 1994. This should create excellent opportunities for the industry to expand its exports to Canada and Mexico. The refrigeration and heating equipment industry is currently experiencing a boom in the production of one of its products. Shipments of air conditioning systems for institutional and commercial buildings have grown dramatically. These units, called chillers, are needed to replace older, less efficient systems that rely on CFC'S. A survey by the Air Conditioning and Refrigeration Institute, "U.S.

shipments of chillers to building owners around the world jumped 32 per cent in 1995 to a record 9,444 units, of which about 40 per cent were used in America to replace CFC chillers..."

Moreover, this surge will continue for several more years because the institute's survey also showed that, "...65,375 or 82 per cent of...chillers in the U.S. were still using CFCS on January 1, [1996] when a ban on CFC production went into effect." Only a few years ago, the outlook for this industry was not encouraging. At the time, producers complained of the potential for equipment shutdowns, the need for employee layoffs, and low inventories. This was primarily due to legislation requiring stringent cutbacks of CFC compounds before the replacements had been invented. Research and development, however, have led to the design of efficient CFC-free refrigeration and air conditioning products, which has helped increase the demand for the industry's output.

Inputs

Over the entire 1967-94 period, labour input increased 1.9 per cent per year, on average. Again, this hides the divergence between pre-and post-1973 trends for the industry. From 1967 to 1973, labour input in SIC 3585 grew at an average annual rate of 7.9 per cent, but from 1973 to 1979, it increased just 0.1 per cent per year. In the final period, 1979-94, employee hours edged up 0.4 per cent each year, on average. In 1967, there were 81,500 people employed by the refrigeration and heating equipment industry. The average hourly earnings for production workers in the industry at that time were $2.93, compared with $2.82 for all manufacturing.

In that same year, 70 per cent of all industry employees were production workers, compared with 74 per cent in all manufacturing. In 1994, the level of employment reached more than 130,000-an impressive recovery from the 1991 level of 115,000 employees. By 1994, average hourly earnings of production workers were $11.80 in the industry, compared with $11.62 in all manufacturing. In 1995, employment in the industry had swelled to a new peak of 139,000. This is in stark contrast to employment in the total manufacturing sector, which last peaked in 1979. Employment levels in the next few years could surpass the 1995 peak for the reasons discussed earlier.

As measured in BLS multifactor productivity studies, capital is the flow of services derived from the equipment, structures finished goods, work-in-process, and materials and supplies inventories that are kept on hand in the firm, as well as the land on which plants are located. Financial assets are not included in the measure. Capital services in the refrigeration and heating equipment industry grew at an average annual rate of 2.2 per cent between 1967 and 1994. Reflecting the industry's tremendous growth through the early 1970s, capital services averaged a 9.8-per cent annual increase during the 1967-

73 period. However, gains slowed sharply after 1973, to just 0.1 per cent per year during 1973-79. This slowdown continued for the 197994 period with capital services increasing at the same rate of 0.1 per cent. From 1967 to 1994, measures of the services of capital structures and land moved similarly to that for total capital, increasing at average annual rates of 2.0 and 2.7 per cent, respectively. That for equipment rose even faster, at an average annual rate of 4.9 per cent. Inventories were steady at 0.0 per cent per year, on average. In the first interval, 1967-73, equipment services rose almost 13 per cent each year, then fell off to a gain of 4.4 per cent annually during 1973-79. Between 1979 and 1994, these services grew even more slowly, at an annual rate of 2.1 per cent.

While inventories as a whole were cyclical for this industry, when viewed in more detail, a different picture emerges. For unitary products, particularly window air conditioning units, inventories change with the seasons and the severity of seasons. A summer that is cooler than average would leave inventories higher than average for the year. Also, the suppliers of materials to the industry sometimes offer incentives, such as attractive financing, that will induce manufacturers to stock up on inventory. For the component products, such as industrial and commercial heating/cooling units for whole buildings, there generally is no inventory. The product itself is so specialized that the materials are not ordered until the buyer has committed to the purchase. In 13 years, the services of structures declined; these annual reductions never exceeded 2 per cent.

For the entire period, 1967-94, the measure for structures increased 2.0 per cent each year, on average. However, the overall increase masks the high pre-1973 gain of 8.8 per cent each year and the drop-off to just a 0.2-per cent gain each year after 1973. Intermediate purchases. Intermediate purchases consist of the raw materials, energy and purchased services used in the production of the industry's output. Materials make up more than 90 per cent of the value of intermediate purchases for the refrigeration and heating equipment industry, with services ranging from 6 per cent to 9 per cent of that value, and fuels and electricity, the remainder. The input of intermediate purchases increased 2.2 per cent each year, on average, between 1967 and 1994, but this overall rate hides the large difference between the pre-1973 and the post-1973 periods. During 1967-73, input of intermediate purchases increased by more than 10 per cent each year, on average, but in 1973-79, this component decreased 3.5 per cent per year. The 1979-94 intervals showed a cessation of the downward trend of the use of intermediate inputs, with an average annual increase of 1.4 per cent each year. The use of intermediate purchases generally follows that of output.

However, when output is increasing faster than the use of intermediate purchases, the result is a gain in intermediate purchases productivity. From

1967 to 1994, intermediate purchases productivity gained 1.4 per cent each year, on average. The rates of change in intermediate purchases productivity were 3.0 per cent for the 1967-73 period, and 3.5 per cent for the 1973-79 period. The last period, 1979-94, shows a complete slowdown in the growth of this measure, to an average 0.0 per cent per year. The price of intermediate purchases for the refrigeration and heating equipment industry increased S. 1 per cent, on average, between 1967 and 1994. Producers are continually trying to discover ways of substituting one group of inputs for another, to reduce the cost of a given level of output.

A rise in price encourages substitution away from the relatively costly input for a cheaper alternative. In this industry, from 1967-73, the price of materials was increasing only 4.4 per cent each year, on average, while the cost of labour was increasing 7.8 per cent per year. The intermediate purchases effect was an average 1.3 per cent annually between 1967 and 1973. In the second period, 1973-79, this trend was reversed as labour became relatively inexpensive while materials became more costly. The intermediate purchases effect declined to an average-2.0 per cent per year in this interval. The last period shows the prices of materials and labour increasing at more equal annual average rates. The intermediate purchases effect was closer to zero, at an average annual rate of 0.6 per cent each year, because less incentive for substitution existed in this period. The 1992 Census of Manufactures details almost 40 categories of materials for the heating, air conditioning, and refrigeration equipment industry. Motors and generators made up the largest portion of the total value of these materials at 13 per cent. The second and third largest shares were for carbon steel and automatic temperature controls.

Refrigerant gases accounted for less than 1 per cent of the value of materials consumed by this industry in 1992, but this understates their importance to refrigeration and heating equipment manufacturers. CFC'S were used as an evaporative agent in many refrigeration and mobile-air conditioning applications. They also were used as a blowing agent to form the insulation that keeps the cold air inside the refrigerated space. CFC'S are very good at both of these functions. Being large, stable compounds, they have a very low thermal conductivity figure and are nontoxic, nonflammable, and noncorrosive. As insulation, CFC'S were blown into liquid plastic and forced, under pressure, into cavities between the walls of appliances.

There, they served as insulators and a stress member of the cabinet itself. Because CFC molecules are large, they do not escape readily through the solidified plastic, as oxygen or carbon dioxide would. The low thermal conductivity of CFC-based insulation allows the compressor to run less often, reducing the energy used by the product. The use of CFC-based insulation increased in the 1970s, so that manufacturers could comply with new regulations regarding the efficiency of their products. The refrigeration and heating equipment industry's inputs and output are regulated, to varying degrees, by the Montreal Protocol; and the U.S. Clean Air Act Amendments, National Appliance Energy Conservation Act, Energy Policy Act, and Toxic Substances Control Act. The refrigeration and heating equipment industry began using CFC'S as inputs in the production process in the 1930s. Decades later, the Montreal Protocol and Clean Air Act Amendments mandated that the industry substitute away from these materials to safeguard the atmosphere. Although the costs of developing the substitutes themselves were borne chiefly by the industrial inorganic chemicals industry, the refrigeration and heating equipment industry required new manufacturing techniques, because the ozone-safe coolants are not perfect substitutes for the originals. Production workers had to be trained to use the new materials, which are toxic, corrosive, and combustible-characteristics that CFC'S do not share. To handle these substitute coolants, new compressor, seal, and blower technology needed to be devised.

The development and adoption of these technologies used resources that might otherwise have gone towards improving efficiency in the production process. This could help explain the slowdown in multifactor productivity growth in the industry during the post-1979 period. After rising 3.6 per cent per year between 1967 and 1973 and 1.9 per cent per year between 1973 and 1979, multifactor productivity increased at an average annual rate of just 0.6 per cent in the 1979-94 period. Initially, the industry substituted hydrochlorofluorocarbons for CFC'S in the production process; HCFC'S do only 2 per cent to 10 per cent as much damage to the ozone layer as CFC'S.

However, their use is to become limited by the year 2003. The industry is already replacing these second-generation coolants with the third, hydrofluorocarbons. HFC'S do no damage to the ozone layer but they are a greenhouse gas and may become limited-use inputs in the future. The fourth-generation coolant may not be a chemical at all. Thermoacoustic cooling is a recent discovery in which sound and inert gas cool an enclosed space. The refrigeration and heating equipment industry will continue to face challenges arising from the need for safer coolants in its products; meeting those challenges might restrain productivity growth in the near future. Output per hour, or labour productivity, in the refrigeration and heating equipment industry increased at an average annual rate of 1.7 per cent between 1967 and 1994. Multifactor productivity for the same period gained 1.5 per cent. The industry experienced rapid growth in output and in both labour productivity and multifactor productivity between 1967 and 1973. A dramatic slowdown in all three measures occurred between 1973 and 1979, after which labour productivity rebounded somewhat.

A major market for this industry's products is in retrofit and reconstruction activities, which have grown consistently in recent years, in part because of legislation at the Federal level. Exports represent a significant portion of the quantity demanded of this industry. Some establishments generate more than 35 per cent of revenues from exports. Finally, a difficult challenge has been met by the refrigeration and heating equipment industry in that substitutes have had to be developed for a group of critical inputs, first chlorofluorocarbons, and then hydrochlorofluorocarbons.

PRODUCTIVITY IN REFRIGERATION EQUIPMENT, AND FURNACES

Output per employee hour in the manufacture of air conditioning, refrigeration, and warm-air heating equipment rose at an average annual rate of 1.3 per cent between 1967 and 1982, compared with 2.4 per cent a year for all of manufacturing. Output climbed 3.4 per cent a year during the period, and employee hours, 2.1 per cent. Strong expansion in the demand for the industry's residential, commercial, and industrial products, and rapid diffusion of basic improvements in metalworking technologies were among factors underlying the rising productivity trend. The improvement in the industry's productivity occurred mostly in the earlier part of the period reviewed. After 1973, output per employee hour did not change, as shown by the following tabulation of average annual rates of change:

- The industry's productivity rate for the 1967-73 period was 50 per cent again as high as for manufacturing, but thereafter the trends in the two rate diverged. Year-to-year swings in the industry's productivity were comparatively moderate. These swings ranged between a 9-per cent increase in 1972 and a 16-per cent decrease in 1972. Year-to-year increases in productivity outnumbered decreases by 12 to 2. In the years when productivity dropped, output dipped less than employee hours. Tnus, in 1975 and 1980, productivity declined 16 per cent and 7 per cent while output dipped 34 per cent and 16 per cent, and employee hours, 22 per cent and 10 per cent. In 1974, productivity rose as a 6-per cent decline in output was outdistanced by a 9-per cent decline in employee hours. Output and demand

The manufacture of air conditioning and refrigeration equipment and of warm-air furnaces involves the production of heat transfer apparatus for residential, commercial, and industrial applications, as well as for hospitals, marine vessels, freight and passenger vehicles, and many specialized applications. Heat transfer equipment here includes unitary air conditioners; room air conditioners; commercial refrigeration equipment; as well as heat pumps and dehumidifiers. The industry, in addition, manufactures compressors and condensers, not only for its own final output, but also for home refrigerators The industry's output rose at an average annual rate of 3.4 per cent between 1967 and 1982. The rate for the earlier part of the period ran four times higher than that for all manufacturing, but dropped below the all-manufacturing rate during 1973-82:

- Among reasons underlying the industry's output growth, and underpinning it after 1973, have been exports. As a proportion of value of shipments, exports by the industry nearly doubled between the earlier and the later period studied here-from 8 per cent to 14 per cent. For manufacturing as a whole, the export share in the value of shipments increased less markedly-from 6 per cent in 1972 to 10 per cent in 1980.

The much slowed expansion in the industry's output from 1973 forward corresponds to trends in the output of its major product groups, which in turn parallel the trends in underlying demand from the industry' most important markets. Thus, the production of heat transfer equipment other than unitary or room air conditioners or warm-air furnaces increased at a rate nearly 10 times higher over the 1967-73 periods than during the 1973-82 span. The increase in the rate had resulted largely from strong demand for motor vehicle air conditioners. Such demand was associated with an increase in motor vehicle output of close to 6 per cent a year in 1967-73. The subsequent tapering of output growth mirrored a falling-off in the annual rate of motor vehicle output by-1.0 per cent for 1973-82. Likewise, output rates of growth of unitary air conditioners and commercial refrigeration equipment slowed after 1973; for warm air furnaces, the rate declined.

This pattern was linked largely to developments in construction. The average annual rate of change in the constant-dollar value of new residential housing construction, for example, declined from around 9 per cent for 1967-73 to 2 per cent thereafter; that for commercial structures, from 15 per cent to 9 per cent; and that for hospitals turned from a 5-per cent annual gain to a 4-per cent annual decrease. Only industrial construction evidenced a contrary trend, with a 10-per cent annual decline in the earlier period giving way to a 3.5-per cent annual rise after 1973. Leaving aside the medium-term swings, the industry's output has been sustained over the longer run by rapidly growing use of central and room air conditioning in homes, as well as more gradual increases in offices and other commercial space, hospitals, and probably in factories.

Increases in the size of homes and other structures generated the shift in demand from room air conditioners to central systems and spurred the demand for warm-air furnaces, which function through the same air circulation system as central air conditioners. In the middle and late 1960's, 28 per cent of all new homes were equipped with central air conditioners; that proportion rose to 43 per cent between 1970 and 1975, and to 66 per cent by 1982. Square footage per new home, to which the size of heat transfer equipment is linked, increased 9 per cent between the mid-1960's and the early 1980's. The proportion of homes wired for room air conditioners more than doubled between the mid-1960's and the mid-1970's, to 53 per cent, but it did not rise much thereafter. Warm-air ducted heating systems in occupied housing units rose by about one-third between 1970 and 1975, but by only 7 per cent between 1975 and 1980. For offices, shopping centres, and hospitals, pertinent data on air conditioning and forced warm-air systems are available only fore some recent years.

A survey conducted in the early 1970's, 91 per cent of all commercial office buildings had central air conditioning, and 67 per cent had forced-air heating systems. For shopping centres, the comparable figures were close to 100 per cent in 1977; and for hospitals and nursing homes, they read 97 per cent and 56 per cent in 1975. These data suggest that industry output is sustained not only by the net increase in such structures, but from replacement and retrofitting with more energy-efficient equipment as well. In 1981, for example, more than half of total residential expenditures on air conditioning and heating systems were for replacement. Furthermore, the introduction of more energy-efficient heat transfer equipment since about 1975 has also bolstered output.

For the same wattage per hour of electric energy input, higher equipment output capacities, as measured in British Thermal Units, have been achieved. Thus, in 1976, the Air Conditioning and Refrigeration Institute listed 56 per cent of new unitary air conditioners as having energy efficiency ratios of between 6.5 and 7.4, and 18 per cent with ratios of 7.5 to 8.4. By 1981, the proportion of the lower efficiency units had shrunk to 37 per cent, while that of the higher efficiency equipment had expanded to 35 per cent. Employment in the air conditioning, refrigeration, and warm-air heating equipment industry numbered 129,000 persons in mid-1984. It rose 32 per cent between 1967 and 1982, or at an average annual rate of 2.2 per cent. Employment reached a peak of 130,000 persons in 1979, and subsequently retreated. This decline was attributable to a 21-per cent contraction in production worker jobs between 1979 and 1982, as compared with a 9-per cent loss in nonproduction worker jobs. Over the longer term, trends in employee hours displayed patterns of acceleration and retardation similar to those noted for production and output trends. Employee hours in the industry rose during the first 6 years of the review period at an average annual rate much greater than for all manufacturing. Subsequently the rate plummeted:

- Production workers accounted for 70 per cent of total employment, which was the same proportion in both 1967 and 1982-nonproduction workers made up the balance. The number of women workers more than doubled over the period, raising their proportion of total employment from 14 per cent to 21 per cent. Underlying this increase may have been a shift in the skill composition of the industry's workers to more assembly-type jobs. The rise in the industry's average hourly earnings also slowed relative to the manufacturing average. In 1967, the former was 104 per cent of the latter, compared with 96 per cent in 1981.

Overtime ran somewhat below the manufacturing average during the review period, suggesting that firms in the industry were inclined to hire new production workers, rather than assign overtime when the workload exceeded certain limits. Turnover rates nonetheless lagged; over the 1967-81 span, they averaged 89 per cent of the manufacturing average for accessions, and 91 per cent of that for separations.

Thus, it appears that employment stability was somewhat greater in the industry than in manufacturing generally. The skill composition of the industry's work force differs from that for manufacturing as a whole. In 1980, craft workers accounted for 17 per cent of total industry employment, compared with 19 per cent for all manufacturing. Operatives, however, accounted for a significantly larger proportion-48 per cent, compared with 43 per cent. The larger component of operatives stemmed from the proportionately greater number of assembly workers in the industry than in all manufacturing.

The proportion of metalworking operatives in the industry was more than twice as high as for manufacturing generally. By contrast, the occupational distribution of white-collar workers was similar to that for manufacturing.

Professional and technical workers made up 8 per cent of the industry's workforce; clerical workers, 12 per cent; and managers and administrators, 5 per cent. Investment in plant and equipment Like manufacturing establishments generally, the air conditioning, refrigeration, and warm-air heating equipment industry installed new production equipment at a fairly high rate over the 1967-81 periods.

However, unlike other manufacturing establishments, firms in the industry spent at a much higher rate during the earlier than the latter part of the review period. For all manufacturing, the reverse held true:

- The industry's high rate of capital spending in the early part of the period resulted from pressures on capacity, related to high output growth rates. With the abatement of output growth after 1973, fixed investment slowed.

The proportion of total fixed investment spent on equipment is as follows:

- The comparatively high proportion of expenditures for equipment is reflected in the data on the modernization of the industry's metalworking machinery, as reported by the American Machinist. The rates shown, however, obscure large year-to-year fluctuations in the industry's capital spending. This instability was far more marked for the industry than for manufacturing generally. For example, in 1975, the industry's plant and equipment expenditures plummeted 41 per cent and in 1977, they soared 56 per cent. Manufacturing recorded a 9-per cent drop, and a 21-per cent rise for the same 2 years.

Fixed assets per employee in the industry were 79 per cent of the manufacturing average in 1980, compared with 76 per cent during 1972 and

1974-76. The rise in the ratio partially reflected the cumulative effects of earlier equipment installations and new plant construction on the value of the industry's fixed assets. More efficient technology Air conditioning and refrigeration equipment essentially consists of a compressor driven by an electric motor, and two coils-the condenser, in which the refrigerant is compressed to a liquid, and the evaporator, in which the refrigerant expands into the gaseous state, enabling it to absorb heat from the space being cooled.

The heat is transferred from the environment with the aid of fins, mounted upon the evaporator coil. Warm-air furnaces built by the industry are mostly gas-fueled forced-air devices. They include a combustion chamber and a motor-driven blower. The sheet metal housing that shields the equipment is manufactured by the industry, but controls and motors normally are not. Advances in the manufacture of air conditioners, refrigeration equipment, and warm-air furnaces have been linked chiefly to technological progress in metalworking machinery, welding, methods of storage and transfer of parts, and assembly. The are also related to improvements in product design.

The production of air conditioners, refrigeration equipment, and warm-air furnaces basically involves the cutting and forming of metal, as well as welding, brazing, and soldering of components. Efforts to improve efficiency usually focus upon these operations, and on plant layout. Auxiliary operations, such as materials handling, painting, testing, and packaging have received increased attention in recent years. The most recent American Machinist inventory of metal-working equipment indicates that, in 1983, 30 per cent of all metalcutting and metalforming machine tools used in the industry were at most 10 years old. In 1968, the proportion was the same for metalcutting tools, but only 25 per cent for metalforming tools.

The industry has steadily improved its metalworking equipment, by and large maintaining the same proportion of new equipment during 1973-83 as during 1958-68. The higher end of the age distribution, however, shows an increase in the proportion of older metalworking equipment in the industry. The share of metalcutting machine tools 20 years and older rose from 25 per cent in 1968 to 32 per cent in 1983, and the share of metalforming tools, from 25 per cent to 37 per cent. However, the relative increase in older machine tools cannot be readily interpreted as a loss in efficiency, inasmuch as the American Machinist inventory does not take into account the retrofitting of older machines with up-to-date components and control devices.

The efficiency of the industry's metalworking equipment has been significantly enhanced by an 11-fold rise in the number of numerically controlled machine tools. In 1983, NC machine tools accounted for 13 per cent and 17 per cent of metalcutting and metalforming tools 9 years old or less. In 1968, when NC machine tools were not yet widely diffused, the proportions were less than 1 per cent. The percentage increase in the number of NC tools understates the increase in the output capabilities which the installation of such tools spells. The American Machinist, the number of machine tools in all metalworking industries declined from 16 per 1,000 population in 1968 to fewer than 10 in 1983. "This represents in part the greater productivity of machine tools, in part the simplification of design of many products, so that less machining is required."

This statement also applies to the industry reviewed here: the number of machine tools in the industry's shops dropped by one-third between 1968 and 1983, while output more than doubled. Thus, the output capability of metalworking equipment in the industry rose nearly threefold over the study period, with that rise likely to be largely attributable to NC-equipped machine tools. Examples of how improved metalworking technology has helped to raise output per hour may be drawn from the sheet metal operations in the industry's larger shops, and from the fabrication of some of the major components of its products. In punching sheet metal, templates were conventionally affixed to the press so as to obtain required shapes.

Templates have been increasingly replaced, however, by taped instructions fed to the press, which greatly speeds output and ensures greater precision of the finished shape. Setup time of the press has been reduced to as little as one-twentieth of the conventional operation. In a related operation, the press, after the sheet metal blank has been placed automatically, is programmed to select 1 of up to 30 built-in punching tools from its turret, and to activate the tool selected. Bending of metal parts has likewise been increasingly automated, the bending apparatus being preset to several sequential settings Setup time here has declined to an estimated 10 per cent of what it had been prior to automation.

Despite their being automated, these metalworking processes continue to require close monitoring by trained operators. The operator may monitor two or more machines at the same time, or may be engaged in such auxiliary tasks as placing and removing work pieces. Some of the more advanced shops in the industry feature such machine tools as high-capacity drills, which may drill all the holes in an air conditioning compressor vessel in one or two operations. Older drilling machines, still widely in use, have much lower capacity and speed. Automatic tool wear adjustment is normally also a feature of NC machine tools, but at times this feature is not desired or used.

Replacement of a tool bit is then left to the discretion of the operator assigned to monitor the entire machining process. In small-lot production, loading and unloading the work piece may be done manually. Improved productivity in the fabrication of air conditioning equipment components during the review period is exemplified by the coil manufacturing process. The coil is the heart of the heat exchanger. The refrigerant is pumped through it to absorb heat from the surrounding space. The coil originates as tubing on a large roll. In the more advance shops, the rolled tubing is automatically straightened, cut to length as specified in, and controlled by, a taped programme, and automatically bent to the shape of a U. This operation has come to be performed by one person, where 10 years or so ago, four persons were required to shear the tube manually and insert it into a bending device. The U-shaped coil is inserted into a nest of aluminum fins. The fins aid in absorbing heat from the refrigerant. The fabrication of fins is usually highly mechanized, precut aluminum blanks being punched to form them, and to accommodate the coils. Numerically controlled punch presses featuring up to 27 spindles are used in the larger shops.

However, the number of blanks that may be punched at a time is limited because punching tends to break rather than cut the metal, and breaking forms rims that cannot be tolerated. Where fins are produced in quantity, punch presses may not be numerically controlled, because longer setup times are usually justified by the longer runs. Loading and unloading of the punch presses has usually been mechanized in the larger plants, so that the fins emerge stacked as nests. The coils are then inserted manually. Manual insertion is still preferred because it prevents "binding." The operator can readily control the pressure he exerts in inserting the individual coils, which is not the case for mechanical insertion where undue pressure may damage the coil. The coils are then brazed together or soldered to form a continuous loop. Brazing or soldering is still performed by means of hand-operated devices to ensure leak proof joints and the continuity of the loop, so as not to "blind-alley" them).

The fabrication of reciprocating compressors provides other examples of the reduction in unit labour requirements which the industry seeks. Compressors, driven by electric motors function to increase the density of the refrigerant to the liquid state. Basically, the reciprocating compressor consists of a piston sitting on a rod connected to the motor; and a cyclinder, against the head of which the piston moves, compressing the refrigerant. Where compressor components are produced in quantity, multistation machinery arranged in circular form has come to be used. Yet, loading and unloading of the workpiece, and transferring it between groups of dial machinery, is still widely done manually. Some establishments began to install automatic transfer lines towards the end of the review period, affording automatic positioning of the workpiece, as well as automation of most other metalworking operations. Transfer lines require usually one-half or less of the labour per unit of the more conventional equipment; so-called "uptime," that is the time during which the machinery is fully operation, is estimated to be 20 per cent higher.

Changes in product design have, in some instances been combined with technological advances. Thus, a cylindrically shaped air conditioning machine has been developed that permits several hundred feet of continual coil to be wrapped around a mandrel in one mechanical process. This increases the heat transfer area, hence the efficiency of the machine. It also minimizes the jointing of coil ends and thus, the leakage of refrigerant. Fins consist of many hundreds of tiny aluminum pieces glued to the tubing's surface. Unit labour requirements in mounting such tubing are estimated at 20 to 30 per cent of those for the manual insertion of U-shaped coils into nests of fins and the fabrication of such fins. Product design and technological advance have also been combined in the case of a thermostatic valve body for automotive air conditioning.

After the valve body was redesigned, it could be fabricated by means of a 43-spindle metalworking machine which combines automatic indexing, milling, drilling, counter boring, tapping, and other operations. Material costs were reduced, assembly facilitated, and quality improved. The machine replaced as many as 11 standard machines run by 30 workers. A fundamental design change in air conditioning equipment and warm-air furnaces during the review period made them more energy-efficient.

The relevant design changes usually involved finer tolerances, hence greater precision machining, especially of compressor components. Precision machining in turn has been facilitated by-and has spurred the adoption of-NC metalworking machinery. Functional testing, furthermore, has been upgraded by such electronic devices as automatic calibration stations, which can be programmed for many settings at a time, and which require little attendance. Assembly appears also to have been improved by the better "fit-up" of the more precisely machine components. Industry structure Industry concentration increased over the period reviewed; in 1977, the 8 largest companies accounted for 51 per cent of the industry's value of shipments, compared with an estimated 45 per cent in 1967. The 20 largest companies accounted for 67 per cent of the value of shipments in 1977, as against 62 per cent in 1967. Moreover, the concentration ratio for 1967 was higher than for 1963.

These increases suggest underlying growth over time in economies of scale, a factor that usually engenders productivity improvement. Employment, too, was concentrated in the larger establishments. In 1977, 50 per cent of the industry's employees worked in 31 of the 860 establishments classified in the industry. At the lower end of the employment size stratification, just over 10 per cent of all employees in the industry worked in 75 per cent of all establishments. It is noteworthy that the size distribution of capital expenditures closely followed the size distribution of employment-such that, for example, nearly one-half of all such expenditures were made by only 4 per cent of all establishments in the industry.In line with the increase in concentration ratios, the larger establishments raised their share of the industry's total employment over time.

Outlook Continued productivity improvement is indicated for the industry. As the American Machinist inventory of metalworking equipment in the industry suggests, diffusion of NC machine tools is far from complete. If past trends in diffusion persist, productivity gains are likely to be generated. Moreover, the larger, more advanced shops plan to install flexible manufacturing systems, which will make small-lot production of larger air conditioning, refrigeration, and heating equipment more efficient. One establishment, which is installing a FM system to produce reciprocal compressors, expects direct labour requirements to be reduced by more than 80 per cent, as compared with conventional production methods. Another establishment, which produces large evaporators in lots of less than 100, also plans to fabricate them by FM methods. Such evaporators require up to 5,000 different metal shapes. In combination with NC machine tools, plant management expects FM to save up to 50 per cent in unit labour requirements, cut lead time by nearly one-half, and cope with declining lot size and more exacting tolerances more efficiently.

Management also foresees significant savings in materials and inventory costs. The cutting of steel, a large-scale operation in the bigger shops, should also become progressively more automated. The cutting and punching of steel is often still done by an operator using templates and judging by sight how to minimize waste in laying them out. Templates an d operator judgment have begun to be replaced by computer-instructed cutting machines, where the computer calculates the most economical distribution of cuts. Templates and operator judgment have begun to be replaced by computer-instructed cutting machines, where the computer calculates the most economical distribution of cuts. The computer memory also records odd pieces of steel that might be used in future work.

With template labour and layout estimation by an operator eliminated, five times as much steel may be processed in the same period as previously. Also, material savings of up to 60 per cent are expected. In welding operations, robots are increasingly being used, but for complex surfaces, skilled welders who may be subject to certification are still necessary. The use of a certified welder is frequently required by a code authority, such as the American Society of Mechanical Engineers, or by a customer, such as the U.S. Navy.

Plant managers generally expect more versatile robots, which sense the complexities of the surfaces to be joined, to become available. But the laborsaving potential of such robots hinges upon the extent to which code requirements are modified. The efficiency of auxiliary operations in the industry is also likely to improve. Thus, while many plants feature partially automated storage of parts and components, work stations are still usually supplied by means of manually operated carts or small trucks. Some plants in the industry which produce in quantity expect to install fully automated storage and delivery systems that convey parts to work stations upon command. Management in one such plant expects labour savings of 50 to 75 per cent, compared with the partially automated system, as well as the near elimination of damage from multiple handling. The occupational composition of the industry's employment is not expected to change very much during the 1980's, except for growth in the proportions of engineers, engineering and science technicians, and computer specialists. Employment in these occupational categories has been projected by the Bureau of Labour Statistics to rise 27 per cent between 1980 and 1990, compared with a 15-per cent increase for employment in the industry as a whole. The proportion of craftworkers and operatives has been projected to remain unchanged.

The projections signify increased reliance upon engineers and technicians in designing and monitoring more efficient production processes. The projections do not, however, indicate an accelerating trend towards either "deskilling" craftworkers or displacing operatives. In 1990, craftworkers will constitute an estimated 16 per cent of total industry employment, and operatives, 48 per cent-the same as in 1980. The proportion of professional, technical, and related workers in the industry is estimated to rise from 8 per cent to just under 9 per cent.

3

Methodology of Business Process Development in Hotel

THE LODGING INDUSTRY

Lodging (or a holiday accommodation) is a type of residential accommodation. People who travel and stay away from home for more than a day need lodging for sleep, rest, safety, shelter from cold temperatures or rain, storage of luggage and access to common household functions.

Lodgings may be *self catering* in which case no food is laid on but cooking facilities are available.

Lodging is done in a hotel, hostel or hostal, a private home (commercial, *i.e.* a bed and breakfast, a guest house, a vacation rental, or non-commercially, with members of hospitality services or in the home of friends), in a tent, caravan/camper (often on a campsite). In addition there are make-shift solutions.

The ability to add value and to create a sustainable hotel project ultimately starts from the first brush on paper and opportunities for this are all the way through to the final touch of paint on the finished product.

The crisis has had a huge impact on all real estate development, including hotels. But due to the gap between hotel supply and demand across the country there remains great opportunities for hotel projects.

Hotels are typically more complex to develop compared with other asset classes, as their design is tailored to the brand operating the business.

The design of these can also have an impact on the overall profitability of the hotel operation, as design deficiencies affect the operation of a hotel and ultimately have a negative impact on the bottom line — and hence asset value.

PRE-OPENING STAFF PLAN

The pre-opening staffing begins with an organizational chart with all positions. Once the titles and staff counts by position are finalized, then spreadsheets are created to include the position titles, start dates, pay rates, bonus, transfer allowances, and number of full-time equivalents (FTEs) for all positions. The pre-opening staff plan is a comprehensive document that states who is hired, when they start, how much they are paid, and whether or not they are allocated a relocation allowance and benefit costs. Each of these pieces is used to build the pre-opening staff plan budget. If hiring has already begun and the opening date changes, the budget must be amended. Hiring a position that does not conform to the plan, such as bringing on a renowned chef one month earlier than planned, also requires the budget be modified.

PRE-OPENING BUDGET

The OPM develops and manages the preopening budget.This budget typically consists of three major categories; labour cost (40 per cent), sales and marketing efforts (40 per cent), and miscellaneous (20 per cent).

The labour cost is taken directly from the pre-opening staff plan. Sales and marketing activities comprise advertising, collateral, public relations, and travel to see clients.

Rounding out the budget are all of the miscellaneous items. These include office space rental before moving into the hotel, utilities (power, water, Internet, and telephone), human resources recruitment (ads, headhunters, drug testing, etc.), training materials, association dues, and licenses and permits (business, liquor, sales tax collection, etc.).

If the hotel opening date is delayed for any reason, the pre-opening budget is affected. Additional costs include labour, office rent, utilities, and marketing efforts. If the opening date changes within three weeks of the original plan, major costs are encountered, as most of the staff is already hired.

OPERATIONAL SUPPLIES AND EQUIPMENT (OS&E)

The largest and most complex aspect of the OPM's responsibility is specifying, quantifying, and budgeting for the operational supplies and equipment (OS&E) list.This budget typically pencils out to $8,000 to $10,000 per guest room for a typical four-star property. The list of goods typically exceeds 2,500 line items. Add a little more for a full-service resort; deduct a little for an in-city business hotel.

The OS&E comprises all of the items that are not nailed down, with the exception of the furniture, fixtures, and equipment (FF&E). The FF&E is typically specified and ordered by the interior designer. Typical guest room items include bedding (frames, box springs, mattresses, mattress pads, sheets, pillows, pillowcases, towels, etc.), clock radios, hangers, laundry bags, laundry tickets, iron, ironing board, ironing board organizer, luggage rack, guest amenities (soap, shampoo, lotion, etc.), hair dryer, shower curtains, and shower curtain hooks.

Housekeeping equipment includes vacuums (guest room and wide-area units), carpet shampooers, carpet extractors, housekeeper carts, laundry bins, garbage trucks, valet delivery carts, and shelving, to name a few of many items. Housekeeping must also keep an inventory of guest request items including humidifiers, dehumidifiers, cribs, high chairs, rollaway beds, bedboards, spare pillows, towels, amenities, refrigerators, laundry soap, and so on.

ON-LINE PRICING: AN ANALYSIS OF HOTEL COMPANY PRACTICES

Both industry cost structure and the perishable nature of the product make effective distribution particularly important in the hotel sector. A hotel room left unsold on any particular night cannot be stored and subsequently offered to the customer at a later date. Thus, selling each room each night at an optimum price is critical to a hotel's long-term success. To achieve this, hotel companies use a variety of different distribution channels to help sell their product, and also manipulate price in response to demand using sophisticated yield management systems in an attempt to maximize revenues. While direct sales are most common, extensive use is normally made of a variety of intermediaries, including travel agents, tour operators, marketing consortia, and representative companies. However, the importance of electronic routes has grown significantly in recent years.

Statistics quoted in the Horwath Worldwide Hotel Industry Studies, direct reservations fell from approximately 39% in 1995 to just 33% in 1999, with the corresponding growth being focused exclusively in electronic channels. And while hotels continue to make extensive use of the travel agent-orientated Global Distribution Systems (GDS), end user consumer adoption of the Internet as a mainstream commerce medium has prompted a change in the way in which the hotel product is being distributed.

Table. Composition of Worldwide Hotel Advanced Reservations

Composition of Advanced Reservations	1995	1996	1997	1998	1999
Direct enquiry	38.3	36.9	35.1	34.0	33.5
Own reservations system	18.9	14.5	14.0	14.7	14.2
Independent reservations system	6.0	5.2	5.3	4.3	5.1
Travel agents	15.7	18.1	19.8	20.7	20.4
Tour operator	12.7	16.5	18.1	16.4	15.9
Hotel representatives	8.4 (Other)	5.7	4.3	6.5	5.9
Transportation company		2.3	2.0	1.6	2.2
Web site/Internet		0.8	1.4	1.8	2.8

The Web has dramatically changed the way people communicate, research information, make decisions, and particularly the way in which they buy goods and services. Travel products in particular have proven to be some of the most suitable for sale online.

The typical profile of an Internet user—affluent, frequent traveller who spends above average on leisure and entertainment—is an attractive market for travel suppliers. Furthermore, from a consumer perspective, in an increasingly wired world, purchasing travel online has become faster, easier, and more convenient than contacting a travel agent or telephoning a supplier directly. As a result, online travel revenues are forecast to grow sharply. For example, online travel sales will more than triple in the next 5 years from US$24 billion in 2001 to US$64 billion in 2007.

Booking volumes are also forecast to climb, with the Travel Industry Association of America estimating that by 2002 between 6% and 10% of all travel reservations will originate on the Web. This will make travel the highest grossing online product, nearly doubling that of PC hardware—the traditional top selling product. E-Commerce analysts Jupiter Media Metrix are even more enthusiastic, predicting that over 22% of all travel bookings will be made online by 2007—an 11% increase over the next 5 years.

Key to successful selling online is the issue of price. Recent research has shown that consumers have become more value conscious. For example, a recent study by BIGResearch found that nearly three quarters of travel consumers were unwilling to buy online unless they felt they were getting a good deal. Furthermore, studies by Gomez, Hospitality Sales and Marketing Association International, the Travel Industry Association of America, Jeong and Lambert, and PhoCusWright have all identified price as being one of the key motivating factors that encourages consumers to purchase travel online.

For example, the PhoCusWright study found that competitive pricing is the best way to attract customers. When travellers who haven't bought online were asked what would encourage them to do so, 64% said that saving money would make them more interested. No other benefit—saving time, getting bonus loyalty club points, more control, or obtaining better information—came close to this level of response.

HOTEL PRICING ON THE WEB

Recent studies have shown that online travel purchasers tend to be price driven. For example, according to Yesawich, Pepperdine and Brown, almost 6 out of 10 leisure travellers now actively seek the "lowest possible price" for travel services. Similarly, a recent Forrester Research study found that 66% of all buyers used an online discount in the past 12 months to buy travel online, and a study by the Joint Hospitality Industry Congress found that there is a real expectation among consumers that Internet prices will be lower than those in the "bricks and mortar" world. Such a perception has developed for several reasons. First, many of the most wellknown Internet retailers compete with traditional outlets based, to a large extent, on price. As a result, there is an assumption among Web users that the same is true for travel products.

Secondly, many consumers are aware of the lower distribution costs associated with Web channels. As Jack Geddes, Managing Director Sales and Marketing Asia, Radisson Hotels Worldwide, has pointed out "Consumers now understand that suppliers are cutting costs through this channel and expect savings to be passed onto them, as well as being rewarded for making the booking themselves".

Such expectations are being reinforced by the budget airline sector, which offers significant discounts for online bookings. Companies such as EasyJet, RyanAir, and Buzz estimate that by avoiding telesales and travel agents, they can make savings of up to 30%—which they pass on to customers in the form of lower fares. Lastly, many hotels use the Web to sell last minute deals—packages at relatively low prices but with short lead times. While such promotions can help dispose of distressed inventory, they have also resulted in the public associating rooms sold over the Internet with cheaper prices.

These factors have combined to make consumers associate online booking with good value. However, in the case of hotel own branded Web sites, industry practice seems to be the opposite of theory. In their 1999 survey, O'Connor and Horan found that, in the majority of cases, rates obtained over hotel Web sites were significantly higher than those obtained by contacting the hotel company's Central Reservations Office. Often the rate quoted by the company's Web site was substantially higher, despite the associated lower cost of distribution.

However, this study was limited in that it only focused on direct sales over hotel chains' own branded Web sites. Hotel electronic distribution is rapidly evolving and a large number of other online consumerfocused channels are now available, with most chains using multiple routes to get their product to the consumer. The availability of so many alternative points-of-sale poses some interesting questions. Is there consistency between the rates and availability being offered over alternative channels? Research has shown that consumers shopping for travel online almost always check more than one site before purchasing. Jupiter Media Metrix, for the hotel product 10% of bookers visit one site, another 43% visit two or three sites, and 22% visit four or more sites. Online purchasers have become increasingly intolerant of inconsistent information, and may react to disparate rates on different channels by purchasing from the company's competitor. Furthermore, if rates are not consistent across channels, is any particular route consistently cheaper? And lastly, if rates are different over alternative channels, is the pricing strategy logical from both the consumer's and the hotel's perspective?

METHODOLOGY AND LIMITATION OF THE STUDY

Hotel Internet use have been limited. Murphy focused on rating the content of hotel Web sites, while Van Hoof and Combrink attempted to measure managers' perceptions of, and attitudes towards, the Internet. Web reservations facilities were investigated in detail in a prior paper by the author. However, the issue of pricing over multiple simultaneous travel distribution channels does not appear to have been the subject of extensive systematic research to date. The objectives, therefore, of this study were to analyse the rates being offered to consumers over hotel electronic distribution channels and to subsequently identify the pricing strategies being used by the hotel companies.

Obviously, an exhaustive analysis of the rates being offered by all hotels would be impossible. However, as the use of both technology and electronic distribution has in the past been lead by the major international hotel chains, an analysis of their efforts was thought to be indicative of developments in the field. As a result, it was decided to focus the study on the Behaviour of the top 50 international hotel brands.

While this strategy means that the findings are not representative of the industry as a whole and thus the results not generally applicable, it does allow an accurate benchmark of trends as they currently stand to be established. The companies were chosen based on the ranking of the top 50 hotel brands published in *Hotels* magazine in July 2000. Two companies were removed from the listing as they are in effect resorts, only distribute their rooms as part of packages, and thus their products are not directly comparable. Furthermore, three companies neither offered online reservations facilities on their own Web site nor were they listed on any of the other channels studied. Thus, the results reflect the findings for 45 hotel brands for which consistent data could be found.

Five major types of electronic B2C distribution channels were identified from the literature and leading examples of each category selected for inclusion in the study. In addition to the chain's own Web site, these included channels that draw their data/ reservations engine from the Global Distribution Systems; those that are based upon the databases/reservation engine of the Switch companies; and pure Web-based channels that require their inventory/ reservations database to be maintained online.

While not collectively exhaustive, these represent the majority of the non-direct-to-hotel reservations. Omitted from the study were the "nameyour-price"/"auction" style Web sites, which, due to their bidding pricing structure, were not comparable and thus could not be included. Voice channels were also incorporated into the study for comparison purposes by analysing the rates offered by the toll-free number to the Central Reservations Office (CRO). Data were collected by iteratively reserving a double room for specified dates in a selected property from each of the brands using each of the distribution channels. Where the product requested was available on the system, both the number of rates displayed and the lowest rate available were recorded for analysis. The hotel company's Central Reservation Office was subsequently telephoned and the same product requested. In the latter case, the first rate quoted by the telesales agent was recorded. This process was repeated for five sets of alternative dates to reduce the possibility of error due to systems malfunctions or other exceptional circumstances. The order in which the channels were polled was also varied to minimize the effect of yield management systems.

NUMBER OF CHANNELS USED

Each of the major hotel brands uses multiple simultaneous distribution channels, with the mean number of channels being 4.68. The most commonly used channels were over voice through the company's Central Reservation Office and through the company's corporate Web site. Those companies that did not use voice were in the economy sector, and, although outside the scope of the study, it could be speculated that their abstinence from using this channel could be a reaction to the high operating costs of this channel. The level of use of a company's own Web site was also found to be high, with nearly 97% of the brands surveyed offering the facility to make an online reservation in this manner. It is interesting to note that this represents a considerable advancement in comparison to prior surveys, which found that only approximately 50% of the major hotel companies provided such online facilities. Thus, there appears to have been major growth in the use of the Web as a direct selling medium by the hotel industry over the past 2 years.

Table. Channels Used by the Major Hotel Brands

Channel	Number	Percentage
Hotel company Web site	44	97%
Microsoft Expedia	38	84%
Travelocity.com	35	78%
TravelWeb	34	76%
WorldRes	14	31%
Voice (CRO)	44	97%

In contrast, usage of the other channels investigated was lower. Approximately four fifths of the major brands used the GDS-based intermediaries Microsoft Expedia and Travelocity, three quarters used TravelWeb, and only approximately one third used WorldRes at the time of the study. These findings are not in themselves surprising. Both Expedia and Travelocity draw their data from the major GDS, and as the majority of the hotel brands represented in the study are business focused, representation on the GDS and thus their subsequent listing on these channels was to be expected. Similarly, TravelWeb draws its data from THISCO (The Hotel Industry Switching Company), and thus any of the hotel brands that use this as their switch service could be expected to leverage their investment by make inventory available for sale over TravelWeb—the switch's consumer-focused

Website. However, the low usage of WorldRes is surprising. With the exception of through a company's own Web site, using WorldRes has the lowest potential transaction cost and thus would appear to be an attractive channel for use by hotel companies. However, in practice, it does not list the properties of many of the major hotel brands.

Examination of its property database reveals a large percentage of independent hotels, bed and breakfasts, and smaller hotel chains, yet the question has to be asked as to why the major brands do not exploit this distribution channel?

Rates Available

With the exception of the toll-free number (where the first rate offered was accepted), each of the channels analysed offered multiple rates to the customer.

Each channel presented an average of five rates in response to the request, with more being offered to the customer in the case of Travelocity than through the other channels surveyed.

Table. Number of Rates Offered to the Customer

Channel	Mean	SD	Maximum	Minimum
Hotel company Web site	4.27	3.6	19	1
Microsoft Expedia	3.66	1.4	5	1
Travelocity.com	6.07	3.3	16	2
TravelWeb	5.62	3.6	17	1
WorldRes	4.58	3.8	12	1
Voice (CRO)	1.00	—	—	—

Presenting a variety of rates to the customer has both positive and negative implications. From a positive perspective, it offers the potential customer a choice and allows them to match their needs with the products being sold. On the other hand, presenting multiple rates without adequate product differentiation can create confusion in the mind of the customer as to what they are getting for their money.

This is best demonstrated by an example encountered in the study, where a property had 17 different rates available for a particular date on TravelWeb, with few (if any) discernable differences identifiable in the rate descriptions. Clearly such a scenario would be confusing and frustrating for any customer wishing to book that property.

In terms of which channel is consistently cheapest, such a broad generalization is difficult to make. However, based on an analysis of the rates found in the study and making allowances for rounding and currency conversions, it can be seen that prices across each of the channels were comparable, with the average price for the requested room being in the range of US$163. There were two noticeable exceptions to this trend. Microsoft

Expedia was consistently marginally cheaper than any of the other channels and the rates found on WorldRes were in general more expensive.

Table. Average Rates Offered to the Customer

Channel	Mean	SD
Hotel company Web site	159	112
Microsoft Expedia	152	116
Travelocity.com	166	134
TravelWeb	162	115
WorldRes	181	168
Voice (CRO)	163	117

Such findings are surprising in that, as was explained earlier, the transaction costs associated with each channel vary greatly. Expedia, as an online travel agency, has a higher cost of distribution from the hotel's perspective, and thus it would be logical to assume that rates offered over this channel would reflect these higher associated costs. Similarly, because WorldRes's transaction costs are relatively low in comparison with the other channels surveyed, it should in theory be offering the cheapest rates if hotel companies were matching their rates to the associated cost of using the channel. However, in practice, in general the rates quoted on WorldRes were the highest found on any the channels surveyed. Clearly, when selling the hotel product online, there does not appear to be a relationship between the cost of using the distribution channel and the rate offered.

However, simply examining broad averages often hides valuable information. If the brands studied are subdivided into classifications based on their targeted market segment, a different picture emerges.

Hotels at the lower end of the market are far more likely to offer consistent rates across all channels used. While it could be speculated that the reason for this might be because economy properties are more likely to have a single fixed price for their product irrespective of demand, it could also be due to a more consistent pricing strategy on the part of the hotel companies involved when addressing a relatively price-sensitive market. Furthermore, it can be seen that consumers at the lower ends of the market are far more likely to obtain lower rates through direct channels. For economy brands, direct sales over the company's own Web site was cheapest nearly one quarter of the time, with a further 46% offering the same rate irrespective of the channel used. Thus, a consumer making a reservation for an economy room on a hotel company's Web site would find the cheapest rate on this channel three times out four. With mid-priced products, the chain Web site is even more likely to give the best rate, offering the cheapest rate nearly half of the time.

However, at the upper end of the market the situation was very different. Hotel company Web sites gave the cheapest rate in less than 10% of cases, but quoted the highest rate in over one third of cases.

Table. Market Sector Analysis

Channel	Cheapest Channel Economy	Mid-Priced	Luxury	Chi-Square
All rates equal	46%	21%	28%	0.016*
Hotel company Web site	26%	47%	8%	0.036*
Online intermediary	26%	21%	31%	0.370
Voice (CRO)	9%	11%	2%	0.600
Microsoft Expedia	14%	11%	22%	0.030*
Travelocity.com	3%	5%	4%	0.750
TravelWeb	9%	5%	4%	0.900
WorldRes	0%	0%	0%	
Channel	**Most Expensive Channel Economy**	**Mid-Priced**	**Luxury**	**Chi-Square**
Hotel company Web site	14%	16%	34%	0.011*
Online intermediary	9%	26%	17%	0.221
Voice (CRO)	31%	37%	21%	0.440
Microsoft Expedia	0%	21%	7%	0.017*
Travelocity.com	3%	5%	10%	0.450
TravelWeb	0%	0%	0%	
WorldRes	6%	0%	0%	0.240

Note:

Columns may not total 100% due to rounding.

*The association is significant at the 95% confidence level.

The evidence is clear. If you want to stay in upmarket hotels, avoid booking on their Web site if you are searching for good value! Instead, the online intermediaries (in particular Microsoft Expedia) offer the highest probability of finding the cheapest rate available for such upper-end properties. It is also clear from the data that a hotel company's Central Reservation Office, accessed through a toll-free number, is not the place to obtain cheaper rates. Irrespective of the market segment, there is a higher probability of obtaining the most expensive rate through this channel, and bookings through this route were almost never the cheapest available. However, this finding is to a large extent a factor of the survey methodology used. With voice, the first rate quoted was the one recorded for analysis. In many cases, other (lower) rates were quoted when the researcher indicated that he did not want to make a booking, suggesting that some degree of haggling would have resulted in significant lower prices on this channel.

CONCLUSIONS

It can be seen that both the range of channels through which hotels can be booked and the complexity of these channels have grown. This study represents the first major attempt to understand hotel company's pricing strategies over electronic routes. Bookings made on five major consumer- focused online travel sites were analysed to determine if a logical pricing strategy could be established. The study revealed that the majority of hotel brands now use multiple simultaneous electronic channels of distribution, making their product available to a relatively wide audience. While the use of voice through a Central Reservation Office has fallen slightly, there has been a growth in the availability of hotel company's own Web site, with 19 out of 20 of companies now making their product available for sale in this manner. The differences between this and earlier published research indicate a major expansion in the use of the Web as a direct selling medium on the part of the hotel industry, perhaps accompanied by a realization of its benefits in comparison with other, more traditional, electronic channels of distribution.

Most companies offer multiple rates to customers over each channel utilized. It is interesting to note the large number of companies that now have consistent pricing across all channels. Research found less than 10% of companies had consistent pricing and cited the lack of integration between the various inventory databases used to manage inventory as a possible cause. Yet over one third of brands now offer consistent pricing across multiple channels, indicating progression in the industry's management of electronic distribution in the interim.

Although no single distribution channel is consistently cheapest, in-depth analysis does reveal a link between the market being targeted and price. Firstly, cheaper prices can rarely be obtained over voice channels, irrespective of market segment. From the data it can be seen that consumers are more likely to find cheaper prices on hotel chains' own Web sites in the economy and mid-price segments. More upmarket hotel brands are, on the other hand, more likely to quote more expensive prices on their own Web site than on other channels. Perhaps this is a reaction by the brands at the lower end of the market to the price sensitivity of their customer, or alternatively a realization that at least some of the cost savings generated by direct selling should morally and ethically be passed onto the consumer. In any case, it represents a more progressive and realistic pricing strategy than that of the upper- end brands, who in many cases are charging their highest prices over the channel that represents their lowest cost of distribution.

And what are the implications of these findings for the consumer? First, it is clear that for those with a taste for more upscale products, the hotel brand's own Web site is not the place to shop, as better value can be obtained in most cases through other channels.

More interesting, however is the fact that, in general, prices have become more or less equal across many of the channels investigated, and thus by implication, across many other electronic distribution channels as well. It is well established that time is a valuable commodity in today's society. Because the number and variety of ways that a consumer can book a hotel room have become undeniably complex, the cost associated with searching through even a small number of the many alternative consumer-focused channels currently available in the marketplace in an attempt to find a cheap price has also grown dramatically. Given that this study has found that many of the rates being offered over alternative channels are more or less the same for the majority of hotels, the question must be asked as to whether spending time and energy searching for the cheapest rate is worthwhile.

CONCLUSION

In order to reduce the risk of developing a hotel, which may not be commercially successful, it is important to seek advice from a hospitality consultant, who will ultimately act as the commercial conscience of the developer.

At the start of the development, prior to building and design stage, the most important question to answer is "is the project viable?" Demand and supply factors for the hotel project need to be identified in order to understand the dynamics of the future operation — to basically understand who will be the target audience for the hotel and build for that. A developer needs to have an understanding of the estimated cash-flow income of the future operation from the opening day of the hotel. This will then provide any potential investor with a comfort level that debt can be serviced from the operation.

When hotels are part of a wider scheme, the design and development of the hotel needs to be in line with the overall development vision of the scheme. In a resort environment, it is important to understand the relationship between hotel, golf, spa, residential and other facilities, and in an urban mixed-use scheme.

The hotel will, more often than not, be managed by a professional hotel operator. It is always of benefit to ask a consultant to run a competitive tender processes (be it tailored or to the wider market) when looking for a hotel company to manage your property, as this provides the opportunity to drive the process in order to achieve the best commercial deal terms available in the market. These contracts typically run for 15-25 years and key terms agreed at the beginning will have a major impact going forward.

Hotels are particularly sensitive to market changes, economic downturns and to alterations in supply and demand — for example when competitive hotels open up next to your own hotel this can severely impact performance. It is better to have all advice and information prior to decisions being taken on concept, design, architecture style, number of rooms, size of facilities, star classification and so on — to avoid the need to either redo all the aforesaid or to face the possibility of building a hotel which no operator wants to manage or which will not be commercially viable.

4

Customer Satisfaction Measurement Practices in Hotels

Every company must be able to satisfy and retain customers. That is the key to its business performance. Your job—as an executive in charge of improving quality, customer satisfaction, or loyalty—may be to enable others to act through training and support. Alternatively, if you're in the quality, customer assessment, or development areas of your company, your job may be to do the work directly—to collect, analyze, or use customer data to improve quality, satisfaction, and retention. Whether you are an enabler or a doer, customer satisfaction and retention are your responsibility. Providing high-quality products and services builds strong relationships with customers and ensures future revenue streams.

Even though you may agree about the importance of customers in driving performance, an important question remains. Does your company align its activities to satisfy and retain customers? Too often the answer is either "no" or "not so well." To help understand the problem, consider how a customer focus has evolved in recent decades.

In the 1970s, quality gurus argued that "quality is free." That is, a tireless pursuit of improvement should not only increase efficiency but also increase customer satisfaction in the process, saving enough on costs and bringing in enough new and repeat business to more than cover any expenditures on quality. This was an underlying concept in the success of many Japanese companies. In the 1980s the experts began to focus more directly on increasing customer satisfaction as an explicit goal. Satisfying and keeping customers, it was argued, is simply less expensive than constantly replacing them. More recently, quality and satisfaction have been viewed as not sufficient by themselves. Companies boast of moving "beyond" quality and satisfaction to focus directly on customer loyalty as the key to profitability.

Yet to argue that quality, or satisfaction, or loyalty is what matters misses the point. These factors form a chain of cause and effect, building on each other so that they cannot be treated separately. They represent a system that must be measured and managed as a whole if you want to maximize results. An example from our teaching experiences underscores the nature of the problem and why companies need to take a systems approach to customer measurement and management. Back in 1993 an executive seminar participant from a Fortune 100 company introduced himself as the "customer satisfaction manager" for his organization. This prompted one of the authors to ask, "What happened to the quality manager?" The participant replied that quality was passé, and that customer satisfaction had become the hot topic in his organization. In fact, being the quality manager had become the "kiss of death" from a career standpoint—a dead-end job! Five years later, a seminar participant from the same company introduced himself as the "customer loyalty manager" for the organization. Again the natural question arose, "What happened to the customer satisfaction manager?" "Oh, him?" It turned out that the satisfaction manager was now the one with the dead-end job.

Many business organizations are beginning to recognize the need to avoid this "Book of the Month Club" mentality and to view customers from a systems perspective. They want explicit linkages that extend from internal processes to customer perceptions to customer satisfaction to loyalty—and ultimately to bottom-line performance. The framework in this book will give executives hard numbers and not just persuasive theories to show that the connection is real and that improving satisfaction and loyalty really does improve profits. And those on the front lines—the quality engineers and service providers—will get specific guidance on what to improve and how to improve it to get the optimal response from customers.

This book will show you how to create an integrated customer measurement and management system that will help you allocate resources and increase profits. To create such a system, you must first understand your company's entire system for generating profit, from internal quality through to business performance. A systems approach acts on the basis of collected and interpreted customer data—but then you have to use the data to allocate resources and create change in the system or else you merely waste time and money.

With an effective customer measurement and management system, you can build organizational value. To do so, you will continually pursue three key activities that underlie a customer orientation: (1) gather customer information, (2) spread that information throughout the organization, and (3) use the information to maintain, improve, or innovate in products and processes.

You need solid information about the concrete product and service attributes or features that customers value, the more abstract consequences and benefits these attributes provide, and ultimately the personal values they serve. The purpose is to understand what your customers want not only in today's products and services but in tomorrow's as well. When you understand your customers at the various levels that motivate their behaviour, you can see their present needs and predict their future needs as well.

To maintain a customer orientation throughout your organization, you need to make sure that customer information gets to everyone who is involved—either directly or indirectly— in improving quality and value and satisfying customers. This both prepares the entire organization for change and provides benchmarks by which to monitor its performance. Finally, you need to prime the organization to act on the customer information to improve product and service offerings so as to increase satisfaction, loyalty, and profitability. This makes it essential to clarify the links among these three factors and understand how your company delivers a compelling product to its customers.

Creating a customer measurement and management system is central to the pursuit of all three of these activities. With such a system in place, you have your customer information in a form that can serve as a basis for both incremental and more revolutionary product and service improvements. The system also makes it easier to share customer information throughout an organization, enhancing its ability to follow through on that information to make product and process changes. It is essential to view customer measurement from a systems perspective that encompasses multiple areas of measurement and expertise (from engineering and design through market research and strategy to finance and accounting) so that you pick up both concrete and abstract details— both what the customers like and dislike and why they react that way—and develop information that will be genuinely useful.

Now you may well be saying, "But we already do a good job of gathering customer information, spreading it, and acting on the voice of the customer." The question is whether you really adopt the "lens of the customer" in this process or fall into the trap of relying on the "lens of the organization."

The lens of the customer shows you your products and services—and the benefits they provide—from your customers' perspective. You see them as they really are in the marketplace, rather than the different and potentially misleading picture you're likely to get from the lens of your own organization. For example, if you run a convenience store chain you may be inclined to view the chain's stores as providing customers with people (service), products (from soft drinks to gasoline), and operations (such as opening hours), each under the management of a different department or business function. The problem is that customers may not share this perspective. Customers view products and services from the standpoint of the benefits they provide and problems they solve, which may not align well with individual business process areas. In this case, customers are looking for safety, convenience, and cleanliness, which are benefits that are not uniquely provided by specific business process areas. Rather, they cut across the people, products, and operating policies of the stores.

Aside from providing a more accurate picture of the drivers of satisfaction and loyalty, adopting the lens of the customer has other advantages. It blurs functional boundaries and provides a common basis and language for communication. The forging of concrete links from area to area within a company is also a key to effective implementation. When an organization reaches a consensus on the importance of customer benefits that are not defined along functional or business process lines, it finds it much easier to engage in the cross-functional activities required to truly innovate and implement change.

We emphasize the word *framework* here. Our aim is to show just what links and models are possible.The actual elements and links in any model vary tremendously from company to company and context to context. After describing the framework, we will illustrate this point using two very different cases in which companies (Volvo and Sears) have developed models to become more customer focused.

The framework includes four general areas: internal quality, external quality and satisfaction, customer loyalty and retention, and financial performance. *Internal quality* encompasses various production and maintenance processes. In the case of a manufactured product, it includes everything from manufacturing processes to the physical characteristics and attributes that describe the product. In a service and retailing context, it includes the service offer, the physical surroundings, and the satisfaction of employees and the resulting service quality they provide.

External quality and satisfaction encompasses what customers see in the purchase and consumption experience: the attributes and benefits that products and services provide and the costs they impose, and the conclusions the customers draw about the company. In the area of customer loyalty and retention, *loyalty* is a customer's intention or predisposition to buy, while *retention* is the behaviour itself (as when a customer returns to a restaurant, comes back to buy the same brand of car, or purchases another financial instrument from the same institution). Although we will use the term *loyalty* at times to encompass both intended loyalty and actual retention, it is important to understand the distinction. When actual retention information is available, it proves extremely valuable in sorting out the drivers of financial performance. When it is unavailable, as it often is, you can use loyalty measures as a proxy for retention.

Quality, satisfaction, and loyalty ultimately affect financial performance, both directly and indirectly. The framework illustrates this point and highlights the possibility that there may be a tension between direct and indirect effects. Consider first the impact of internal quality. Producing a high-quality product or service at an attractive price indirectly affects financial performance through its effect on external customer perceptions of the purchase-consumption experience. But internal quality may also have a direct effect on costs and revenues. According to the "quality is free" argument, improvements in internal quality can increase productivity and lower internal costs and thus directly increase profitability. Recent research suggests, however, that this link is likely to be more positive for products and less positive or even negative for services. Why the difference? Services are produced and delivered at a time and place that is typically dictated by the customer. Thus improving service quality often requires an increase in personnel and operating or contact hours, which raises operating costs.

The external quality, value, and customer satisfaction component of the framework also has both direct and indirect effects on costs and revenues. Indirectly, a positive overall experience predisposes customers to stay loyal toward a product, service, or provider, which generates future sales. Satisfaction thus contributes to financial performance through its effect on loyalty and retention. But satisfaction also has direct effects, independent of loyalty. The cost of maintaining a customer account—or fixing a product—is a direct function of how happy the customer is. Satisfied customers are less likely to demand expensive product repairs or replacements or to invoke service guarantees. Also—even outside the world of TV commercials—people do talk about the products and services they buy, and your company's entry into that stream of word-of-mouth publicity is through perceived quality and satisfaction rather than through loyalty. Satisfaction is *news*—something to talk about—while loyalty is a background state that goes without saying unless something happens to damage it.

The direct effects of loyalty and retention on performance include revenues from repeat purchases, reduction in costs of finding new customers (to replace lost customers), and revenues generated through cross-selling. Another direct effect is the price premium that loyal customers often pay. Because loyal customers are not actively shopping for alternatives, they tend to be insulated from price incentives and offers such as coupons, price cuts, and free merchandise.

The recent turnaround at Volvo Car Company provides a good example of how a durable goods manufacturer views the links described in our framework. In 1991, Volvo was performing poorly in the global automotive market. It ranked as low as twenty-sixth out of thirty-four brands in the J. D. Power Initial Quality Study in the United States, and sales and profitability were suffering. In its comeback effort, Volvo began to develop a customer orientation from a total quality management foundation.

Formerly, Volvo had emphasized changing internal quality to improve productivity and reduce costs. Its management realized, however, that just focusing on internal quality was insufficient. Internal improvements had to matter to the customers before they could create improved external quality, customer satisfaction, and loyalty.

Volvo's approach is just one example of the variety of tailored models that are consistent with the framework. Like Volvo, Sears has attempted to radically transform itself into a more customer-focused organization. But since Sears is a retailer that competes primarily on service, its model has evolved quite differently. Internal quality at Sears is primarily about its people and the service they provide. The Sears model draws directly on a service-profit chain that links internal quality (including employee satisfaction and loyalty) to service quality, and the satisfaction generated by service quality to loyalty and financial performance.

In developing its model, Sears has discovered both direct effects of satisfaction on financial performance and indirect effects through loyalty, which is consistent with our framework. A quantitative employee-customer-profit model at Sears has helped the company to establish very specific links that have enabled it to improve financial performance. The model shows, for example, that a 5-point improvement in employee attitudes (on a 0 to 100 scale) drives a 1.3-point improvement in customer satisfaction, which in turn drives a 0.5 percent improvement in revenue growth.

The Volvo and Sears models share a common logic, but each model is uniquely tailored to the organization's own situation. Both models link internal quality through to profitability. At the same time, each reflects the nature of a specific company, its customers and offerings, and the contexts involved. When you look at your own company, you will see that the same logic will work for you when you develop a similar understanding of your own customers and what you can offer them.

The best measurement system can only provide information— it can't make decisions for you. People make decisions, whether it is the convenience store executive who sets corporate priorities, the front-line service manager who translates these priorities into policies and procedures, or the service worker who translates policies and procedures into concrete actions. At all three levels, decision makers are much more likely to choose to do something that will help the store chain succeed if they understand what matters to customers and how the job at hand can enhance that value.

The process of moving from information to decisions draws heavily on *importance-performance analysis.* According to this analysis, the most cost-effective areas of product and service performance to improve are those that are important to customers *and* on which, at the same time, the company is performing poorly. Executives and managers must identify these priority areas of high importance and low performance. As an output of this selection process, they can categorize and display the drivers of satisfaction and loyalty using a strategic satisfaction matrix.

The matrix identifies four categories of performance drivers with different market action implications. Again, the aspects to improve first are those where impact or importance is high and performance is weak. This focuses resources and quality improvement efforts likely to have the greatest impact on satisfaction and thus on loyalty and profitability. Those aspects where performance and impact are both high reflect a firm's competitive advantage. It is essential to maintain if not improve performance on these drivers. When impact and performance are both weak, on the other hand, there is no need to waste resources on improvement.

More interesting is the low impact–strong performance category. This may be an area where resources have been wasted in the past because the benefits and attributes are not important to customers. Alternatively, this category may contain drivers of satisfaction that customers see as basic and necessary—so much a part of the product or service that they ignore it as long as it's there when they want it, like electric power or water on tap. Although such drivers are important in an absolute sense, they have little to no impact on satisfaction because there is little variance in their performance. The danger is that a reduction in performance quality would increase the impact on satisfaction (this danger is often referred to as a "slippery slope"). Another possibility here is to find a new target market segment for the product or service. For example, if the quality of an electrical system is so constant that it has no impact on satisfaction in one application, the system might be used in applications where minor fluctuations in this quality are more important and therefore likely to have a real impact on satisfaction.

There is also a danger that something in this category may become important in the future. For example, few customers considered "environmental friendliness" to be an important factor until recently, but more and more people are beginning to pay attention to this aspect of the goods and services they buy. In a growing variety of fields, companies that predicted the importance of this area and prepared their business accordingly clearly have an advantage over those that did not.

The circular nature of the process reflects the continuous nature of a customer orientation. Customer needs, competitive offerings, and business technologies change constantly, so customer focus is an ideal of constant growth rather than static achievement. The cycle in is thus a continuous process of planning, researching, analyzing, deciding, implementing, and learning. This includes identifying the system's purpose or goals within a more balanced set of corporate performance measures (including financial goals, employee satisfaction goals, process improvement goals, knowledge and learning goals, and so forth). The chapter explores the key customer and market segmentation issues upon which the system is based, including the distinction between internal and external customers.

Chapter Three tells how to conduct qualitative research to guide the development of the measurement system. Conducting interviews and focus groups and observing customers provides you with the lens through which customers view products and services. This lens is the basis for your quality-satisfactionloyalty modeling.

Chapter Four tells how to use the lens of the customer to develop a customer monitoring system. It discusses ways to develop and administer surveys that assess the attributes and benefits your products and services provide and the overall levels of customer satisfaction and loyalty that result. The goal is to customize the measurement of quality, value, satisfaction, and loyalty for a particular customer segment, company, and context.

Chapter Five tells how to analyze satisfaction and loyalty data to provide the information you will need to set priorities for improvement. Again, the purpose is to identify both the relative importance and performance of key satisfaction and loyalty drivers. It provides guidelines for identifying the area or areas where importance is high and performance is low, which offer the most potential return on quality improvement efforts. We develop a statistical approach to help you estimate your system or model linking quality to loyalty and financial performance. We also provide concrete examples.

Chapter Six tells how to evaluate system outputs to make decisions. As emphasized earlier, management must take part in categorizing the output of a customer analysis into a strategic satisfaction matrix. Just where boundaries are set between highversus low-impact drivers and strong versus weak performance depends on a variety of factors, including what you can achieve in the time available, your cost structure, and your overall strategy. Interpreting model outputs also requires appropriate bench for evaluating both performance and importance. We will end Chapter Six by describing how to translate customer priorities into their means of accomplishment.

Who should collect your customer data, analyze it, and use it to set priorities and allocate resources? It often seems logical to delegate the satisfaction and loyalty measurement operation to outside research firms and consultants. This is especially true early in the process of becoming a customer-oriented organization, because outside specialists offer specific skills related to collecting and analyzing customer data that you do not have. Unfortunately, if you delegate the system, your company does not take ownership of it, and you and your people may fail to learn or acquire the skills necessary to measure and manage customer data on your own. The consultant's bills, heavy as they are likely to be, are only a small part of the cost of handing off a customer information system.

Bear in mind that when customer information is the key to strategy, it should reside within the company. Your best teachers about what is right and wrong with your products and services are your own customers. Direct contact with customers and customer data is a critical part of learning what it takes to satisfy customer needs. No matter how good the consultants are, they will always function as filters.

An important part of establishing a customer orientation as a core competency is creating, over time, internal specialists to measure, model, and manage quality, satisfaction, and loyalty. Early in the process, external experts are apt to be a necessity. They can provide the interviewing, surveying, data warehousing, statistical analysis, and interpretation skills that you may lack or not yet want (or be able) to invest in. Over time, however, continued reliance on external specialists becomes costly and also fails to develop customer measurement and management as a core competency. Internalization of the process allows you to adapt to changing market needs and competitive environments in a cost-effective fashion. More important, your organization accepts ownership of the process and the data—and the decisions that emerge.

This is not to say that all parts of the process should be brought in-house in all cases. You may not want to try to run a survey that involves computer-aided telephone interviews or a Web-based system with highly specialized personnel (such as trained interviewers) and potential economies of scale. Even in the most customer-savvy organization, it may be best to outsource certain parts of the process. At the same time, a truly customer-oriented firm should own rather than rent the ability to observe and to talk to customers, formalize survey instruments, analyze and interpret customer data, and use the output to make resource allocation decisions.

Over the last three decades business organizations have evolved from a focus on quality to a focus on customer satisfaction, and onward to a focus on loyalty as a means of creating value. A customer measurement and management system views each of these areas as an indispensable link in a chain of causes and effects that runs from internal quality through to profitability. The goal of this book is to help you and your organization create an integrated customer measurement and management system for making effective resource allocation decisions and increasing profitability. In the process of building a system, organizations develop internal specialists capable of gathering, analyzing, and interpreting customer data. Truly customer-oriented companies should, over time, add these skills to their core competencies.

A systems approach to customer measurement and management also requires that you tailor the system to your unique purpose, customers, and contexts. As an illustration, Volvo's model incorporates the positive effects of improving internal quality on both productivity and customer perceptions of quality, satisfaction, and loyalty. In contrast, a major retailer such as Sears incorporates the central role that satisfied employees play in delivering quality and value to customers.

These measurement systems and models are not substitutes for decision making. Rather, they provide the information you need to make resource allocation decisions and manage the process. The system provides information on how the company and its competitors are performing in different areas and how important the areas are to customers. When combined with cost and strategy considerations, the system allows both enablers and doers to create organizational value through a continuous focus on customers. To maximize the value generated by the system, make sure your company's own staff perform the bulk of the work of collecting and interpreting customer data, so that you get the full benefit of the insights generated by the effort.

Before you dive in and start conducting customer interviews or surveys, you must know how your measurement system will be used. This chapter focuses on the strategy and planning for such a system. Since a customer orientation builds on internal quality, we'll start with a brief overview of quality management and its role in driving company strategy and customer measures. We'll then discuss two related approaches to translating strategy into action: policy deployment and balanced performance measures. Then we'll focus on the process of getting started on developing a customer measurement and management system—or improving an existing one—which involves taking a look at the breadth and depth of the proposed system and the role of market segmentation in it.

In our customer satisfaction framework, internal quality is the first in the chain of events that drives financial performance. It's important not to underestimate the role of *total quality management* (or TQM, also known as *company-wide quality management,* CWQM, and as *total quality control,* TQC)—nor to exaggerate it. For longterm survival, businesses have been forced to improve their abilities to change and innovate. But internal quality management is not in itself sufficient to assure success. Internal quality improvements must be linked to improvements in external quality, satisfaction, loyalty, and financial performance. And the links must be established in an environment of constantly evolving customer preferences, markets, competitors, and technologies.

The broad principles and methods of quality management apply directly to the development of a customer measurement system. The concept of quality should unify all of a company's activities. After all, only your customers can ultimately define quality for you! In the end, it doesn't matter how well the production system works, how well marketing functions are performed, or how good the company's strategy is. If no one buys, there will be no revenues.

Quality experts emphasize three basic strategies for successful quality management: use reference models or benchmarks, set priorities for quality improvement, and focus your resources.

Do not try to do things completely on your own. Instead, make use of reference models or benchmarks when they're available. Benchmarking is particularly important in developing a customer measurement and management system.

Process benchmarking—finding out how things are done— works as well in developing a customer measurement and management system as in any other area of business. When you can manage it, arrange visits to firms with strong reputations to gauge their practices and learn what they are doing, see how they are doing it, and understand what is possible. Devote some time to reverse engineering their products as well. And don't limit the benchmarking to competitors—in a general area such as customer measurement, you'll find individuals or organizations in many fields who excel in areas that you are interested in improving.

Benchmarking on their processes can help you to learn how to conduct better customer interviews, develop and administer more effective surveys, and analyze customer data in more productive ways—and they're likely to be much more willing to share information with you if you're not trying to sell the same offering to the same customers.

For *output* or *performance benchmarking,* you will measure your product or service against direct or indirect competitors on various dimensions such as internal or technical quality, external or perceived quality and value, and overall customer satisfaction, loyalty, and retention. As noted in Chapter Six, external benchmarks will help you interpret your findings regarding your own customers and decide just where to devote your resources to get the most mileage from your improvement efforts.

Set Priorities for Quality Improvement

The second basic strategy of quality management is the universal law of priorities. In a quality context, it is often said that 20 percent of parts, processes, or people account for 80 percent of quality problems (often called the *Pareto principle*). Each customer and each market will react differently to the various drivers of satisfaction and loyalty, so one of your primary goals in customer measurement is to identify the drivers that are most important to improve. As described in Chapter One, you need to find out where the impact on customers is high and your current performance is poor. Your goal should be to set priorities and *optimize* rather than *maximize* your quality and satisfaction improvement efforts.

Focus Your Resources

Once you have chosen the area or areas to change, the third basic strategy of quality management is to concentrate your resources to maximal effect. The goal is to create a company-wide focus on the things that matter most for performance and survival. This is one of the most important yet also most often neglected aspects of quality management. Increasingly, managers face a common problem in that their customer measurement systems point out specific needs for improvement, but their organizations don't respond. The manager knows what area or areas to attack, but has difficulty getting anyone to do anything about it. This is where the lens of the customer shows its usefulness.

Once the concept spreads through an organization the independent actions of each individual and department are much more likely to fit into the overall improvement effort.

Two Ways to Translate Strategy into Action

Since no amount of information will do you any good if no one will act on it, creating an environment where resources get focused on quality management is in many ways the key element of the process. One basic approach to this problem, called *policy deployment,* has proven very effective where a company has a clear priority regarding what policy to deploy. A variation known as *balanced performance measures* allows a company to determine and deploy a balanced mix of quality improvements.

Policy deployment, or hoshin planning *(hoshin kanri)* as it is sometimes called, is a powerful quality management process that converts a company's strategy into operational change and effectively moves different units within the company in the same direction. Customer policy deployment, in particular, aims to move the entire organization to focus more on customers in order to increase their satisfaction and loyalty.

Policy deployment includes four major steps:

- *Mission and Vision:* Clearly state the organization's philosophy, mission, and vision (also called the *president's diagnosis*).
- *Goals:* Understand exactly where the organization is today and where it wants to be in the short, medium, and long term with regard to specific criteria or goals.
- *Communication Strategy:* Communicate the mission, vision, and goals throughout the organization.
- *Priority Setting and Implementation:* Set priorities, align the incentives, and implement quality improvement projects accordingly (using project management).

Making customers a priority became a strategy for Volvo's survival in the intensely competitive global automotive industry. Back in 1991, the question was how to create a customer orientation in a traditionally engineering-driven company. Volvo quickly realized that policy deployment was a natural means of building on its quality management foundations to move the company from an engineering focus to a customer focus. Here is a summary of how Volvo implemented the four major phases of policy deployment:

- *Volvo's Mission and Vision:* "To be the world's most desired and successful premium car brand."
- *Volvo's Goals:* "To be number 5 in customer satisfaction (according to the J. D. Power IQS study) in 1995 and number 3 in 1997."
- *Volvo's Communication Strategy:* Stop keeping secrets about customer complaints; give employees an open information system and a broad

view of the customer value-added process that encompasses the vehicle sales and service experience throughout the life of the vehicle.
- *Volvo's Priority Setting and Implementation:* Use quality teams to focus on the two hundred highest-priority areas (out of two thousand possibilities identified in an initial review), and reward team members based on the degree to which Volvo met its corporate goals as well as on the degree to which the team met its own goals.

Once mission statements work their way through various levels of management, they often end up reading like the Boy Scouts' oath. Companies want to be all things to all people. In contrast, Volvo's vision was specifically to be the most desired successful specialty car brand. While abstract and forward-looking, the vision nonetheless pointed to a particular segment of the automotive market in which Volvo wanted to excel. Quantitatively,

Volvo's goal was defined in terms of placement in a specific independent survey—to be number 5 in its industry by 1995 and number 3 by 1997. Although any measurement system has its strengths and weaknesses, by defining customer satisfaction using the J. D. Power IQS study, Volvo effectively defined where it was (twenty-sixth out of thirty-four makes) and where it wanted to be at different points in time. Volvo effectively aligned its mission and vision to concrete measures and goals.

Volvo's next step was communication. Stellan Flodin, the senior vice president in charge of quality, and Jan-Olof Nilsson, senior vice president of Business Area 900, led the effort to create a communication process and culture of openness across the company. Volvo abandoned its hush-hush approach to quality and customer data in favour of a more open system in which information was made available to anyone who could influence customer satisfaction. This was critically important at Volvo because its employees perceived their company as doing quite well. Internally, they had been improving products and processes from year to year all along. But externally, relative quality was falling and the company was losing ground to competitors. This decline was a well-kept secret until Volvo decided to change policy and speak freely about its problems.

Many of the problems reported in the IQS studies involved customers' experiences with sales and service, so it was essential that Volvo encompass the entire value-added chain (from production to delivery and dealer service) in its policy deployment process. Over a period of about two years, the company created an environment in which individuals from very different value-adding areas worked together to solve a variety of customer problems. Reported quality problems came to be viewed as opportunities to learn and improve rather than as negative reflections on any particular area, team, or individual.

As noted, Volvo's customer data revealed over two thousand areas in which quality improvements might be made. The final stage of the process, project management, set priorities and put quality teams to work improving approximately two hundred of the most glaring problem areas. On the Volvo 850, for example, customer data revealed that the manual transmission alone generated a surprising number of complaints (about twenty per hundred vehicles). For example, many customers said the manual gear box was too stiff, and people of below average height added that the stick shift was too far away and difficult to reach in some gears. A project team was therefore deployed to improve the quality of the transmission. Additional customer surveys allowed the team to translate customer perceptions into design and part changes that, when introduced, decreased the incidence of complaints by over 50 percent.

A key to making all this happen, however, was that Volvo aligned the project teams' and individuals' goals with overall policy goals. Team members were compensated based on whether their teams met project goals (such as reducing transmission problems per hundred cars from twenty to ten to five over time) and whether Volvo met its overall corporate goals such as reducing overall problems per hundred cars to reach the number 5 position by 1995 and the number 3 position by 1997.

The policy deployment process that Sears is using to create a customer focus is similar to the process at Volvo. The main difference is that, whereas Volvo built on its knowledge of quality management to implement policy deployment from the top down, Sears is using the development of its employee-customerprofit chain (the idea that satisfied employees make for satisfied customers and thereby increase sales and profits, described in Chapter One) to drive the deployment process from the bottom up. The process has been more implicit than explicit.

Retail-service companies have not gone through the same quality management revolution and training as manufacturing companies such as Volvo. But once Sears's employee-customerprofit chain was developed, it became an important tool to drive change in the company's mission, vision, goals, and communication. Everyone from senior managers to store employees had to be taught the logic of the model and its implications, including how the company's competitive environment had changed. The company held town hall meetings and used learning maps to help employees grasp the logic behind the model so that they, in turn, could apply it at the store level. In the end, the deployment process has helped build a leadership model that incorporates the various aspects of the employee-customer-profit chain. The leadership model is to make Sears a compelling place to work, shop, and invest.

Yet the deployment process has progressed more slowly at Sears than at Volvo. The process at Sears has been more data driven, working from the bottom up. Only after the employee-customer-profit chain was developed did Sears executives confront many of the challenges in deploying policy, from a lack of buy-in among top executives to communication problems among their retail employees. And arguably, Volvo has been more successful at implementing its customer orientation and turning the corner on profitability. After some initial success, financial performance at Sears remains weak.

These results aren't surprising, and they provide a useful warning to those in service industries. Product companies tend to have a history of quality management when they begin to implement customer policy deployment, and this gives them a strong head start. Few service companies have gone through the same quality revolution, although there are important exceptions. Disney, Fidelity Investments, and USAA, for example, have long-standing commitments to quality management and its principles. Disney has used policy deployment in the development of its theme parks for many years. But most service firms simply did not get the wake-up call that hit manufacturing firms in the 1970s and 1980s, when they were confronted with competitors producing higher-quality products in less time and at lower cost.

If you manage or work in a service industry such as telecommunication, insurance, or banking, very likely your company is now experiencing or will soon experience the same type of global competition and cost pressures as your counterparts in the manufacturing world. Technology such as the Internet now provides a basis for delivering cost-effective global service. The warning from product companies is clear. If you hope to continue to prosper, establish a culture that emphasizes quality as your foundation for using customer information to drive organizational change.

Balanced performance measures or BPMs share many of the principles of policy deployment. But whereas policy deployment has always been an explicit means of translating strategy into action, BPMs were initially developed as a way of balancing the needs of multiple stakeholders in an organization. Rather than focusing mainly on customers, BPMs recognize that a customer focus must be balanced against the needs of other stakeholders, such as owners, employees, and suppliers. A popular approach to developing BPMs is the balanced scorecard.

Companies use the balanced scorecard to assess their performance and strategy in a highly integrated fashion. The scorecard's four main components are the company's financial perspective, the customer perspective, the internal business process perspective, and the learning and innovation perspective.

The *customer perspective* includes those customer measures that are most important for the company to improve, such as targets for customer satisfaction or account penetration. The *financial perspective* includes targets the company sets with respect to both financial (market value) and accounting (revenue and profit) measures. The *internal perspective* includes internal quality and business process measures, such as the number of hours the company spends talking with customers about current or future projects, or the level of employee satisfaction. The *innovation and learning perspective* include goals and measures for investments in training and new product or service development. For each perspective, goals and measures are developed and drilled down to operational levels for teams and individuals ("personal scorecards"). As balanced performance measurement systems evolved through the 1990s, their relationship to policy deployment has become clear. For example, in more recent versions of the balanced scorecard, a company's vision and strategy drive a management process that includes strategy feedback and learning, clarifying and translating the vision and strategy, communicating and linking rewards to performance measures, and planning and setting targets. These stages obviously parallel the four main steps in policy deployment described earlier. Yet important differences remain. Whereas a full policy deployment moves an organization in a completely new direction, such as focusing more explicitly on customers, BPMs balance various stakeholders' needs. In this sense, BPMs are a weak form of policy deployment. They more or less presume that the organization is headed in the right direction and align its activities accordingly. A balanced scorecard approach keeps an organization on course through an integrated management and budgeting process.

BPMs also lack any guiding framework or model of the drivers of financial performance. The approach focuses generally on synergies among the various perspectives or stakeholder needs. As emphasized in Chapter One, it is important that you build your measurement system on an evolving understanding of the drivers of financial performance that is tailored to your company and competitive environment, as Volvo and Sears did.

Although this book's focus is primarily on the customer perspective, balanced performance measures do serve as a reminder that the measurement and management process described here can be applied to other stakeholders as well. In the Sears model, for example, employee attitudes and beliefs are critically important in driving employee behaviour. The processes and tools described in this book for developing the lens of the customer can certainly be applied to develop the lens of the employee, supplier, or equity stakeholder as a basis for developing and administering surveys, analyzing data, and setting priorities for improvement.

When you embark on a strategy of customer-driven quality improvement, questions will arise about how to set up a system to collect the data you need to work with. Many of these questions can be broadly categorized as relating either to *system breadth*— the range of internal and external customers and market segments that you want to measure—or to *system depth*—the level of detail and nature of the information that you gather.

Companies typically serve a range of very different customers both inside and outside the organization. Internal customers may be in the same physical location, as when marketing and finance are customers of information services, or in different locations, as when manufacturing plants are customers of the home office. External customers range from wholesalers and retailers to end users. The customer chain shows three levels of customers: plant customers, retailing customers, and end users. We have kept this example simple to make the relationships easy to see on paper; in practice any given organization or network is likely to have a much larger number of customer levels, as any individual might be considered someone else's customer. And it isn't enough to track exchanges of funds for goods or services, as even external customers don't necessarily pay to assume that role—regulatory agencies are customers for reports, for example, and people downstream (literally or metaphorically) from traditional end users are the ones likely to be customers for ecological and recycling efforts.

To determine just which customers should be your primary measurement and management focus, refer back to the framework in Chapter One. What links in the customer chain drive your financial performance? Where are the links from quality to satisfaction to loyalty and profitability the strongest? Those are the places where you're likely to get the most mileage out of any investment in improved quality. Even without a detailed measurement system, you probably have some knowledge or understanding of where to start looking.

Think about the nature of the competition and customer choice at each level. The logic of a customer orientation (the idea that quality, satisfaction, and loyalty drive profitability) is based on two critical assumptions. First, the customer is relatively free to choose products and services. This assumption holds for most industries in the developed world today—customers face a dizzying variety of brands of cars, soap, phone service, and most necessities and luxuries, and if one alternative doesn't satisfy there's always another to try. This assumption doesn't always hold true, however—when customers face significant switching costs in moving from one provider to another, or there is only one supplier available, they are essentially hostages. That is, when it's expensive or difficult to find another supplier, only a very dissatisfied customer will switch to a competitor. Airline customers are often held hostage to the hub-and-spoke system of air travel, where flying on other than the hub airline imposes significant costs in terms of time and convenience. However, no company can count on keeping its customers hostage indefinitely. In the gas and electric supply business, for example, many customers still have few options to choose from—but recent deregulation means that the situation is changing rapidly, and customer satisfaction and loyalty are likely to become drivers of profitability soon.

The second important assumption in the logic of a customer orientation is that the important customers are the ones who will generate new business if they're satisfied with their experience—buy replacements for past purchases, buy new offerings, or inspire potential customers to try the company's wares. Investments to satisfy more transient or one-time customers may not generate future revenues or cost savings. The benefits of increasing satisfaction are thus greatest at the level in the customer chain where your customers have both a choice and a potential to reward you with future revenues at lower costs. Related to the notion of customer choice is the relative *push* versus *pull* of your products and services through the customer chain.

Consider a service provider such as Fidelity, which places investment instruments through a variety of independent retailers. In one region, the end users—the individual investors— may have strong brand attitudes and perceptions that have been created over a long period of time through experience, advertising, and word of mouth. In this case, the most important customer in the chain is probably the end user who goes to a retailer (whether an agency or a Web site) in search of a particular offering. The choice in this case resides primarily with end users who pull the product through the chain. Although all customers are important at some level, relatively speaking, the satisfaction of the retailer is not as critical in this case as the satisfaction of the end user. To satisfy and retain their own customers, the retailers need to make the Fidelity offerings available to them.

Elsewhere, investors may be much more likely to follow the advice of the retailer about which brand to purchase. The retailer may be more established and trusted in the end user's mind than any individual brand. If investors are more likely to defer their choice to a trusted retailer, Fidelity is in a position of pushing the product or service through the chain. In this case, the most important thing to measure and manage may be the satisfaction of the retailer and its willingness to push the brand on to the end user. The same logic applies regardless of the product or service—if the offering is seen as interchangeable at the end-user level, you have to give the retailer a reason to favour your brand over others.

At each level in the customer chain, the market segmentation scheme is the key element in your strategic market plan to build a customer measurement system. Market segmentation is the process of identifying and targeting unique populations or *segments* of customers and developing tailored marketing strategies to meet the individual segment needs. To identify and target segments, take the following steps:

- Group customers into segments based on customer needs, benefits sought, or personal values served.
- Identify or describe the segments according to their behaviours, lifestyles, or demographics.
- Evaluate the attractiveness of each segment in terms of, for example, profit potential, risk, capacity utilization, and core competencies required to serve the segment.
- Determine strategically which segments to target and pursue and, as a result, which segments to measure, analyze, and manage separately.

These steps bring you to a framework for just which customers to measure, analyze, and monitor. Because the drivers of satisfaction and loyalty may be very different from segment to segment, be wary of averaging across segments. Averages can be deceiving. If customer data are aggregated too highly, they provide a profile of an average customer who simply does not exist. If the segments are different enough, they will require separate survey development and analysis. Even when the same survey is applicable to more than one group of customers, be sure to analyze importance and performance levels separately for each group.

SEGMENTATION IN A HOTEL CHAIN

Consider, for example, the needs of business customers and vacation customers at "Wolverine Inns" a fictitious name for a major mid-priced hotel chain we worked with recently. The chain recently segmented its franchisees according to which segment of customers they are most likely to serve, based on the idea that downtown properties cater more to the business customer segment and leisure-area properties cater more to the vacation customer segment.

The matrices are used to set priorities for quality improvement. The company's satisfaction and loyalty survey covers eight general quality areas or customer benefits (reservation process, staff, facilities, grounds, bathroom, room, breakfast, and perceived value) and each area is rated on a variety of attributes. For the moment, just look at the impact and performance aspects of the eight types of benefit. Later we will take up the issue of setting priorities among the attributes that provide each benefit, such as the friendliness, helpfulness, efficiency, and grooming and appearance of the hotel staff.

The vertical axes show how each type of property performs on each of the eight benefits using a weighted average of customers' attribute ratings (on a scale where 1 is poor and 5 is excellent). Both downtown and leisure-area properties, for example, perform very well on the quality of the reservations process. The horizontal axes show the relative importance of each benefit as revealed by its statistical impact on overall satisfaction.

For example, the impact score of.75 for quality of the room for the downtown properties shows that as room quality increases by 10 percent, satisfaction increases by 7.5 percent (10 percent ×.75). (This example is based on standardized scale values.)

The results reveal vast differences in the drivers of satisfaction across the two property types. Business customers who frequent downtown Wolverine Inn locations look for the hotel to simply provide a clean and comfortable room. They use the hotel for a place to get a good night's sleep and have little interest in its other services. In contrast, a much wider variety of factors drive satisfaction for the vacation customers who frequent the chain's leisure-area properties. The quality of the room is secondary to the quality of service and advice that the staff provides. The quality of the grounds, bathroom, and breakfast are also more important for the vacation customer. As hotel manager at any given property, you would certainly want to know impact and performance levels for your target customers. Assuming the described results for individual hotels, the downtown manager would see improving the quality of the rooms as the greatest priority, given its high impact and currently moderate performance. In contrast, the manager of the leisure-area property would see improving the quality of the staff as relatively more important. Neither manager would have much incentive to do anything about perceived value—the customers' view of the price they are paying for the experience—even though it is far and away the lowest performance area in both cases, because the survey results show that neither group of customers cares much about it. Lowering prices would be costly for the hotel and would make it more difficult to sustain improvements in areas that matter to the customers, so it's best to avoid this step unless the hotel has an incentive to change its customer base to one that regards the current price level as a barrier rather than a minor irritant.

After deciding which customer levels to include in the measurement system and what customers or market segments to include, the next step is to ask what level of generality or detail about the lens of the customer the system should contain. Customer satisfaction is a complex matter, made up of the way the customer perceives the concrete attributes of a product, the benefits the customer derives from those attributes, and the personal values that the product supports. All these elements reside with the customer and are beyond the company's direct control, so we refer to them as *external quality factors.* Measurement systems vary in the amount of detail they provide about external factors such as these.

For example, macro-level measurement systems such as the American Customer Satisfaction Index (ACSI) only include very general differences in external perceptions of overall quality and value as drivers of satisfaction and loyalty. Quality is itself measured using customer ratings of the levels of customization and reliability provided, while value is measured using customer perceptions of the price or prices paid for the quality received. The purpose of measurement systems such as the ACSI is, however, to provide quality, value, satisfaction, and loyalty benchmarks across a very wide range of firms, industry groupings (including products, services, retailers, and government and public agencies), and even countries. Such broad-based comparisons require a measurement system that emphasizes generality and comparability as opposed to depth and detail.

If your goal is to improve or radically reinvent goods and services, you'll need a more detailed and comprehensive information system. It should include information on the range of concrete attributes and abstract benefits that might drive satisfaction and require improvement. Chapter Three will return to the convenience store example and discuss perceived convenience, merchandise quality, and safety as just three of the benefits that directly affect customer satisfaction. In subsequent chapters we will discuss how to develop these more detailed or in-depth measurement systems for the purpose of measuring and managing customer data for a particular product or service and market segment. Remember that the information in the measurement system is designed to leverage either incremental (evolutionary) or innovative (revolutionary) activities, or both. For example, when Volvo discovered that its customers found its manual transmissions difficult to shift (an attribute-level problem), it translated the problem into one of changing certain parts that immediately reduced complaints. In contrast, when product or service designers are pursuing major innovations, they shift upward from the attribute level to more abstract customer benefits and personal values as input to the design process. Developing a fuel cell or electric vehicle, for example, requires matching the benefits and consequences that the new technology provides (such as zero emissions and moderate performance) with the benefits and values that are important to target customers (such as a willingness to trade off vehicle performance for environmental impact). Product or service design is then a process of developing a whole new configuration of product and service attributes to better serve customer needs.

We are often asked when to engage in revolutionary innovation rather than more evolutionary continuous improvement. The key, of course, is to avoid focusing on one to the exclusion of the other, but rather to balance both activities. Masaaki Imai, who was instrumental in developing the *kaizen* or continuous improvement process, emphasizes the importance of maintaining a balance among three activities: maintaining the quality of existing products, services, or processes; achieving kaizen or continuous improvement; and achieving innovation. The temptation, Imai argues, is to focus only on innovation as a means of making rapid changes and leapfrogging the competition. This ignores the long-term benefits that continuous improvement brings to a company.

When all three activities are balanced, the result is a formidable competitive advantage. Disney is a great example of an organization that consistently manages to balance all three activities. The regular development of new characters for use in movies, television shows, and theme parks is a constant source of innovation. At the same time, Disney works to maintain or keep improving every stage of its customers' experience. The combination has created a legendary service organization that is built on a quality foundation *and* reinvents itself on a regular basis.

Measuring quality, customer satisfaction, and loyalty should be an ongoing, repetitive process. It is difficult, however, to make general recommendations about just how frequently to measure. The frequency varies from company to company and depends on the audience, the stability or volatility of the product or service, and the nature of the market. For instance, if you have relatively few customers it may not be desirable to survey them too often. Needless to say, your customers should never feel that the process is burdensome. And once you do a survey and set some priorities, be sure to implement the changes before you launch another survey. Otherwise, your customers will ask the obvious question: "Why should I bother filling out this survey when you didn't pay any attention to the last one?"

A product's life cycle also affects the frequency of measurement. You need frequent contact with customers early on, when the market is evolving and changes to the product or service can have a great impact on a company's success. Consider the battle between Ericsson and Nokia in the cellular phone market. The early adopters of cellular phones were businesspeople. They simply wanted a reliable phone, which gave Ericsson the edge. But Ericsson did not keep up with the evolution of customer needs in the market and emergence of new market segments that demanded more features and design improvements. This allowed Nokia to achieve a greater advantage as the market evolved.

Later in a product's life cycle, customers are much harder to attract, more valuable to keep, and more costly to lose, so again you want close and frequent customer contacts. And, of course, it is always important to listen carefully to customers when the threat of competition has increased. The general point is that contact with customers should become more frequent during certain critical stages of the product life cycle and market dynamics.

Keeping these contingencies in mind, we recommend a customer satisfaction survey at least yearly. More frequent surveys are likely to have little effect on your improvement efforts when the product and the market are stable. If competition is really active and is moving quickly in a market, it may be necessary to carry out more frequent studies—perhaps even on a quarterly basis. But make sure you have enough resources to process and implement the findings, or the efforts are wasted. It is often a good compromise to measure every six months in times of change.

Finally, remember that there's a difference between customer measures and surveys as the basis of a measurement and management system and more informal surveys or methods designed to take a quick pulse or to identify problems as they occur. The latter methods typically focus on the most recent episode or transaction with a customer (such as the latest stay at the hotel or visit to the bookstore), and are often loosely structured (an informal interview by the manager or an open-ended "opinion" card). Their value toward allocating resources and deciding strategy is limited. At the same time, they may be a valuable source of information for service managers or front-line service personnel to catch and resolve certain classes of problems as they occur.

Providing external quality and customer satisfaction depends directly on the quality of your company's internal processes, operating policies, strategies, and plans. Whether your company provides products or services (or both), quality management provides a solid foundation for developing and deploying strategy and measuring quality through the lens of the customer. As you move through subsequent chapters, you will see the three basic strategies of quality management. We will describe the use of reference models or benchmarks to interpret and analyze customer data. We will show you how to optimize rather than maximize customer satisfaction and loyalty by setting priorities for quality improvement. Finally, we will describe ways to maximize use of available resources to implement the change. Policy deployment and its variants, including balanced performance measures, are important tools for creating a more universal and consistent focus. These approaches provide companies with a means of translating their customer strategies into action.

Just where to begin building the system requires decisions regarding which customers to include, or system breadth, and how much detail to provide, or system depth. You want to include the kinds of customers that drive business performance. To do this, you will need to ask "which of our internal or external customers are both a source of future profits and have a choice about where they take their business?" To drive profitability, produce and deliver high-quality products and services to satisfy and retain these customers. When including customers in the measurement system, remember that customers do not all value the same things and behave in the same way. Build your customer measurement systems on an understanding of how your customer base at any given level (such as retail or end-user) is segmented.

Segmentation is a process of identifying individuals or populations of customers with unique needs and wants. By paying attention to segment differences you will avoid the pitfall of setting priorities based on "average" customers who don't exist. In your planning process, also consider just how much detail you will need to measure and how you will use your measurement system. At a general level, macro-level customer measurement systems provide for broad-based comparisons and benchmarking but give only general guidance about what companies should improve (such as product or service quality or value). In this book, the focus is on measurement systems that are more specific to the company or segment; they provide detailed information regarding concrete product or service attributes as well as information about more abstract consequences and benefits. By continually improving the concrete attributes of existing offerings and finding completely new ways to provide customer benefits, you can leverage your customer data to create a truly exemplary level of performance and competitive advantage.

To link internal quality to profitability, you have to find out how customers see the products and services they purchase and consume. Your first step (and the subject of this chapter) will be to develop a model of how customers view your firm's products, services, and activities—the "lens of the customer" that will guide the rest of your efforts. As discussed earlier, people inside an organization too often develop customer surveys from their own perspective, or how they believe customers view their products and services.

The result is a survey or measurement instrument that embodies the lens of the organization rather than the lens of the customer. You'll often see airline surveys organized in this fashion, for example, full of questions broken out by organizational activity (check-in, preflight service, food and beverage, flight crews, and cabin environment). A survey that aligns question areas with organizational responsibility in this fashion does have the advantage of producing recommendations that are fairly straightforward to implement. If the survey results and prioritysetting process indicate that flight crews are most in need of improvement, then the responsibility for making improvements within the organization is clear.

Unfortunately, this type of survey may warp or entirely miss issues that cross organizational boundaries, as when flight crews get blamed for being short-tempered about carry-on baggage that should never have been allowed into the cabin in the first place. Customers tend to form opinions regarding such benefits as service, convenience, and safety that cut across the functional areas of an organization. It is essential, therefore, that the measurement system be based squarely on the lens of the customer. In addition, having a survey instrument that better captures the customers' perception of the company makes the data easier to analyze. We are able to explain more variation in key customer evaluations and behaviours, such as satisfaction and loyalty, when the questionnaire is based on the customers' view. For an airline, such a questionnaire might address a whole range of activities from seat reservations through boarding to baggage claim under the heading of convenience, and everything from the gate lobby staff to the seat cushions under the heading of comfort.

The concrete attributes of a product or service and the abstract benefits it generates occupy different levels in the customers' lens. This distinction is very useful but may take some getting used to.

The rectangular objects at the left-hand side represent the concrete aspects or dimensions on which customers can readily report performance via survey measures (such as whether a sales staff keeps its appointments and returns telephone calls and e-mail messages). The circular objects to the right of the attributes represent the relatively abstract or *latent* variables that capture the benefits or consequences that the attributes provide or, at an even more abstract level, the personal values that they serve. For simplicity, we will refer to all the abstract drivers of satisfaction and loyalty as *benefits*.

As in a traditional marketing perspective, the customer satisfaction model embodies the view that products and services compete primarily on the benefits they provide or the needs they fulfill. The concrete attributes of the product or service are only the means to these more abstract ends. Letters, e-mail messages, and faxes all, for example, provide the benefit of communication. You can thus view benefits as the primary drivers of satisfaction in the lens. Notice, however, that benefits may be measured using different numbers of concrete attributes.

Satisfaction in the model is defined as a customer's overall evaluation of the purchase and consumption experience with a product, service, or provider. This definition is quite different from transaction-specific definitions of satisfaction that capture a customer's immediate reaction to a particular episode or experience. Why discard the immediate response in favour of a more cumulative or overall definition of satisfaction? Although it seems more remote, the latter turns out to be more directly tied to customers' repurchase intentions and behaviour. Customers' repurchase decisions are affected by their entire purchase and consumption history with a company or brand, not just the last trip to the restaurant or last shipment from a supplier. Although we list loyalty, broadly defined, as the desired outcome of satisfaction, there are other constructs we could have shown there as well. Customer satisfaction may also lead to an enhanced reputation and greater brand equity for the company, which will in turn attract additional customers who are disposed to develop loyalty of their own.

The also see overall satisfaction and loyalty in circles, treating them as abstract constructs that can be measured in concrete terms. Overall satisfaction is reflected in different concrete satisfaction measures, which might include a satisfaction scale, how the product or service performs overall versus customer expectations, performance versus an ideal product or service in the category, and performance versus "best in class" competitors. Similarly, loyalty may be measured using a variety of behavioural intentions (ratings of the likelihood that customers will return, will purchase other products and services from the company, or will speak positively of their experience to others) or actual behaviours (such as whether customers do return, how often they return and how much they purchase when they do, and whether they bring or refer additional customers).

Note the dotted arrow that runs from an attribute-benefit cluster directly to customer loyalty. This captures the possibility that customers' intentions or decisions to repurchase are affected directly by certain benefits. In a recent study of satisfaction with hair care providers, for example, we found that the quality of the haircut, the relationship with the stylist, and the atmosphere of the salon all affect loyalty via overall satisfaction. However, the timeliness and ease of scheduling an appointment have direct effects on loyalty in addition to their effects on satisfaction. Price can also affect loyalty directly— customers are likely to weigh price or value much more when evaluating loyalty than when evaluating satisfaction. "I love his work, but I can't afford to go back every month" You can't develop the lens of the customer by sitting around and reflecting on how customers view the world. Instead, you need in-depth, qualitative research to show you the issues from the customers' own perspective. Keep in mind that the goal of conducting qualitative research (such as interviews and focus groups) is not to immediately set priorities for quality improvement— it is to identify a comprehensive range of issues (benefits and attributes) that potentially drive satisfaction, loyalty, and profitability. The customer sample that you use at this stage of the research should represent a good cross-section or range of customers from the population or target market of interest, but it need not be truly random as you're not looking for statistical validity at this point. The lens or model that results from this qualitative research provides the foundation for more systematic survey research, which in turn becomes the primary basis for setting priorities when you get to that stage of the process.

Marketing books offer a wide choice of qualitative methods that you can use to identify product and service attributes and the customer benefits they provide—one-on-one interviews, group interviews or focus groups, protocol methods (having customers "think out loud" while using or evaluating a product or service), and a variety of observation techniques. Here, we focus on one qualitative technique that is particularly well suited to the development of a customer model or lens: the *critical incident technique* (CIT).

The CIT can be used to identify satisfaction drivers for a range of internal and external customers. It typically involves an interview in which individuals or groups of customers are asked to provide a list of the things that they like and dislike about the product, service, or company in question. According to Bob Hayes, an expert on the CIT approach, "A critical incident is a specific example of the service or product that describes either *positive* or *negative* performance. A positive example is a characteristic of the service or product that the customer would like to see every time he or she receives that service or product. A negative example is a characteristic of the service or product that would make the customer question the quality of the company."

The critical incidents themselves should be as specific as possible in describing a single feature of the customer's purchase and consumption experience. Hayes argues that a good critical incident should cover a single behaviour or characteristic, and should either describe the service provider in behavioural terms or describe the service or product using specific adjectives. Consider two examples from the case study in Appendix A, which describes CIT interviews with tire retailers. One retailer noted positively that "the range (variety) of products is good"—pointing to a particular characteristic of the tires (the available range) using a specific adjective (good). Another retailer noted negatively that "regional representatives arrive too seldom"—pointing to a specific behaviour of the local salesperson (waiting too long between visits).

If the critical incidents are too general, the interviewer needs to ask additional questions to clarify what the customer really has in mind. For each specific incident, it is also useful to ask the customer for comments on the significance and consequences of the incident. Such questions will elicit valuable information for the next stage of the process, categorizing the incidents into attributes and benefit groupings. When encouraged to elaborate, for example, the retailer who praised the product range pointed out that carrying a range of tire products allowed him to offer "a tire for almost every customer that walks into my store." The one who said the regional representative arrived too seldom said that "he should come every month ...just to see how things are going."

Overall, the CIT process involves a number of steps that are helpful to describe using an activity-based flowchart. Step 1 is to compile and assess whatever relevant secondary research or knowledge pertaining to the lens of the customer already exists within the company. (One should avoid, of course, any biases from the lens of the organization.) Perhaps similar studies have been conducted in slightly different research contexts that shed light on how customers view the product or service. Step 2 is to make initial visits to different customers early in the process. We have found this important for two reasons. First, the visits will provide firsthand observations of the

QUALITY-SATISFACTION

You'll usually need several sources of data to establish all the links from quality through to profits. Consider the experience at Sears and Volvo. Sears uses one survey to measure internal quality in the form of employee perceptions and attitudes and a second survey to measure external quality and satisfaction from the customers' perspective. Information from both sources is then combined with financial performance information for individual stores to trace the links in the employee-customer-profit chain. Volvo tracks internal quality with engineering-based measures of vehicle performance, and uses customer surveys to track external quality.

Now we focus on ways to develop and administer the survey that measures customer perceptions of quality, satisfaction, and loyalty. The lens of the customer—built from the qualitative research in Chapter Three—will serve as a blueprint for your survey, identifying the attributes to include and the order they should appear. To make the survey results useful, however, you will also need to specify and include measures of satisfaction and loyalty so as to be able to combine the individual customer responses into a meaningful pattern of causes and effects.

Step 1: The Preliminaries

As in any other activity, if you don't know what you want to get out of customer measurement, it's going to be hard to tell if you've found it. So before you develop the survey itself, you need to figure out what information is required—which is a function of what you're planning to do with it—as well as how to segment your customer base, what survey method or methods to use, and how to sample the population.

What Information Is Required?

Start by restating in simple terms what you want your customer survey to tell you, and what you plan to do about it. This might be as generic as "We want to know what our customers want so we can give them more of it—and what they don't want, so we can avoid including it, " or it might be tailored to your particular business. Then look back at the lens of the customer and list the attributes and benefits it identifies as having the potential to drive customer satisfaction and loyalty.

Then list some direct questions about customer satisfaction and loyalty. From a statistical standpoint, these are the primary dependent variables that the model is to explain based on customer perceptions of attribute and benefit performance. Make sure that the things you're asking about are at least partially under your control, so the results will be meaningful and useful. There is no point in finding out that your customers are uniformly unhappy that every day they get a day older, unless you're in the business of providing some way to preserve youth and prolong life. So consider just how the results will affect areas and individuals in your organization and what actions you may need to take based on the results.

How to Segment Survey Respondents?

The next step is to figure out which market segments to include in the survey—and just how to classify respondents into those segments. The choice of segments should be based on their importance in your strategic market plans. Beyond the choice of key segments (such as "daily" and "weekly" convenience store customers), another important question related to segmentation and sampling is whether to include current, past, or potential customers in the research. Companies are often content to focus only on current customers. Unfortunately, if current customers are systematically different from those you've lost or those you would like to pursue in the future, your results from a currentcustomer survey could be misleading or incomplete.

Market segment classifications may be based on information collected prior to the survey. Existing research may already have determined which customers are classified into which segments. If survey respondents can be identified and classified into segments beforehand, then it is perhaps unnecessary to have segment-related information in the survey itself. Otherwise it will be critical to include information in the survey that allows you to sort or select customers by segment. The sorting or selection criteria may be direct or indirect.

The Indirect Approach

Using the indirect approach, you might include descriptive items in the survey such as demographic variables (age, sex, income level, education level, ethnic background), geographic variables (city, country, or geographic area), and experience-related variables (frequency of purchase or consumption of the product or service, confidence in evaluating the product or service, and so on). These measures would then be analyzed *after* the surveys are administered to develop distinct clusters or groups of customers that differ on the variables of interest (such as male versus female or frequent versus infrequent convenience store customers).

This approach is indirect in the sense that the descriptive measures are only proxies for identifying more needs-based segments. A disadvantage of this approach is that it can lead to the inclusion of so many descriptive variables that the survey becomes long and cumbersome. An advantage of the approach is that it provides a database that can be used to develop and identify new segments. This allows you to *cut,* or sort the data, in various anticipated and unanticipated ways. Descriptive variables are typically collected near the end of the survey. If a customer feels sensitive about answering particular questions (such as age, income, or education level), encountering such questions up front may bias the responses to the whole questionnaire or lead the customer to give up on it entirely.

The Direct Approach

Using the direct approach, you provide an existing segmentation within which customers place themselves in a needs-based segment. Often companies have some existing knowledge of the major segments or populations in their customer base. If simple descriptions of each of the different segments can be included in the survey, customers can indicate directly which segment they most identify with. For the convenience store survey, for example, independent research conducted prior to the survey helped us define five major segment profiles. We then used the profiles to develop descriptive statements for each segment:

Segment 1: I tend to visit a convenience store several times a day for snacks as well as meals.

Segment 2: I am a parent who occasionally goes to a convenience store mainly to buy fill-in items, emergency items, or things for the kids.

Segment 3: I visit a convenience store daily to buy one or two items such as a soda, coffee, cigarettes, or candy.

Segment 4: I go to a convenience store once or twice a week to buy a snack, soda, or coffee.

Segment 5: I shop at a convenience store less than once a week, mainly to buy snacks and party items or items for a trip.

In the resulting convenience store survey (presented in Appendix B at the end of the book), we asked survey respondents to indicate which of these statements best described their behaviour. The primary advantage of this approach is that it is based directly on an existing segmentation scheme. This greatly simplifies the analysis of the survey data. The responses are simply sorted according to their segment identification and analyzed. The disadvantage of using existing segment profiles is that it assumes that the profiles provide an accurate description of the underlying segments. If the nature of the segments changes between the segmentation study and the quality-satisfaction-loyalty survey, the results of the latter will be skewed in unpredictable ways.

We recommend using a hybrid of the direct and indirect segmentation approaches when possible. Using existing segment profiles simplifies subsequent analysis and bases the analysis squarely on a segmentation scheme. But it is helpful to include some additional descriptive questions. The convenience store questionnaire, for example, augments the segment-level questions with a small number of demographic questions used in U.S. census questionnaires. The hybrid approach allows for some exploratory analysis using the demographic variables to sort or cluster respondents into new segments. The demographics also provide descriptive details of the segment profiles, such as whether "daily" convenience store customers tend to be male, female, older, younger, and so on.

Prior to developing the survey, you also need to decide just how to communicate with customers and administer the survey. The choice of survey methods has important implications for the nature of the questions and scales involved. There are various approaches, the more common being one-on-one interview surveys, telephone surveys, Web-based surveys, and written surveys. Each method has its strengths and weaknesses. The choice of methods should depend on the context.

One-on-one interviews are well suited to business-to-business applications, where the population of customers is relatively well defined (such as those customers who purchase a certain type of chemical or part). Conducting personal interviews is a good way to increase response rates; it shows customers that you are deeply interested in their opinions. This is important if your organization has a reasonably small number of key customers that you want to take special care of. A disadvantage of one-on-one interviews is that they can become difficult to manage when the sample of respondents is large.

Problems also arise when the individual conducting a survey interview has a vested interest in the results of the survey, as when the salespeople's bonus system is tied to the data that they collect from customers. Anyone who has purchased or leased a new automobile in the last few years might remember the pleas from salespeople to "give me 10s on the survey—my bonus depends on it!" It is crucial to maintain independence and objectivity in these cases through the use of a third party within the company (such as a manager or a salesperson who does not serve that customer) or an independent data collection agency to conduct the actual interviews.

Telephone surveys, particularly those using a computeraided telephone interview or CATI system, are particularly well suited to end-user products and services where representative samples of consumers are needed from a large population. The convenience store survey script in Appendix B is taken from a CATI application. The advantages of telephone interviews include their relatively low cost per completed interview and the control the interviewer has over who is responding to the survey (compared, for example, to written or mail surveys). A human interviewer can clarify any misunderstandings or problems that a respondent may have in answering a survey question. And when they encounter respondents who are simply not able or willing to respond to the survey, trained interviewers can quickly say thank you and terminate the interview. The disadvantage of the telephone interview approach is that interviewers may generate unpredictable effects of their own. They must be carefully trained, as the way questions are stated is likely to have an impact on how customers respond.

Through the use of randomization techniques (such as random-digit dialing), telephone interviewing typically yields more representative samples of customers in a population than you get with other methods. Using this approach, time zones and area codes can be systematically sampled. The American Customer Satisfaction Index survey, a large national survey, uses this approach to obtain valid cross-sections of U.S. consumers. The survey samples are checked against census data using demographic profiles to ensure that they are properly balanced with respect to age, sex, income and education levels, and ethnic background.

Internet-based surveys are growing in importance as the population of Web users becomes more representative of specific customer groups. Web surveys offer significant advantages in that data can be collected, transferred, and updated continuously online. And unlike CATI survey participants, Web respondents have a written version of the survey available on the computer screen to help keep the questions and scales clearly in mind—and they all see exactly the same questions, which eliminates the danger of interviewer bias. Web surveys have already become the preferred method of data collection in those industries where Web samples are representative of the customer base (as for certain financial services and online retail operations).

Yet many customer populations continue to contain large percentages of individuals from lower income and education categories that do not have direct access to the Web (such as convenience store and mass merchandise retailer customers). This situation is likely to change in the near future. Infrastructure changes, such as the diffusion of broadband cable, will broaden the population of Web users in the years to come. Even now, creative solutions can be used to give more customers Web access for the purpose of conducting a survey. For example, a kiosk system can be placed in a location that all customers could access (such as a convenience store or an employee lounge). A crosssection of customers could be encouraged to use the kiosk using personal communication or incentives (such as store coupons). Easy-to-read touch-screen displays can be used to collect, transfer, and even analyze the data on-line. Another alternative is to use printed versions of the survey that can be handed out or mailed to customers and later scanned and processed on-line.

Written surveys, particularly mail surveys, remain a popular approach to data collection. An advantage of written surveys is their relative low cost *per targeted respondent,* or survey sent. Written surveys can be mailed or distributed efficiently to a relatively large number of customers. The problem is that response rates tend to be low for this approach. Because of the low yield, direct mail often proves more expensive than telephone or Webbased surveys and the respondents are not as representative of the customer population. The quality of the survey data also suffers in that, compared to phone or interview surveys, written surveys offer less control over the interview itself. Written surveys may be passed along for others (subordinates or other family members) to fill out and there is no easy way to clear up misunderstandings or ensure that the respondent is responding carefully to the questions.

One solution to the weaknesses inherent in any one method of data collection is to combine elements of more than one approach. For example, one-on-one or small group interviews can be used to explain the purpose of the survey and motivate participation.

To ensure anonymity, written surveys could then be left with the respondents to fill out and return after the interview. Another successful approach in retail contexts is to use store intercepts in combination with written, telephone, or Web surveys. The store intercepts are used to explain the survey and motivate participants to participate in it, while the follow-up survey (in writing, by phone, or by Web page) allows respondents to participate at their convenience.

Sampling is the process of selecting respondents or customers from a population for inclusion in the survey. Naturally, then, sampling starts with the customer population or populations of interest. Your market segmentation scheme and the specific segments that you have decided to include in the research largely define your customer population.

The wide variety of techniques for sampling from customer populations fall into three General categories:

- Census samples
- Judgment samples
- Statistical samples

Census samples involve gathering information from every possible member of a population, such as all of an organization's customers—or all customers in a given segment. Census samples are perfectly representative because the sample and the population are one and the same. Census samples are feasible primarily when the population size is relatively small (such as potential purchasers of jumbo jet engines or highly specialized industrial tools). If you define your population as all customers who have recently recorded transactions, your own records can supply a census sample of current customers.

When the population of customers is too large for a census sample, judgment or statistical samples are called for. Judgment samples involve—as you would expect—using your judgment to decide who should and should not be included. One common method of judgment sampling is to take a list customers and pick people well dispersed with respect to age, sex, income, education, and so on. The drawback is that the inclusion of respondents in the sample is at the discretion of the researcher. This makes it difficult to generalize any results to the population at large. At the same time, this approach is useful when the goal is simply to identify potentially important issues, as when conducting qualitative research. Recall, for example, that the primary goal of using the CIT (critical incident technique) method is to find out what attributes and benefits to include in a more systematic survey.

Statistical sampling involves using statistical probability to determine a sample. Hayes tells us that the primary differences between judgment and statistical sampling are that statistical sampling involves the use of random selection to include cases or respondents in the sample, the ability to statistically determine an appropriate sample size, and the ability to determine how representative the sample is of the population. Thus statistical sampling allows for greater generalization of the study results to the population as a whole. Examples of statistical sampling methods include random-digit dialing of customers (as through CATI systems) and systematic sampling from a customer list (start at a random point and then pick customers at set intervals, say, every tenth or hundredth name, until you have the number you need for your sample). Respondents in the ACSI survey, for example, are selected using random-digit dialing. Naturally, the choice of a sampling method or methods is a function of both the size and accessibility of the customer population or populations of interest and the purpose of the research.

Once you've cleared away the preliminary survey questions, the next issue that you face in developing the survey is just how to measure benefit and attribute performance and importance. With respect to performance, the survey results should provide reliable and sensitive measures of customer benefits, customer satisfaction, and loyalty. When measuring importance, you must choose between direct customer measures of importance (using, for example, scales or other rating tasks) and derived importance or impact measures based on statistical analysis. There are two important factors to consider when you measure perceived customer benefits, customer satisfaction, and loyalty.

First is the abstract nature of the constructs involved. Recall from Chapter Three that customers do not obtain satisfaction directly from the concrete attributes and features that describe product and service offerings. Rather, satisfaction and loyalty are a function of the benefits and consequences that the attributes provide. These benefits (such as convenience, safety, and service quality), being abstract or latent constructs, cannot be observed or measured directly using single survey items and scales. The same is true for such overall evaluations as customer satisfaction and loyalty. Abstract or latent variables are reflected in a variety of concrete measures. Benefits are reflected in the attribute ratings that make up the benefit, satisfaction is reflected in a variety of overall performance ratings, and loyalty in a variety of behavioural intentions.

The best way to empirically measure these latent variables is to use multiple concrete *proxies,* or survey measures. For example, qualitative research shows that a convenience store customer's perception of convenience is reflected in ratings of store location, hours of operation, speed and efficiency of employees, and the availability of parking. A latent variable can be measured using a weighted average or *index* of these survey measures. The convenience index of a convenience store thus becomes a weighted average of a customer's ratings of store location, hours of operation, speed and efficiency of employees, and the availability of parking. Overall satisfaction becomes a weighted average of a customer's ratings on such measures as satisfaction, overall performance versus expectations, and overall performance versus a "best in class" competitor.

The second factor to consider when measuring perceived customer benefits, customer satisfaction, and loyalty is the distribution of the data as it relates to your need for *sensitive measures*—measures that can differentiate among fairly small differences in the underlying conditions. This is an ongoing problem in customer surveys because perceptions of quality and satisfaction almost never fall on a normal distribution. That is, there are typically no bell-shaped curves in the data. In a competitive economy, only those competitors with relatively high quality and satisfaction ratings tend to survive. As we know this results in quality and satisfaction data that is strongly *skewed* (where most of the responses are bunched near the high end of the quality and satisfaction scale and the tail of the distribution trails off toward the low end of the scale).

The measurement challenge is to be able to distinguish among customers that are crowded together at the high end of the scale. To illustrate the problem, consider what happens if you use a very insensitive measure of satisfaction. When asked yes-or-no questions (say, Are you satisfied?), the overwhelming majority of customers answer yes. In a recent study of airline passengers we found 95 percent of customers responding yes when asked to evaluate their satisfaction on a yes-no scale. Unfortunately, yes-or-no questions give you no way to distinguish among customers that range from moderately to very satisfied.

The sensitivity of the scale improves when you move to a 5-point scale (where 1 = poor performance or very dissatisfied and 5 = excellent performance or very satisfied). Research on quality and satisfaction scales suggests that using a 10-point scale is better still. Going beyond 10-point scales, however, is not beneficial as respondents have trouble using all the scale points.

Most sensitive of all is the use of multiple 10-point scale questions to form an index. Consider that any given survey measure is composed of two sources of variation, that which is supposed to be measured (what statisticians call the "true score") and that which is not meant to be measured (the "error"). The *true score* is what the various items in an index have in common, while the *error* is more a function of the biases or problems inherent in individual survey questions. By averaging the measures into a single index, you can increase the amount of true score and reduce the overall error variance (relative to an individual survey measure or question) as error from the individual questions is canceled out. As a result, in statistical analysis and modeling, when you use indices in place of single item measures, you explain more of the variation in satisfaction and loyalty, and the relationships involving quality, satisfaction, and loyalty are stronger. In state-of-the-art quality and satisfaction modeling, the use of indexing to measure abstract or latent variables has become the norm.

Consider a simple example of the value that indices bring to an analysis. When you assess the financial health of your company, you know that any one marketing, accounting, or finance measure (customer retention, return on investment, return on capital employed, stock price) is an imperfect reflection of overall state of the company. Taken together, however, the measures provide a more accurate picture of financial health than is possible using any single measure.

The next step is to decide whether to use direct or derived measures of attribute and benefit importance. Many satisfaction measurement systems rely heavily on the "gap" model, in which the measure of what needs improvement in quality or satisfaction is the difference between customers' direct ratings of attribute importance and direct ratings of performance (performance minus importance). There are three kinds of direct measures commonly used in marketing research:

- *Direct scale ratings:* Respondents rate the importance of a product or service's attributes on a scale ranging, for example, from "not at all important" to "very important."
- *Point allocation methods:* Respondents distribute importance "points" (say 100 points) among a given set of attributes where the proportion of points allocated to an attribute indicates its importance.

- *Paired comparison ratings:* Respondents rate the relative importance of attribute pairs.

Paired comparison ratings can place tremendous burdens on respondents because of the number of attribute pairs involved. They have also been heavily criticized for producing arbitrary measures of importance.

Direct scale ratings are considered more accurate (less biased) than point allocations and easier for respondents to provide than either point allocations or paired comparison ratings. These factors make direct scale ratings the more popular choice, so the remainder of this discussion will focus on this method of assessing customer responses.

The primary advantage of direct importance scale ratings and the gap model is their ease of implementation. They require minimal analysis (plotting averages and taking difference scores) and can be easily understood at various levels in an organization, from front-line service personnel to CEOs. Yet there are several problems associated with using direct measures. The method assumes that customers understand what you mean by "important" and also that they know just what attributes are important to them—and are willing to tell you about it. In the end, we find that asking customers directly to rate the impact that an attribute has on their satisfaction and loyalty is an extremely difficult task. Direct importance measures often result in socially acceptable or status quo answers and poor discrimination. Using direct scale ratings, for example, respondents have a difficult time differentiating among those attributes that are most important to them. We have rarely found significant differences in importance among the top-rated fifteen to twenty attributes in a survey. Research also shows that the importance measures or weights that people report and those that they use when making a decision often differ dramatically. The insight that direct ratings provide drops off as the number of attributes increases.

We illustrate both the strengths and weaknesses of the gap model using a study in which we examined the drivers of satisfaction for a pharmacy. Approximately a hundred customers evaluated twenty-nine attributes of a retail pharmacy.The mean values of rated attribute importance are ordered from least to most important and plotted question by question (where 1 = not at all important and 10 = very important). The corresponding attribute performance measures are also plotted (where 1 = poor performance and 10 = excellent performance). The key attributes to improve are those where the "gap" (performance minus importance) is lowest.

On the positive side, gap models are relatively easy to implement, analyze, and explain. The analysis simply involves plotting the two dimensions, importance and performance, and examining their differences. This often makes gap models a good option for companies that are just beginning to develop a customer orientation. The models identify the "low-hanging fruit"—the obvious gaps that need to be closed—and get the company into the habit of monitoring customers. The prioritysetting logic is also the same as for the strategic satisfaction matrix. Attributes on which both importance and performance are rated high are core competencies, while attributes with high importance and low performance need improvement.

However, a major problem with the approach is that customers rate most everything as important. The conclusion is that the company needs to improve most of the items with low performance ratings, and it's hard to tell which ones would make the most difference to results. Basically, importance scales are effective at highlighting the *least* important attributes but ineffective at highlighting the *most* important attributes. The direct importance ratings are simply not diagnostic. It is primarily the *performance* measures that drive the priority-setting process.

Another problem with direct importance measures and the gap model is that the survey has a tendency to grow. Because the approach requires at least two ratings for each attribute, the survey becomes nearly twice as long as a survey where importance measures are derived by other (statistical) means, as described in the next section. One question is required to rate an attribute's performance and another to rate its importance. Direct importance ratings may be the only option when the customer population (or the sample size) is too small or ease of implementation is an overriding concern. Where feasible, however, it is much more economical to take the statistical approach and add good dependent variables, such as satisfaction and loyalty, for use in a regression analysis.

Importance measures do not need to be measured directly. They can be derived statistically from attribute performance ratings and ratings of overall satisfaction. Because statistical estimations are more objective and less biased, they are often superior to direct customer ratings. Statistical analysis provides estimates of importance as the impact that one variable has on another. Customers indicate how they perceive a product or service to perform on a number of attributes as well as their overall satisfaction and loyalty. Variation in performance and satisfaction across customers allows the researcher to estimate (using regression or regression-based statistical techniques) the impact that different aspects of quality and value have on satisfaction and loyalty. Statistically determined importance ratings can avoid many of the problems that you encounter with direct importance ratings.

But the quality of the statistical estimates can vary significantly. *The important question is whether or not the estimation builds on the lens of the customer!* The lens should be viewed as a blueprint for both survey development *and* analysis. A major problem facing regression-based estimates of impact or importance centres on the correlation among the drivers of satisfaction. If attribute ratings are too highly correlated, that is, if changes in one rating tend to follow changes in another without regard to outside factors—what statisticians refer to as lacking sufficient *independence*—the statistical estimates of impact may be poor.

The lens of the customer, which is based on thorough analysis of qualitative research, shows just which attributes go together in the customer's mind. By combining multiple attribute ratings together into benefit indices, the lens provides a means of reducing correlation among the satisfaction drivers; it increases their independence. The result is a set of benefit and attribute importance weights that are superior to those that can be collected directly from customers.

Once you go through the background analysis outlined thus far, you'll be in a position to develop a survey instrument you can use with confidence. The process described here follows the flowchart which we have found useful in developing and administering our own quality-satisfactionloyalty surveys. The first part of this chapter covered Step 1 (the preliminary decisions regarding what information to collect and how to collect it), so the discussion here starts with Step 2 and goes through the rest of the process. Appendix B at the back of the book provides a sample output in the form of a finished survey script from the National Association of Convenience Stores (NACS). We refer to this survey throughout the process to illustrate our recommendations.

The primary purpose of the opening statement is to persuade your targeted respondents to take part in the survey. There are three main messages that can be communicated in an opening statement to help maximize the response rate:

- Emphasize the importance of the topic or problem area to respondents.
- Emphasize that the primary purpose of the research is to better understand the problem.
- Emphasize that the organization or entity conducting the research will use the results to improve the situation.

In the convenience store survey, the emphasis in the opening statements is on the latter two points. The statements point out that the survey is meant to understand what quality areas are important to convenience store customers and that the results will be used to guide quality improvement efforts.

The opening statements may also include screener questions needed to identify customers. The convenience store survey screens respondents to include those individuals who have visited a convenience store within the last three months. The screener in the survey also provides an explanation that convenience stores do not include grocery store chains, drug or discount stores, or mass merchandisers. If asked, the interviewer explicitly defines a convenience store as "typically a small franchised market that is open long hours." These explanations and definitions were added as a result of pretesting and revising the survey. Once respondents have been screened and agree to participate, their first task is to evaluate attribute performance levels. In some cases the ratings may only apply to the product, service, or retailer of interest (say, stores in the Seven-Eleven chain). In other cases the ratings may apply to multiple competitors (say, Seven-Eleven, Quik Stop, and other widely known chains). Before providing the information, the survey must instruct respondents on how to perform the task. This includes who or what is being rated and how to use the scales.

The types of scales and their explanation depend partly on the method used to collect the data. If, for example, it is important to explain multiple anchors on the scale (such as what a 1, 2, 3, 4, or 5 actually means in the context of the survey), it is easier to do this in a written or Web-based survey where respondents can refer to the written anchors. It is more difficult to do so in a telephone survey. Because the respondent has no written list to refer to, the emphasis is typically on keeping only the two endpoints in mind. In the convenience store survey, for example, it is explained that a rating of 1 means poor performance and a rating of 10 means excellent performance.

Keep in mind that the choice of scales and the need to label scale points depends on the researcher's approach to measurement. Given the abstract nature of the constructs and the need for sensitive measures, we strongly advocate using indices to measure customer benefits, customer satisfaction, and loyalty. The use of indices gets you away from very concrete, individual scales where each point on the scale is ascribed some meaning. Indices resemble temperature scales—they just show that the reported value is higher or lower than some benchmark. The meaning you attach to the index levels is based on how a product or service performs against competitors and over time. By deemphasizing concrete scale points in favour of more sensitive indices, you have less need to ascribe meaning to anything more than the end points. We recommend using 10-point scales, where 1 is poor and 10 is excellent, to evaluate performance across data collection methods.

The next sections of the survey present all of the attributes the lens of the customer research recommended for evaluation. The lens of the customer provides a blueprint as to how the attributes are organized— how they go together in a customer's mind. The survey should leverage this lens and present the attributes in clusters defined by the benefit categories (quality of the service, product offerings, store layout, and so on). Particular to the convenience store survey is the inclusion of two questions at the beginning of this section to assess customer perceptions of store reputation. As described in Chapter Three, these ratings will be used in combination with overall satisfaction to explain customer loyalty.

Satisfaction is the customer's overall evaluation of his or her experiences with a product or service provider. In your subsequent analysis, it will be a major dependent variable that you will explain using your measures of attribute and benefit performance. Satisfaction is a latent variable that will be manifested in a variety of more concrete performance ratings. As we have said, it is critical to combine multiple measures of satisfaction in a satisfaction index. In addition to a simple rating of satisfaction, other measures include evaluations of overall product or service performance against different benchmarks. You might ask customers to evaluate performance versus their expectations, versus an ideal product or service provider in the category, or versus a "best in class" competitor.

Notice that we do not advocate using any one of these as a proxy for satisfaction. Rather, satisfaction as a latent or abstract construct is what all of the various evaluations have in common. The measures simply represent different benchmarks that customers use to evaluate performance and from which an index can be constructed. The convenience store survey has respondents evaluate performance using three different questions. The first asks them to express overall satisfaction, the second asks for an evaluation of performance versus expectations, and the third seeks an evaluation of performance versus an ideal product or service in the category. These questions were modeled directly on those used in the ACSI survey, which have been shown to provide a very reliable and sensitive measure of satisfaction. An added benefit of using the ACSI questions is that it allowed us to benchmark the survey results for convenience stores against other industries and firms included in the ACSI survey.

Whereas satisfaction measures apply more or less universally across industries and contexts, loyalty measures do not. As discussed in Chapter Three, the desired outcomes of satisfaction are highly specific to the nature of the business, product, and service involved. Volvo, for example, has specified a range of desired customer outcomes, from the repeat purchase of a Volvo vehicle to the purchase of Volvo financing, Volvo insurance, the purchase and use of a Volvo gas card, and the spread of positive word-ofmouth advertising. If your customers are retailers who turn around and sell your product to end users, loyalty may take the form of the *push*—the sales effort they make on your behalf—as in the "Råtorp Tire Company" case in Appendix A.

If your product is a once-in-a-lifetime purchase (a piece of jewelry or a collector's item), loyalty may involve the customer's willingness to buy other products or services from you (cross-selling) and to tell other potential customers about your offerings. In an industrial context, the level of satisfaction may have little effect on whether a customer buys at least some of your products and services. At the same time, it may have a great effect on just how *much* they buy (account penetration). Another desired outcome may include the trust that customers place in you and their resulting commitment to maintaining a relationship.

Our point is simply that, whereas satisfaction measures are more or less universal, loyalty measures must be customized. In the convenience store survey, the desired outcomes for the store chains and franchisees are rather straightforward. They include enhancing the customers' likelihood of visiting the store again in the future and their likelihood of recommending the store to others. The measures used in the Råtorp Tire Company survey were quite different. As in the convenience store survey, they included the likelihood that the customer (in this case a retailer) would continue to purchase, but they also included whether the proportion of products ordered from the manufacturer would likely increase or decrease in the future (account penetration) and the degree to which the retailer would recommend the manufacturer's products to its customers (push).

Descriptive questions (including market segment profiles and demographic questions) are typically added near the end of the survey. As noted earlier, the main reason for this placement is that the questions, being more personal in nature, are apt to lead a respondent to terminate the survey if asked early on. Once the interviewer has developed some rapport with the respondent and the interview has the momentum provided by answering the performance, satisfaction, and loyalty questions, descriptive information is often easier to get.

The primary purpose of the descriptive questions is to group customers by characteristics such as age and income level for later analysis, so as to track their representativeness and discover possible new segments. Recall that the convenience store survey contains both a direct question regarding segmentation and a group of indirect demographic questions that can be used to segment or describe customers. The direct question presents the five segment-defining statements listed toward the beginning of this chapter and asks respondents to select the one statement that best describes their use of the convenience store. As noted earlier, the primary benefit of having respondents selfselect into preexisting segments is the ease of subsequent analysis. The drawback is that it presumes that the segments do not change or evolve significantly over time.

A golden rule of survey research is to conduct one or more tests before you put any survey into the field. The primary purpose of preliminary testing is to identify and resolve whatever problems respondents might have in answering the questions. Pretesting tells you whether the survey is able to collect the desired information, and where you need to reword questions to make them simpler and easier to understand. If the pretest is weak and major revisions are required, the revised survey should be tested again before being put into the field.

Pretesting is not just the domain of those who administer the survey; it can raise questions of strategic relevance to top management as well. Another rule we like to follow is to involve both those directly involved in the survey process and those who will use the information to make resource allocation decisions. In pretesting the convenience store survey, for example, we learned several lessons. One was that many people were unclear as to just what a convenience store was in the first place. Does it include gas stations that sell some other merchandise? Grocery store chains that sell gasoline? This led to the inclusion of more specific screening questions and definitions that the interviewer could use as needed.

Pretesting also raised questions about what benchmarks the customer should use to evaluate the competitiveness of a convenience store's prices. Should the benchmarks be limited to other convenience stores, or should they include other stores that sell similar merchandise (such as grocery stores for bread, milk, and soft drinks). Based on top management input, it was decided to let customers compare prices to other stores at which they may buy similar merchandise. The reason was that executives at the various chains were very interested in the gap between perceived and actual price differences between convenience stores and other types of stores. Whereas convenience stores are often perceived as having relatively high prices, actual price differences are often small or nonexistent.

Just how the survey is arranged and conducted is largely a function of the method of contact. Telephone surveys often involve random-digit dialing or random selection from a customer list.

The interviewer makes a pitch for participation and, if the time is not convenient, can arrange for a better time to call back. Before collecting survey data in a one-on-one interview, the respondent is usually called and an explicit appointment is made. Recall that store intercepts are also a valuable tool for selling the survey—persuading people to take part in later administration either by phone, Web, or mail. Web surveys may use an e-mail message to introduce and gain interest in the survey and then instruct the respondent on how to access the survey. Customers may also self-select to participate in surveys that are available on a company's Web site.

Just who administers the survey is a function of both the sheer number of respondents and the need for objectivity. We suggest that people within the sponsoring company administer the survey themselves as long as the number of respondents is not too large and administrators can remain objective. As argued in Chapter One, a truly customer-oriented company should not routinely leave the job of collecting customer data to outsiders. But for a large-sample survey, it will be more cost-effective to use a professional data collection firm. If the interviewer's compensation is a function of customer responses (the number of "10s" on the survey), the objectivity of the responses and resulting data will be compromised. If a more objective interviewer cannot be found within the company, it would again be best to use a third party to collect the data.

The development of a quality-satisfaction-loyalty survey builds directly on the lens of the customer. Survey development should not be a process in which people from different parts of a company sit around and decide what they would like to see on the survey. Rather, the lens of the customer provides a blueprint for deciding which attributes to include and the benefit categories to use for organizing them. Even before developing a survey it is important to understand what populations or market segments to survey, what data collection method or methods to use, and how to sample from the target populations.

In leveraging the lens of the customer, the construction of a quality-satisfaction-loyalty survey should follow certain guidelines. Benefits, satisfaction, and loyalty are abstract constructs that cannot be measured directly using any one concrete survey item. They are best measured using an index of multiple measures or proxies. Indices also provide for more sensitive measures than single survey items, so they can explain more of the variation in satisfaction and loyalty and are better at identifying important satisfaction drivers.

The importance that customers place on attributes and benefits has traditionally been determined by two different approaches: direct measures of importance and those derived from statistical analysis. Among the different direct measures, direct scales (ratings from "not important" to "very important") are often preferred. They are straightforward to collect and as good as or better than other direct approaches (such as point allocation or paired comparisons). Yet, when done properly, statistically derived measures of importance are better than direct measures at objectively capturing the impact attributes and benefits have on satisfaction and loyalty. It is important for statistical analyses to leverage the lens of the customer when grouping variables for analysis. Otherwise, even the most rigorous statistical estimates may be a poor reflection of reality.

With the lens of the customer in mind and the data collection methods chosen, you can complete the survey instrument in a systematic way. First, assess attribute performance by benefit category. After that, obtain overall evaluations of satisfaction. Then select loyalty measures and customize them to fit the product, service, or context. To some, loyalty is simply a matter of whether a customer comes back to buy the same product or use the same service. To others, loyalty is a matter of how much more customers will buy (account penetration) or what else they will buy (cross-selling). After adding descriptive questions to help identify market segments, pretest the survey to identify any unforeseen problems. Arranging and conducting the survey yields the data that serves as input to the next phase of the process. In Chapter Five we focus on using this data to derive the information needed to set priorities and improve product and service quality.

W hen it comes to analyzing your customer survey data, you have a lot of options. We recommend a variation on *principal-components regression (PCR)* that is relatively simple to use and provides as much detailed information as you need to make quality improvement decisions. It combines two statistical methods: principal-components analysis and regression analysis. *Principal-components analysis* is a data reduction tool that shows what any group of survey measures have in common, so you can develop the benefit, satisfaction, and loyalty indices. *Regression analysis* relates these indices to each other and lets you determine the benefit, satisfaction, and loyalty impact scores.

As in earlier chapters, we present a flowchart to illustrate the necessary steps used to apply PCR to the lens of the customer. To support our recommendation, in Appendix C at the end of the book we compare results achieved using this method against the results of other approaches.

We begin by describing just what information you can and should be obtaining from your analysis. After describing our data analysis method, we end the chapter with a discussion of how to link survey data to financial performance measures, illustrating the links with examples from Volvo and a major hotel chain. These financial links, which highlight the payoff from investments suggested by customer measurement, will help you inspire people to make real quality improvements based on the information the survey process develops.

When you analyze satisfaction and loyalty data, you're really looking for answers to two relatively simple questions. Where does your company need to improve quality or value to increase satisfaction and loyalty? And once satisfaction and loyalty are improved, what are the payoffs? The basic assumptions are that improved quality leads to increased satisfaction, which in turn makes customers more loyal, and that you get more profit from loyal customers than from those who don't care where they get the product or service you're selling.

Now, how do you quantify the links? The prerequisite is that your measurement system should provide sensitive *and* reliable measures. Your goal is to provide managers with truly diagnostic information—with levers they can push to improve quality and satisfaction. You don't want results that suggest that everything (or nothing) is important, or results that show differences (as among competitors) or changes (over time) that are not valid and meaningful. In other words, you want a system that produces results you can trust. Finally, you want to be able to predict what happens when satisfaction increases. How likely are customers to come back and how much more revenue or profit will they generate?

To make your measurement system a reality, you will need to analyze your survey data to produce multiple levels of information in the system. The circles labeled "satisfaction" and "loyalty" are the key to understanding your customers' overall consumption experience. Best measured using indices made up of multiple concrete measures, these abstract constructs are important in benchmarking performance versus competitors and tracking performance over time. These benefit-level indices are the heart of the lens of the customer. They provide an overall view of how you are performing in quality areas as defined by your customers. But because these indices are abstract, they cannot be acted upon directly. Action requires moving down to the level of the underlying concrete attributes.

Attribute values are obtained directly from the quality-satisfaction-loyalty survey ratings. Each is measured using a 10-point scale like the ones in the convenience store questionnaire in Appendix B. For the benefits and attributes, 1 is poor performance and 10 is excellent performance. But setting priorities requires you to measure impact as well, that is, the extent to which a change in an attribute will lead to a change in satisfaction, loyalty, and other desired customer outcomes. As there are attribute and benefit levels of performance, so there are also attribute and benefit levels of impact. The benefit-level impacts (obtained from the regression analysis described later in this chapter), indicate how much impact each benefit has on customer satisfaction. It is helpful to focus initially on these benefit-level impacts to gain an understanding of the consumption experience. Looking at the attribute or question level impacts (obtained from the principal-components analysis also described in this chapter) will help you relate your improvement efforts to the everyday activities of the company that have the highest payoff. Attribute impacts are more the focus of continuous improvement efforts, while benefit impacts are the focus of innovation efforts—attempts to find completely new ways to deliver the benefits that customers value.

A benefit-level impact of 0.5 shows that a 1-unit change in that benefit index is associated with a 0.5-unit increase in the satisfaction index. Once you have impact information at every level of the model, you can quantify the change that improving an attribute or benefit would make in loyalty (and subsequent profitability, once this data is added to the model). The impact of changing an input to the model (an attribute) on the output of the model (loyalty or profitability) is simply the product of all impacts in the chain of causes and effects. (Where there is more than one path or chain of cause-and-effect relationships, it would be the sum of the different impact chains.)

If you are familiar with traditional PCR, you will see that our approach to principal-components regression has some unique features. Traditional PCR factor-analyzes all the attribute ratings simultaneously to produce a set of independent components or factors. It ignores benefit clusters of the type we recommend you develop using qualitative research to create the lens of the customer. The problem is that the approach is too data driven; the factor analysis dictates the lens. In contrast, our approach uses the benefit groupings or clusters in the lens as a theory or model to structure the PCR analysis. This approach provides the technical sophistication and diagnostic information that your analysis requires. The main alternative to using our version of PCR is *partial least squares* (PLS). Both our PCR approach and PLS use the lens of the customer as a guide to structure the analysis. PCR is a two-step approach in which the benefit, satisfaction, and loyalty indices are first estimated using a series of principal-components analyses. The researcher then uses these indices or latent variables in a series of regression models to estimate a causal chain of events (as from quality through to financial performance). PLS performs both of these steps for the researcher. It estimates an entire causal chain or model using an iterative estimation procedure that integrates aspects of principal-components analysis and multiple regression. Researchers in the areas of quality, marketing, and consumer research regard PLS as the state of the art in customer satisfaction modeling.

The disadvantage of PLS is that it requires special software and training, and the software is neither user-friendly nor easy to find. If you have mastered PLS, by all means use it. At a conceptual level, our flowchart and procedure for evaluating the quality of your analysis still applies. Otherwise, we recommend that you use PCR, which is straightforward to do using easily available and user-friendly software packages. In Appendix C we demonstrate just how similar the results are with PCR and PLS. Comparing the two approaches we find a 0.99 correlation in estimated benefit-level impacts and a 0.98 correlation in estimated attribute-level impacts. In other words, the results are virtually identical. The following sections describe how to analyze a customer satisfaction model using our PCR method.

The sole purpose of analysis is to make sense out of the data you collect. This section includes a step-by-step guide to analyzing data sets that you can use if you're in charge of performing or managing the data analysis. Even if you're remote from the actual research and your responsibility is to create an environment where customer data will be developed and used, the guide will still be useful as it will demystify the process and, as a consequence, make you more constructively critical when evaluating the output of an analysis.

The first major accomplishment will be to create the latent variables for benefits, satisfaction, and loyalty. Then the process will go on to derive the actual values for the impact of one level of the model on the next, and to establish benchmark values for the benefit, satisfaction, and loyalty indices. The combination of impacts and indices will provide the cause-effect chain.

Once you've built the lens of the customer for your products or services and seen the valuable information it can help you produce, it's tempting to sit back and ask, "Well, now what do the numbers say we should do?"

But it's not that simple. The critical next phase of the process is to use the information to set priorities for improvement. And don't underestimate the importance of obtaining top management input to your action plans at this point. This may require some persistence. Too often managers view measurement systems, including the quality-satisfaction-loyalty model we present here, as a means of avoiding tough decisions—but "the numbers" don't pay the bills, and they don't make decisions, either.

Managers who are in charge of implementing their company's strategies and hold the authority to budget and who allocate resources to improve quality and satisfaction cannot absent themselves from the process. The numbers simply help managers base their decisions on facts.

Here in this chapter we close the loop. We first discuss management's role in using the output of the measurement system to set priorities for improvement. We then discuss how to implement the priorities. We bridge the gap between the customer benefits and product or service attributes that need improvement and the internal changes they require.

As we said in Chapter One, setting priorities requires both impact and performance information for the various drivers of satisfaction and loyalty. But to set priorities, you must make some critical decisions regarding just what constitutes high versus low impact and high versus low performance. These decisions require you to consider a number of factors beyond the information in your impact-performance chart, including your strategy and competencies as well as relevant benchmarks, costs, and market dynamics.

Recall that the basic logic is to categorize the various benefit and attribute drivers of satisfaction into one of the four cells of the matrix, each of which is associated with its own market action implications. Generally, the essential areas to improve are those where impact or importance is high and performance is low. Customers are essentially telling us that we are falling short in these important areas. Improvements to these areas will effectively focus resources where they have the greatest impact on satisfaction and subsequent loyalty and profitability. This is also the cell in which you are most competitively vulnerable. If competitors do an excellent job in these areas, they will lure your customers away.

Those areas that are important to customers and in which your performance is strong represent your core competencies and competitive advantages. It is essential to maintain if not improve performance on these drivers. The implications for the opposite cell, where impact is low and performance is weak, are also clear. Generally, there's no reason to waste resources on improving these areas. According to the customers, performance here just doesn't matter.

The implications for the remaining cell, in which impact is low yet performance is high, are less straightforward. This may be an area where resources have been wasted in the past because the benefits and attributes are not important to customers. In one recent application, for example, we found that customers at an IKEA furniture store in the United States rated traditional Swedish amenities—a child-care facility and a Swedish bake-shop—very positively. Nonetheless, these amenities had little to no impact on satisfaction and loyalty. From a cost-benefit standpoint, we concluded that having the amenities was not costeffective for the U.S.-based store.

Alternatively, benefits and attributes in the low impact-high performance category may contain drivers of satisfaction that customers consider to be basic and necessary (as in Kano's model described in Chapter Five). Customers may find these benefits and attributes everywhere they look and take them for granted. Although important in an absolute sense, these features offer no differentiation because there is little to no variance in their performance across customers and competitors. Airline safety is a classic example here—as long as the planes aren't falling out of the sky, passengers tend to regard one airline as much the same as another. That doesn't mean that any airline can afford to ease off on safety! The same sort of consideration can apply in less dramatic circumstances as well. In the IKEA project, we found that "ease of assembly" was also rated highly and had little impact. Our conclusion here, however, was to make certain that we assure continued high performance on this benefit. Withdrawing resources and reducing performance would only serve to put us on a "slippery slope" and decrease satisfaction. The area would quickly return to the high impact–low performance category. Another possibility in the high performance–low impact quadrant is to find a new target market segment for the product or service. It may well be possible to find new customers who would especially value these benefit areas (such as customers who would value the child-care and bakery facilities in the IKEA store).

But data analysis does not determine where to draw the cell boundaries. Managers must draw the lines and decide just where the improvement should occur. Again, the impact-performance charts are a primary input to this decision process, but there are several other factors that you need to consider.

Your strategic market plan leads you to focus on particular segments of customers to leverage core competencies. But what if your customer data analysis suggests that you improve in areas that are inconsistent with your basic strengths? Management must decide whether or not the areas that need improvement are those in which core competencies and a competitive advantage can be achieved. If not, you may be pursuing customers you can't please with your strengths, at the risk of alienating customers who currently value your offerings. Perhaps you should reconsider your entire strategic market plan instead.

At the same time, the information may be very valuable in deciding on network partners who can help provide customers with the benefits they need. Think back to the convenience store survey, which revealed that safety is the primary driver of satisfaction for customers. In practical terms, safety is not something that a convenience store can completely control, so the implication may be to network and collaborate with those who can have more effect. In some cities, for example, convenience stores provide an area where local law enforcement officers can take a break, make phone calls, and do paperwork. This win-win solution saves the officers time and creates a greater atmosphere of safety than the stores could provide on their own.

It is also critically important to benchmark both impact and performance when using this information to set priorities. In the Råtorp Tire Company case (Appendix A at the back of the book), impact-performance charts are supplied for three main competitors in the market. As the reader quickly finds out, making decisions for Råtorp requires a careful consideration of impact and performance levels for the competitors as well. In an absolute sense, impact may be high and performance low in a given area, suggesting the need to make improvements. But what if your closest competitor shows even lower performance and higher impact? It may be a mistake to improve that area if there are others that also call for attention. Relatively, it may be a competitive strength, at least in the short run.

At the same time, do not ignore the absolute levels of impact and performance. Over the long haul, the absolute levels of performance and impact highlight your vulnerabilities, as well as those of your competitors, and suggest where new competitors may enter or improve to take customers away.

In Chapter Five we briefly discussed how to incorporate cost considerations into the analysis. When you tie your model and analysis to increased profit per customer, you then have some idea that the costs typically incurred to improve quality are covered. But in most cases, managers must consider the relative costs of making improvements when deciding which areas to improve. Remember that the goal is to optimize rather than maximize satisfaction and loyalty. If two areas show equally low performance and high impact, managers should ask, "Which is more cost-effective to improve?" One source of cost information is management itself. Another is through the use of tools such as QFD (quality function deployment, described later in this chapter) that translate product improvements into internal change and explicitly consider cost information.

Finally, consider where your market is headed over time. Just what factors will become more or less important? For personal computers, will processing speed become less of a differential advantage going forward? For convenience stores, will prepared foods become a greater source of differentiation and impact? Both social and technological forecasting are important bases for predicting these market dynamics, but are beyond the scope of our discussion.

Appendix A at the end of the book concludes with a prioritysetting exercise that makes use of the Råtorp Tire Company information discussed in Chapter Three. The exercise provides the output of a survey and data analysis for Råtorp and its two main competitors. We strongly encourage you to work through the data in the case and set priorities for Råtorp. Based on the data, consider what you expect the competition to do as well. The case will force you to consider several factors, including what Råtorp's strategy should be, how the benchmarks influence interpretation of the results, how the competition is likely to evolve over time (such as the role filled by import brands), and what the improvements might cost. The case emphasizes that the task of moving from information to decisions is far from trivial. It requires significant reflection and input from managers in a position to set and implement a strategic market plan.

Once you have targeted which benefits and attributes to improve, you have to figure out just how to improve them. In effect, you need to build a bridge from your model of customer perceptions and behaviours to your internal metrics, parts, processes, and people. When you do this, you'll soon find that—as with any bridge—the traffic on this one flows both ways.

The framework integrates aspects of two leading approaches to improving quality and satisfaction: *quality function deployment* (QFD) and customer satisfaction modeling (as detailed in Chapter Five). Together, the two approaches illustrate qualitatively different steps in the overall process of translating satisfaction into its means of accomplishment. Our satisfaction models translate overall satisfaction down into the customer benefits that drive satisfaction and into the product and service attributes that provide the benefits. These are the uppermost stages of the framework. The lower stages, taken from QFD, translate these attributes further down into their means of accomplishment or production.

It is important to consider what we mean by *translation* in the framework. Consistent with the arrows is a process of moving from the most abstract information of interest to the most concrete. Customer satisfaction is customers' overall evaluation of their purchase and consumption experience. Moving downstream in the framework from satisfaction to production is, therefore, a process of translating abstract, subjective evaluations into concrete, objective means of accomplishment.

In contrast, the process of moving up in the framework from concrete processes and attributes to abstract benefits and overall satisfaction is more of an inductive or *change monitoring* process. After determining what changes to make, it is important to track the changes back upstream in the process. Did, for example, the changes we made internally have a subsequent effect on customer perceptions and satisfaction? To what degree did our improvements to production processes improve process operations, parts deployment, engineering or design characteristics, and ultimately attribute and benefit performance? As we see, the combination of translation and change monitoring forms a two-way traffic that is essential to close the loop on the quality improvement process.

A central point of the framework is that QFD picks up where satisfaction modeling leaves off. The product and service attributes that are the output of the priority-setting process represent the input to QFD. The four houses or phases of QFD thus represent phases four through seven of an overall translation process. The translation is, however, different for pure products than for pure services. For products, targeted attributes must be translated into engineering or design characteristics, parts characteristics, process operations, and finally production requirements. Because services are co-produced by customers and employees at a time and place of the customer's choosing, service production is a different beast. In service applications of QFD, targeted attributes for improvement must be translated into service qualities (for example, hotel arrival), service functions (airport shuttle service), service process designs (number of shuttles, routes, and personnel), and operating policies and procedures (daily schedules and contingency plans).

An important implication of the framework is that for a given product or service, there are at least seven conceptually distinct stages in the overall translation and change monitoring process. It highlights the difficulties and challenges that we face even after a satisfaction model is analyzed and priorities are set. Our goal here is not to exhaustively discuss the implementation phases, but rather to introduce you to QFD as one tool that has helped thousands of companies around the world to link their customer data to product and service improvements. A thorough treatment of how tools such as QFD are used to implement product-driven product and process changes is beyond the scope of this book. It is, in fact, the subject of our next book in the UMBS Management Series.

The work is usually documented in a series of matrices. Its primary benefits are reduced design costs and development time. Other benefits include improving communication and cohesion within a product development or improvement team and solidifying design decisions early in the development cycle.

Generally there are two variants of the QFD methodology. The first is the four-phase system captured and presented in more detail later. In this approach, QFD starts with an input list of customer-desired attributes. These attributes are often ordered hierarchically to handle the large number required to describe a product (such as an automobile door system). At a higher level of abstraction are the benefit categories similar to those used in our satisfaction model (such as that a door system "operates well"). At a lower level of abstraction are the more concrete attributes (such as that a door system is "easy to close from the outside").

The QFD translation process begins in Phase 1, the "House of Quality, " where attributes are translated into engineering characteristics. In subsequent phases—often called *houses*— engineering targets are translated into parts characteristics; targeted parts characteristics are translated into key process operations; and key process operations are translated into production requirements or work instructions. As mentioned, this system is altered when applied to services. The second variant of QFD recognizes that the four-phase system that only fulfills a portion of the planning that is needed for a new product. Separate matrix systems are required to incorporate product quality deployment, technology deployment, cost deployment, and reliability deployment throughout the planning, design, trial, manufacturing, and service phases of product development and launch.

5

Strategic Marketing Plan for a Hotel

HOTEL SALES ORGANIZATION AND OPERATIONS

SALES AND OPERATIONS

Sales is the critical link between marketing and operations.While hospitality professionals may espouse marketing, all too often it becomes ignored in the daily hustle and bustle of operations. It is the role of sales to help bridge this gap and find ways for the key customer-contact members of the hotel to keep the promise of marketing.

Selling starts by the professional sales managers prospecting, making contacts, establishing relationships with clients, uncovering their specific needs and wants. But it doesn't end there. Sales is also the host or hostess greeting restaurant patrons. Sales is the front desk clerk welcoming a guest at the local Holiday Inn or at the Waldorf-Astoria in New York City. Sales is the housekeeping staff delivering the extra set of towels requested by a guest. Sales is the sommelier in a gourmet restaurant recommending wines to complement an entrée choice. Sales is the front office cashier saying, "Thank you for staying with us. We hope you enjoyed your stay." It is amazing how a simple thank-you can express appreciation for a customer's patronage and bring them back.

All client-contact personnel of a hospitality organization perform personal selling either consciously or unconsciously. This includes staff who does not regularly have guest contact, such as the credit manager. One of the authors nearly lost a $100,000 annual account when a poorly trained credit manager called the client to collect a payment that had not yet been billed. A well-trained and motivated employee who understands how a hotel works is key to successful selling. This is accomplished through the hiring and training process, and although the many facets of human resources are beyond the scope of this stage, its importance to guest satisfaction cannot be overstated.

In this particular context, however, the hotel's human resources department can perform services on behalf of the sales department by recruiting sales associates who understand the nature of the hotel industry and its place in the broader category of the services segment of business. Services are different from products and require specialized knowledge and training to be competitive.

Because hospitality is very much a part of the services industry, it is useful to understand how services differ from products. Those characteristics that are unique to the services industry product include perishability, simultaneity, heterogeneity, and intangibility.

Perishability refers to the short shelf life of the hospitality product. If it is not sold today, the potential revenue from the sales of that product is gone. A hotel room has a 24- hour shelf life. A restaurant seat has a twohour shelf life. Manufactured goods have a much longer period of durability. If a television set is not sold today, it can be sold tomorrow or next week. The potential revenue from the sale of that product is not lost. But a Tuesday-night hotel room cannot be resold on Wednesday.Tuesday has come and gone. If the hotel guest room goes unsold Tuesday, the potential revenue lost from that vacant room cannot be recouped.

Simultaneity means that production and consumption occur at the same time. How can you produce a guest experience without the guest? Our customers, in a sense, are part of the assembly line.They need to be present for final production of the product offering.A vacant guest room produces nothing. Yes, the carpeting is installed; the bed is made, the bathroom plumbing works. But it all just exists until a guest arrives to use it. Simultaneous production and consumption is a unique challenge for successful operations in hospitality management. The guest needs to be present, because many of the facets of the service involve performances by hotel staff. A related service characteristic in hospitality is *heterogeneity*. Heterogeneity refers to the variability of service delivery. Guest service agents have their moods. Customers have their moods. All have personalities of varying shapes and sizes. Hospitality is a very peopleoriented business. Service personnel change from shift to shift, typically on an 8-hour schedule. Though operational manuals exist in most hospitality establishments, rarely are policies and procedures followed in an exact manner. Guests' "personalities," too, can change throughout their stay, and it may have nothing to do with how they were treated by service personnel. Dealing with heterogeneity in service operations is dealing with reality.

Mistakes will happen. But more importantly, mistakes can be addressed. Often a simple apology can win back a customer regardless of who was at fault when a mistake happens. *Intangibility* is a fourth major characteristic of service businesses. Some consider it the most important component to recognize. Intangibility refers to the highly intangible nature of the service product offering. Intangibility is a feeling; it is having a sense about something that one cannot fully articulate.

The intangible nature of the service product cannot be prejudged. Consumers cannot really see, touch, smell, hear, or taste a service product prior to consumption. They can only anticipate. One can test-drive a car before an automobile purchase is made to see what it feels like to drive. But a hospitality customer cannot test-drive a hotel weekend package or a restaurant meal prior to consumption. The intangibility aspect of hospitality emphasizes that service delivery is critical to customer satisfaction.

Most customers have an idea of what to expect. But, in the end, they are really not sure of what they are buying until the hospitality experience actually takes place. Finally, after the service has been consumed, the guest has only the memory of the performance.

The foregoing unique characteristics represent the foundational challenge to the hotel's sales staff: they must find a way to promise performance and experience in such a way that the hotel's operations departments can deliver on the promise. If the essence of marketing is finding and keeping a customer, then the sales promise is fundamental to that effort. Operations' most important role is the keeping of that promise to the customer— having that customer walk away with a positive and memorable experience and want to return again.

MANAGEMENT OF THE SALES PROCESS

Sales management is effectively directing the personal selling efforts of a hospitality establishment. It involves managing the sales process from both an individual and team perspective. In other words, sales management addresses the logistics of sales solicitation and the development of sales account executives to enhance their sales productivity.

Sales account executives need to manage their day-to-day activity, sales teams need to coordinate their efforts, and customers need to feel that they are working with a professional and well-managed organization.

There are several components to hospitality sales management. These include sales organization, sales account management, recruitment, training and development, goal setting, and performance appraisals. Sales organization refers to departmental and individual organizational issues and inventory management. The following part focuses on the sales organization aspect of hospitality sales management.

Sales Organization

Sales organization can be viewed from three perspectives. These include departmental organization, individual planning of sales activity, and inventory management. A sales department needs to be organized, and sales managers within that organizational setup need to coordinate their efforts. Sales managers need to plan or organize their individual activities on a daily, weekly, and monthly basis.

Allocating the sale of inventory to various customer segments needs to be managed, as well. These are important issues in hospitality sales management.

Departmental Organization

Organizing a sales department means determining who is going to do what. Sales solicitation needs to take place, administrative tasks need to be completed, and managerial decisions need to be made on a regular basis. In medium- to large-size hospitality establishments, a director of sales and/or a director of marketing coordinates these efforts. In smaller operations, it is not unusual to have one individual responsible for all of the above. For most bed and breakfast operations in the United States and Canada and the small boutique hotels in Europe, for example, the owner and/or manager of the establishment typically handle sales activities.

Sales organizational setup for a midsize urban hotel targeting business clientele. The sales managers in this example are organized by target market and by geographic territory. Sales manager 1 is responsible for corporate accounts located in the immediate downtown and surrounding area. Sales manager 2 is responsible for national corporate accounts. This refers to companies based in other areas that conduct business or have the potential to conduct business at the hotel. Both of these sales managers solicit group and transient business from their account base

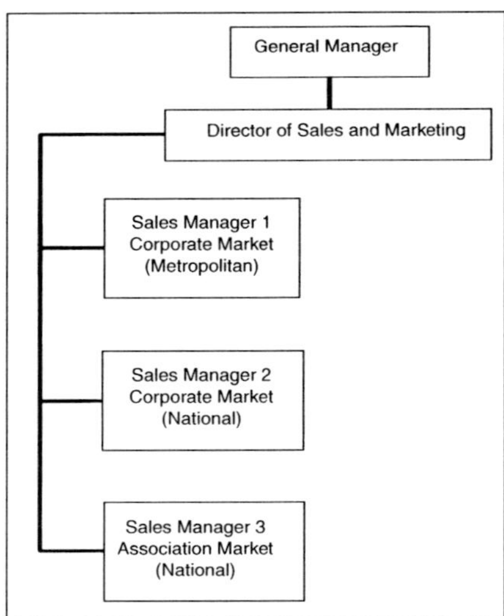

Fig. Organization of an Urban Hotel Sales Department

Sales manager 3 targets meetings and convention business from national association accounts.This business may include executive board meetings, committee meetings, regional conferences, and annual conventions.

In this example, once group events have been booked they are turned over to the conference services department for service delivery. Both the sales managers and director of conference services report to the director of sales and marketing. The sales team meets weekly to discuss issues pertinent to achieving the department's sales objectives.

Weekly sales meetings are very much a part of a sales department's organizational structure, be it a sales force of two or twelve sales account executives. They are critical for effective communication within the department.

At these meetings, each team member highlights his or her weekly activity with regard to new prospects uncovered, tentative bookings, verbal definites, cancellations, etc. (Verbal definites are bookings where clients have verbally committed their meeting or function to the facility but a signed contract is not yet in hand.) In other words, sales managers share with each other progress reports on various accounts they are currently working on. Thus, each team member gets an upto- date informal report on the status of all current sales activity.

For example, one sales manager may be working on a tentative booking but considers it weak because of strong competition for this particular account. Call this Group A. Another sales manager may have a new prospect with similar space requirements interested in the same dates. Call this Group B. Assume, however, that the property has the capability of booking only Group A or Group B over the same dates because of space limitations.

When these types of issues surface at sales meetings discussion will occur raising the following types of questions:

- What is the likelihood that either group will eventually book its business at the property?
- What is the estimated profitability and/or contribution margin for each group?
- Is either group a regular client?
- What is the likelihood of repeat business from either group? In other words, what is the long-term profitability for each?
- Can either group consider alternative dates? What would incite them to move dates?
- Do convention history reports match their current space allocation requests?

These are just a sampling of questions that need to be raised and answered. It is a never-ending process in hospitality sales management to search for the best fit for both the buyer and seller.

The organization of sales management is the process of directing the personal selling efforts of a hospitality establishment. It involves effectively managing the sales process from both an individual and team perspective.

Sales or account managers need to manage their day-to-day activity; sales teams need to coordinate their efforts. Sales account management involves developing, maintaining, and enhancing customer relationships. Sales managers develop expertise for specific market segments, industry segments, and/or customer accounts, and common traits among successful sales account executives include self-confidence, high energy, empathy, enthusiasm, and a sense of self-worth.

This stage introduces the foundation for hospitality sales and marketing. First and foremost, sales flow from marketing. If management doesn't have a marketing mindset, then sales efforts will be all for naught.

Marketing is giving the targeted customers what they want, when they want it, where they want it, at a price they are willing and able to pay. Sales is direct communication with potential customers letting them know we have what they want. In many respects, sales is the link between marketing and operations.

Operations is essentially the delivery component of marketing and the final determination of a happy customer. Marketing begins, transcends, and ends with the consumer. Sales makes sure it happens.

SALES AND MARKETING

Sales and marketing are related concepts, and each is an art and a science. Sales flow from marketing. Marketing, well stated by Lewis "is communicating to and giving target market customers what they want, when they want it, where they want it, and at a price they are willing and able to pay."The primary focus of sales is on the communication aspect of marketing. It involves direct personal selling to potential customers that you and your organization have the right product, in the right place, at the right time, and at the right price—be it a hotel, a restaurant, a casino, or contract food services.

Marketing is getting and keeping a customer, a macro approach to managing a successful business. In a broad sense, marketing is the development and delivery of a successful product, that is, the development and delivery of a satisfied customer. Hotel sales comprises finding that customer and matching his or her specific needs with the right product offering, a micro or one-on-one approach to customer satisfaction. For example, a meeting planner from Texas Instruments is planning an annual sales meeting to be held in Dallas. From a macro perspective, this planner has selected the city and is searching for full-service lodging accommodations for 200 TI sales representatives for a five-day conference. From a micro perspective, he or she visits several hotel alternatives and meets with the hotel sales representatives to find the best "fit." Various aspects of the meeting being planned are discussed including dates, rates, guest room accommodations, function room requirements, food and beverage services, and so forth. It is the job of the hotel sales manager to learn the specific needs and wants of the planner and "create" the right product, place, time, and price for a successful conference.

A successful conference is what the planner is really buying, not bricks and mortar. Thus, successful selling is understanding the real needs of the buyer, communicating how your product and service can best respond to those needs, and then delivering it. In another context, McDonald's Golden Arches markets fun, simplicity, good service, and a good price.

McDonald's sells friendly service, good value for price paid, convenient locations, and those delicious golden chicken nuggets on which many of us grew up. Ronald McDonald is an ancillary product, a public relations endeavor, which augments and supports the idea or concept of kids and why they are special.

Public relations, advertising, and special promotions often support the selling effort. Advertisements for the Ritz-Carlton Hotel Company are directed to their business traveller clientele. Such advertisements incorporate both the selling and marketing aspects of this upscale hotel chain. The company is simultaneously selling hotel rooms to busy business executives and marketing a hotel that "remembers your needs," and is hallmarked by the vision implicit in their slogan "ladies and gentlemen serving ladies and gentlemen."

A travel agent, a corporate travel manager, or a secretary, however, may have handled the actual purchase of the hotel room. Thus, the Ritz-Carlton advertisements support the sale, but they do not actually make the sale happen.

BUILDING MARKET LEADERSHIP: MARKETING AS PROCESS

The hotel business has changed enormously over the last 30 years, embracing special niche forms of lodging, new ways of segmenting markets brand proliferation and consolidation, new tools for acquiring customers distribution innovations and globalization. These changes in markets and in ways hotels relate to and capitalize on them have put new demands on marketing.

Marketing, as addressed herein is not the sales and marketing department; I mean marketing in its broadest sense of how hotels respond to and seize on market opportunities.

Definition? Marketing is a process of creating and sustaining productive relationships with desirable customers. Its goal? To produce such relationships more effectively than competitors do. Let's examine the definition and its implications.

Marketing is:

- *A process*: A process, a series of functions and actions for approaching and dealing with opportunities. *Marketing,* as used herein, is not a job but a way of proceeding to create and operate a hotel focused on customers and competitors, a way that incorporates all members of the hotel staff and its support.
- *Of creating*: The essence of marketing is creation: imagination, insight, willingness to change and evolve, and, yes, discard.
- *And sustaining*: Loyalty over time and repeat customers are the key to productivity and optimal contribution margins.
- *Productive relationships*: A relationship must be two-sided, with

benefits for both partners in the relationship. In the case of customers, the benefits are wants and needs consistently fulfilled and full value received; in the case of staff, professional satisfaction and operating profits sufficient to fund improvements provide attractive compensation, and provide returns on investors' or owners' capital.

- *With desirable customers*: Not all customers are equally desirable; we want those who are willing to pay, growing in numbers, making multiple purchases, and whose needs we are able to fully satisfy. And the goal?
- To produce such relationships. *Production* implies inputs, outputs, and the measurement of productivity. Marketing productivity has been lagging for the last decade; the rising costs of acquiring customers must be reined in.
- More effectively than competitors do. Marketing success is judged in relative terms, using competitors and similar hotels as benchmarks. As a creative process, especially in a field like hospitality wherein innovations are unprotected and easily copied, the benchmarks and goals are always moving targets. Besting the competition is the constant challenge.

It will be clear that successful marketing of a hotel requires the orchestration of a wide variety of talents and skills, of which sales and marketing personnel are only a part.

Chain hotels approach the process one way; independents must do so another. But in either case, market success depends on an effective integration of marketing and operations at the property level under the direction and leadership of a marketdriven general manager.

HOTEL PRICING

CURRENT PRICING CRITERIA

"Our pricing is market-driven, not costbased," says Scott Farrell, corporate director of distribution with Fairmont Hotels and Resorts, a Toronto-based chain of luxury properties. When the chain is setting its prices, it starts with comprehensive market research. Based on the data, the correct price for each marketplace is determined. If there is a major shift in a market, then the prices will adjust for that. However, if there is a major shift in a demand curve, then a shift of price may have no effect.

It may actually leave more money on the table. For example, if the airlines go on strike, a significant shift in the demand curve would result. Under such conditions, decreasing the rate by $50, for example, would only result in a $50 loss. If there is an opportunity to go after a new targeted market with a specific offer, enabling the chain to capture a greater market share, then lowering the rate serves its purpose. Generally, however, lowering rates across the board is not the preferred pricing strategy.

PRICING: WHO IS IN CHARGE

While independently owned properties make their own pricing decisions, in case of a chain it is usually corporate headquarters (HQ) that sets pricing guidelines. Often, individual properties are still responsible for the actual pricing.

Because they are held accountable, they must balance corporate guidelines with their autonomy to set their prices. Caroline Shin, member of the revenue management team at Starwood Hotels and Resorts Worldwide, which operates a number of upscale brands, such as Sheraton and W Hotels, stresses the cooperative nature of this relationship. Successful pricing strategies arise from an ongoing interaction of both sides. Corporate HQ provides sophisticated tools and in-depth market analysis that would be beyond reach of individual properties. Property managers, on the other hand, offer their experience and knowledge of regional specifics that may have gone unnoticed by the corporate team."The people who have been in the property understand the dynamics of that market, and they have developed pricing intuition," explains Shin. Some experts view intuition as a valuable part of the pricing mechanism, and even managers who are technically savvy check the numbers against their gut feeling.

PRICING: SCIENCE, ART, AND INTUITION

Pricing distribution and revenue management techniques are a mix of science and art. Recent research shows that two-thirds of managers making strategic decisions under pressure and time constraints use a combination of analysis and intuition.

The advent of modern technology, such as yield management software packages, has further strengthened this link. "Even the most sophisticated analytical model for forecasting, may it be for hotel pricing or for thermal dynamics of a nuclear plant, still needs variables based upon assumptions," says Shin, who used to work as a nuclear engineer.The more business- savvy hotel management becomes and the more they understand the hotel dynamics and the market, the more can be gained from training them how to define their experiencebased intuition and put it into numbers. In this respect, an interaction between the corporate revenue management team and individual hotels is paramount. "Every time I go out to a property, I learn something new. It only helps me when I build my analytical models to almost translate what they know into numbers," confirms Shin. The better hotels can do that, the better models they can develop. Nonetheless, inaccurate historical data remains a major limitation.

No model is ever going to be perfect, though.What seems to work best is to teach hotel managers how to use the model and to understand the direction of the pricing decisions they need to make. That is the scientific part.The art piece comes into play when they infuse the model with their knowledge and intuition.

Staff training is an important part of this process. "We can't just have Ph.D.s sitting in one room coming with all these models and we just roll it out. At the same time, we can't just have people with intuitions run around and set prices," says Shin.

Revenue management teams must make sure that hotels understand how to employ the models in their daily pricing decisions. When science is applied, the revenue team can go to their experts, ask probing questions, and get solid results. Even though intuition is a part of this process, it is based only on a hypothesis that could have been triggered by a discussion with a customer, knowledge of what is happening in the marketplace, or historic trends. That is why pure intuition is not sufficient. "Managers must have reliable data to support their hunches," cautions Scott Farrell.

CUSTOMER NEEDS

Customer satisfaction is a crucial part of marketing, pricing, and yield management. Any pricing strategy established by the hotel management must attract customers willing to pay the specified rate.While price is a determinator of the customer profile the hotel is looking for, it is also an indicator of the quality of services and the market segment the hotel is competing in.

Therefore, yield management uses information about targeted customers' purchasing Behaviour and product sales to develop pricing strategy together with inventory control that delivers products that are better matched to customer needs, create greater demand, and, on that account, produce greater revenues. Lieberman states that yield management is the process of maximizing profits from the sale of perishable assets, such as hotel rooms, by controlling price and inventory and improving service through systemization.

An exact definition of the target market is essential. There is a definite and firm perception in the psyche of the customer, who views the price as the value forthcoming. Therefore, the eventual satisfaction of the customer is the paramount task of the pricing mechanism. This is the make-or-break factor of the entire hotel, especially if the value expected does not match the price.

TRADITIONAL APPROACH

The single most important criterion of success in any business, including hotels, is profit.The purpose of this object is to discuss the importance of hotel pricing and its influence on yield or revenue management, especially in terms of profit generation, and because of inherent dangers to the industry worldwide, integrity of the established pricing structure. Historically, price has been determined by the triangular relationship of cost and demand in the context of competition. The actual pricing structure is developed with one of these three components as the deciding factor while the other two play supplementary roles.

The traditional pricing strategy was largely cost-driven. Many hotel operators tended to favour the rule-of-thumb method. This approach, also called the $1 per $1,000 rule, states that hotels should charge approximately $1 per night for every $1,000 of room cost, based on an average 70 per cent occupancy.

Although popular in its day, the calculation of cost was commonly misunderstood. Another widely used quantitative method was the Hubbart Formula, developed in the late 1940s as a guideline issued by the American Hotel Association. It focused on computing an average room rate that would cover operational costs and yield a reasonable return on investment. These quantitative methods are fairly static and therefore suited for a stable economic environment. Qualitative pricing approaches, such as percentage increase of previous-year rates adjusted for inflation, payroll increases, and new cost of supplies, reflect more realistically the projected cost.

Other qualitative techniques are less exact but, by being competition-oriented, they offer more flexibility. The Pied Piper or Follow-the-Leader method uses competition as the basis for rate setting, while the Gouge 'Em approach tries to lure business away from other properties by undercutting their prices. If there is no competition to speak of, Hit or Miss fluctuation of rates tied to profitable occupancy levels could be employed.

The drawback of competition-driven pricing is its sole focus on rate comparison, ignoring differences in operating expenses and customer- perceived value. An effective approach, therefore, calls for a mix of methods adjusted for different situations. The fundamental question remains:What should be the driving force in formulating a sound pricing strategy? In today's dynamic business environment, which discards the traditional view that market demand for room rates is largely inelastic, demand orientation seems to provide the best fit.

ROLE OF TECHNOLOGY

While the approach to hotel pricing is still ruled by supply and demand, speed and sophistication of room-rate yield or revenue maximization is now much increased due to two technological factors: yield management software and Internet bookings.

Yield management software packages enable hotels to use a higher number of roomrate levels, or buckets, and to control inventory for rate availability in real time. Each level may consist of several room rates open under given conditions to yield a maximum profit. Traditionally, hotels used between three and five rate levels; otherwise, the adjustment became too complex for the human brain to work with. The introduction of software removed this barrier, and some hotel chains now use up to ten rate levels.This allows implementation of much narrower ranges for each bucket, thus optimizing price elasticity. This further means the software model recognizes the point at which the same number of bookings can be achieved at a higher rate.

Online monitoring of room inventory in real time facilitates the timing of the adjustment. So far, the biggest limitation is the reliability of historical data. Even in its imperfect form, the system has made a difference. However, hotel managers are fully aware that it takes years to develop brand recognition and quality but just a push of a button to damage or even destroy it, if the pricing is not set up knowledgeably. As the technology becomes more sophisticated, it will eliminate such questionable practices as overbooking, which aims at compensating for last-minute cancellations by taking in more than 100 per cent reservations. Besides the question of whether overbooking is ethical and, in some countries, even illegal, better technology would definitely improve the quality of service provided by properties that engage in this practice.

Another area where technological advancement had a great impact on hotel pricing is the Internet. Its use as a booking tool has created a new level of pricing transparency and tiered competition. It also penetrated the negotiation of corporate rates. Many hotels see the effect of the Internet as both good and bad.The good side is that website bookings are growing every day. As more customers become familiar with their favourite hotel websites, hotel companies have started investing heavily in website development and upkeep, which gives them several advantages. First, the cost of online bookings is lower than for bookings made through other distribution channels. Companies do not have to pay commission because the booking is direct, circumventing all intermediaries. Online booking also provides an opportunity to monitor inventory in real time without reliance on a distributor willing to share and regularly supply data. Last but not least, it generates loyal customers by making them eligible for bonus points, which they cannot earn if they use an Internet intermediary.

That is exactly where the flip side of the Internet lies. The intermediaries are getting more powerful and growing significantly in volume. Because most of them show all hotel rates on their website, they make the information accessible to any computer user. One way to meet the challenge of more powerful intermediaries, especially if hotels need to move inventory, is to utilize auctions where the name of the hotel is not disclosed to the customer until the transaction is finalized. Such action, however, calls for extreme caution so that it does not damage a hotel's reputation or threaten its strategic partnerships.

As intermediaries become bigger, rate transparency will increase to the point where it will drive the market, especially when computer literacy and Internet access become the norm.

Moreover, the Internet allows nonbranded hotels to compete more heavily with the branded hotels because they can now be displayed just as readily.

Without significant advertising expense, they can compete on price. For some markets this does not matter, especially when the brand is powerful enough to charge the premium and get the business.

In highly competitive markets, however, the competition creates an additional strain for the individual property. Many branded hotels must now compete with other brands through the traditional distribution channels and with nonbranded hotels on the Internet, which, in principle, lowers hotel rates. A frequently adopted strategy is to invest heavily in website development and customer loyalty programmes, assuring excellent website functionality and that customers are rewarded for booking directly through the hotel website rather than through the website of a thirdparty intermediary. Both Fairmont and Starwood, for example, utilize their high-quality loyalty programmes in this way.

Internet booking also changed the way corporate accounts are negotiated. Because many companies now require that their employees make business travel arrangements via the corporate website, the placement of a hotel or a brand on this booking tool is of strategic importance. Being listed first in the accommodation part, for example, may bring in a higher volume of business and thus substantiate a lower negotiated rate.

THE ROLE OF CREATIVITY IN PRICING

Creativity, either of an individual or a team, can and often does lead to innovative pricing ideas. However, its application must be specific, not just directional. It is not enough to state,"We have to do something about our occupancy level." A pricing campaign must target a number of sold rooms or generated revenue that is required in order to break even or to do better. This specific approach injects efficiency into allocating marketing money to areas where it is most effective and in periods when it is desired.

If there is no task direction or overall pricing leadership, the most creative idea may book only ten roomnights instead of one hundred. It may generate more customer loyalty, but that is something the hotel may not need at the moment, although it could be an acceptable outcome in a low-season month. Pricing leadership helps team members understand the hotel's current situation and direct money and creativity to do exactly what is needed. Creativity comes up with the idea, which serves as a vehicle, but spending marketing money the smart way is a matter of experience in innovation, which turns the idea into a successful product. Creativity also plays a large part in employee satisfaction, and it lowers turnover.

In a sluggish economy, some hotels start paying attention not only to profit as the bottom line but also to revenue. This means they monitor closely the accrued cost as well as the generated revenue, thus achieving the maximum yield. Interestingly, contemporary price leadership may take different forms.

It could mean, for example, elimination of smoking rooms throughout the property. Many U.S. motels are revamping rooms, ripping off cigarette- damaged furniture and carpets, and designating them as nonsmoking. This saves on maintenance and adds to overall packaging flexibility when the business is hurt by lackluster demand. This tactic means drapes, carpets, bedding, and other furnishings must be replaced less frequently; it also mitigates fire risk and enhances cleanliness and overall safety.

THE ROLE OF HUMAN RESOURCES IN PRICING

Some large chains recognize that pricing is a complex issue and that they need to get better at it.There is a new focus on analysing the culture of pricing and how it can be improved. This approach is reflected even in the kinds of people chains are hiring. Although the majority of staff involved in strategic pricing are in the hotel industry and have a background in revenue management, others are in the airline industry and have indepth travel revenue management experience. Some chains have sought access to this experience by hiring from outside the hotel industry. This is to encourage diversification of thinking and new ways of thought—completely out of the box, as the traditional team members are joined by researchers doing a different kind of optimization analysis. The goal could be as radical as trying to manage risk or optimize towards the railroad industry and its scheduling.

On the surface, these tactics have nothing to do with revenue management *per se*.A lot of experience in optimizing difficult travel, however, can only be gained by bringing in people with different backgrounds in consulting or with in-depth Internet experience. In order to move pricing and revenue management to a different level of thought, a new mix of people is necessary. For this approach to work, adequate training must be in place. In this respect, basic HR functions, such as hiring and training, have an impact on pricing. What is necessary is not only to train personnel in quantitative core skills but also in strategic thinking. For example, when a hotel does not want to take a specific piece of business, it must ask such questions as:What is the revenue? What is the rate? What am I displacing by this decision? Where do I think this will go? How does it help my RevPAR? Hotel managers must become more analytical so they can use all the new tools now available. When reports are created, team members must be taught how to use them.A lot of training must be provided for corporate executives, general managers, and regional revenue directors as well. They all must be trained to think more strategically and to understand analysis and the reports so they can help their individual properties.

LONG-TERM STRATEGY TOR THE INTERNET

Because hotels cannot expect that Internet distributors will go out of business, they smartly conclude that a partnership with the devil is better than a fight with him. Besides using their own websites, hotel companies are also making sure that the cost of their transactions goes down continuously so they can compete even at lower rates—while maintaining a good relationship with their carefully selected online intermediaries.

There is a large number of distributors to choose from. On one end of the spectrum is, for example, Expedia, which allows participating hotels to control their rates, meaning a hotel can change its rates any time it wants.At the other end are companies, such as Hotel Reservation Network that bind hotels contractually to a locked rate that cannot be changed. Some hotel chains do not want to partner with these distributors because they like pricing flexibility and want to make sure their rates yield as much as possible.

Adaptation to new technology has been the biggest component of change for intermediaries as well. Companies that do not have the most current technology working in real time or allowing hotels to yield rates in real time are usually not considered a suitable distribution partner for some chains. On the other hand, companies that invest in real-time technology to yield rates are ideal partners because, as the industry sees it, they work with, not against the industry by permitting hotels to raise or lower rates in real time. "They work with us," says Caroline Shin.

"They give data to us very frequently so that we understand the travel pattern bookings on their website.Then we compare it with what is happening on our website and also what we are getting outside the Internet to make sure that our market mix is set appropriately." Pricing flexibility, compatibility with the desired hotel image, and protection of its strategic partnerships, together with cost, play important roles in selecting an intermediary.

PRICING: SUPPORT AND PROTECT

The corporate pricing structure is also in place to support and protect members of the chain in a number of areas including pricing and partnerships. The corporate office sets guidelines for hotels in terms of pricing structure and the market segments they deal with. Fairmont Hotels and Resorts, for example, focuses on four segments: transient leisure travel, group travel, business travel, and wholesale. The corporate structure provides guidelines about how the segments fit with each other, how they cross over, and where they reside in the overall pricing structure.

This information is necessary because every segment acts differently. Most market segments are dynamic and require frequent rate adjustments. One exception is the wholesale market, where pricing is still largely done the traditional way: A wholesaler provides a net rate, marks it up, and sells it to the general population.There may be a hidden cost, however, if the distribution chain includes an operator acting as a middleman between the wholesaler and the supplier.

When setting up the overall pricing structure, one starts with the retail rate, which is a bucket of premium or best available rates charged on the open market. They usually do not carry any restrictions, such as cancellation fees, and they are fully billable. Depending on the level of occupancy, one of these rates is available on any given day when the hotel is not fully booked. It is up to the yield management system to identify which BAR to offer. All other rate types, such as discount rates and prenegotiated rates, are determined in relation to the retail rate. For instance, a corporate rate for a high-volume client will be probably set lower than the BAR rate that is estimated to sell most during the period when the contract is in place. This way the rates are nested within each other in a manner that makes economic sense.

The corporate pricing guidelines follow two main criteria: to maximize revenue and to protect key partnerships.While the hotel sales force negotiates contracts with key partners, such as longstanding corporate accounts or wholesale volume accounts, they make sure to protect these partnerships and provide them value. At the same time, they take every opportunity to maximize revenue. One cannot survive without the other, reiterates Scott Farrell. However, it is up to the hotels themselves, with guidance and additional research, to determine in their marketplace what their pricing structure should look like.

A diversified corporate team, with a mix of people with a hotel industry background and others skilled in optimization modeling, fulfills an additional function. It acts as a risk prevention mechanism, a necessary prerequisite for managing the risk inherent in pricing. Any chain with a wide variety of hotels must make sure the properties are covered in all kinds of situations. One risk containment scenario might be that the chain, in response to a changing demand curve, acquires a type of business that the brand has not catered to traditionally.

Caroline Shin explains, "Sheraton did not take on airline crew business because we did not want crew members lingering in the lobby; it affected our brand image. But we thought maybe we could start taking that when our RevPAR index or occupancy slips to a certain point. So we are trying to change the standards of different market segments we are willing to take."

On the international scale, another risk management plan would be analysing operational cost and determining whether to close down part of the hotel if market research shows occupancy will not be high enough. When PESTEL (political, economic, sociocultural, technological, environmental, legal) analysis indicates demand will drop precipitously for an extended period instead of hoping for the best and running a full house with a full staff, the hotel may decide to shut down floors or restaurants and save cost until the market picks up again. Selection of the appropriate strategy will depend on the market specifics and protection of the image. A property may opt to close down several floors over the weekend if it caters mostly to business clientele staying during the week. It would not, however, suspend room service, although unprofitable, if that is considered an integral part of the offered product. In a worst-case scenario, the chain may decide to sell properties in global risk areas when it determines the external circumstances make it difficult to raise occupancy on an ongoing basis.

BETTER UTILIZE YOUR DISTRIBUTION CHANNELS

The Internet creates a new level of transparency as it allows the opportunity to maximize profitability.There is now a multitude of channels to choose from. Understanding the cost of each channel in relation to the value of provided service has an impact on the quality of pricing decisions. Therefore, it is necessary to determine how much revenue bookings through an Internet intermediary generate and whether or not they justify the accrued cost.There is also a tremendous risk involved.

As discussed earlier, one of key guidelines of corporate marketing is that partners are protected. Just because there is a new Internet site it does not mean a chain can use it and advertise a lower rate, which would undermine a partnership of many years. In terms of cost, the chain must review its pricing strategy not only by market segment but also by distribution channel. "Several years ago, we would not consider the cost of distribution in our ROI.Today we do," concedes Scott Farrell.

Another challenge is to keep up with new Internet sites. The chains must reevaluate constantly and prioritize their yield so as to choose which channels to keep or drop. Fairmont Hotels and Resorts, for example, applies the 80–20 rule. They focus on the 20 per cent of the online wholesalers that capture more than 80 per cent of the business. As Scott Farrell puts it,"Why would I play with the other 10–12 per cent? I only have so many hours in a day to manage. I may as well work with the lion's share."

QUALITY ABOVE ALL?

Criteria for selecting an online distribution partner vary by price levels as well. Budget and economy properties are driven mostly by financial considerations, while upscale and luxury hotels are more concerned with compatibility.

As for chains, they ask two basic questions:

- How can the partnership increase our brand recognition or a brand reach, and
- How much is it going to bring us in terms of revenue or profitability?

Their choice has to match the brand first, and then it has to drive the revenue. If the brand is equaled with quality, online providers that project a connotation of cheapness will not be considered at all.The quality image refers not only to the hotel asset itself but also to how and where this asset is sold.

Fairmont Hotels and Resorts, as a quality brand on the luxury side, cannot compete on price. The quality of their product and the offering of the experience must be considered by the customer at the price being offered. When their hotels play with price, the corporate office watches closely. Scott Farrell explains, "If our property wanted to shift their rate by $50, I would ask why? Give me the case behind it and tell me what you are going to do to make up the additional $50 you are going to lose. If they come back to me and say they are moving their rate from $300 to $250 while driving a certain volume, I would make them go through the process of determining what incremental volume they will need to make up for the $50 in loss." In other words, pricing decisions must be driven by ROI, not only a feeling. Feelings and experience may be involved, but properties must present a strong case based on the estimated ROI and what they plan to get out of the proposed strategy. It allows them to go into the pricing change with their eyes open. They also must consider how the competition will respond.A carelessly lowered rate may lead to a price war.

PRICE ELASTICITY

Contrary to the traditional view that hotel rates are, in the long-term, generally inelastic, price elasticity is receiving a lot of attention nowadays thanks to yield management. Its goal is to take advantage of and to cover the entire spectrum of the customers' ability to purchase. Price elasticity allows hotels to capture customers who do not mind paying the high rate as well as those who are more priceconscious. This can be done in a number of ways. By using different room categories, a luxury hotel can have on the same day suites available at $500 and entry-level rooms at $200. Every room rate category has a different value proposition associated with the incremental revenue. If the variance between a standard room and a deluxe room is $75, the latter should provide an adequately greater value to the customer. The result is a clear product differentiation, which can be also achieved by stay restrictions or by the use of fencing. Examples of physical differences, or fences, are room type, view, amenities, and location.

Nonphysical fences may mean different customers, transactions, or consumption characteristics. These bear many similarities with airline pricing strategies, which differentiate the product by, for example, cancellation restrictions or last-minute availability of a prenegotiated corporate rate. The result is nested pricing, allowing properties to have a very high rate available on the same day as a rate that is more attractive to the lower-end customer.

NEW AREAS OF PRICING AND YIELD MANAGEMENT

Hotel pricing strategies traditionally have been limited to setting and adjusting room rates and other ongoing activities. In order to survive in the current dynamic, competitive, and even dangerous global environment, hotels and resorts are taking on other types of business, some of which are one-time projects. Organizing shows, festivals, and conferences or undergoing renovations requires a new type of core competency. Therefore, in addition to mastering current pricing strategies, hotel practitioners must acquire project management skills, such as those that are taught and practiced by Project Management Institute. Mastering these skills will make hotel team members capable of maximizing yield from project-type functions the same way as they optimize revenue from room rates.

SPEED AND STRATEGY

The speed and immediacy of exposure via the Internet have reshaped how marketing campaigns are conducted. Having eliminated the delay of exposure to marketing collateral material, such as brochures or newspaper advertisements, hotels can conduct targeted discount mini-campaigns on their own websites when the yield management system indicates a drop in occupancy for specific dates. In a similar manner, brand recognition can be enhanced by a carefully orchestrated online auction. The South African hospitality group Protea was among the first in the industry using this method by offering their prospective guests the opportunity to bid on a limited number of weekend getaways in their properties that needed to boost occupancy.

By setting a minimum bidding price, the integrity of the hotel image was protected. Similar auction systems, used to encourage room-night sales during slow periods, are nowadays available in the United States and Canada via several Internet intermediaries. For chains in particular, a long-term strategy in distribution pricing is paramount. It stipulates the criteria and accepts or rejects short-term adjustments depending on what is happening in the industry, what is new in the technology, and who the new players are.

In terms of corporate hierarchy, pricing is formulated and executed on three levels:

- Strategy,
- Tactics and execution, and
- Measurement.

Strategy comes first, followed by tactics meant to support that strategy and their execution. Finally, the achieved outcome is measured against the set benchmarks. If the strategy is sound, it will last longer than the other two steps. Frequently, new tactics must be implemented; these drive the execution and the measurement. This requires a development of proprietary criteria for measurement and their continuous adjustment to changing conditions.

DIVERSIFICATION: THE IMPROVEMENT OF THE PRICING PROCESS

As noted, exclusive hotel industry experience may lead to ossification due to one-sided judgment and the inability to see beyond the familiar. From this perspective, experience is both an asset and a liability. It is human nature to take for granted the way things are done after being in the same environment for a while. Therefore, hotel chains are continuously creating and refining pricing strategies to accommodate not only different market segments but also different situations a hotel may face based on occupancy levels. Corporate HQ tries to identify these different situations and associated variables. "It is almost like a bag of goods, a bag of pricing strategies that should be tested," says Caroline Shin. Hotels are given the full menu and encouraged to try a certain strategy if they are in a specific situation. Depending on the region, an individual property may use one set of strategies more than another. In a weak economy, however, the chains have to work harder and be more flexible because the market is overflowing with demand.

Adapting step by step, a hotel may apply a different strategy every week.The problem for the corporate office is to identify situations a hotel might be in and seek remedy. For example, if group bookings are low this week but competitors are full, how can the property make up the difference with transient or leisure business? The general manager may ask the corporate team, "What pricing strategies can I use in order to fill my house?" Then he or she may ask, "What else worked before for other hotels, and what may work for me based on my market specifics and market characteristics?" That way he or she can test each strategy using the provided tool and personal experience.

EXMAR

PRODUCT DESCRIPTION

EXMAR is a process, supported by a set of associated services, for developing Strategic Marketing Plans.

It assists companies by:

- Guiding them through a logical marketing planning process
- Prompting and defining key data requirements
- Displaying information graphically to aid understanding of the business
- Providing advice at key stages
- Allowing 'what-if ' analyses
- Automatically outputting the report resulting from the analysis.

There are a number of techniques and methodologies incorporated in EXMAR including:

- Gap Analysis
- SWOT Analysis
- Ansoff Matrix
- Boston Box
- Directional Policy Matrix
- Market Segmentation
- Perceptual Maps
- Porter Matrix
- Objective and Strategy setting.

BENEFITS OF EXMAR

The competitive differentiation derived from EXMAR has been the subject of extensive research by Cranfield School of Management and can be summarised as follows:

- Provides a planning framework which ensures consistency across divisions and each division covers all the key aspects of the planning process
- Takes the 'number crunching' out of marketing analysis
- Gives new insights into the markets particularly through the market segmentation techniques
- Gives powerful graphical display which makes large volumes of data understandable
- Enables easy 'what-if ' iterations as strategy options are explored
- Facilitates team work and multidisciplinary involvement in the marketing planning process
- Improves marketing skills within the company
- Focuses planning on the customer
- Gives a clear vision of markets and the company's position in them
- Adds value to marketing database investment.

THE MARKETING PROCESS

Professor Malcolm McDonald of Cranfield University School of Management, a world authority on marketing planning, has produced numerous publications on the marketing planning process over the last 10 years. His best selling book, *Marketing Plans - How to prepare them: How to use them*, now in the Fourth Edition, describes *The Ten Steps of the Strategic Marketing Planning Process* as follows:

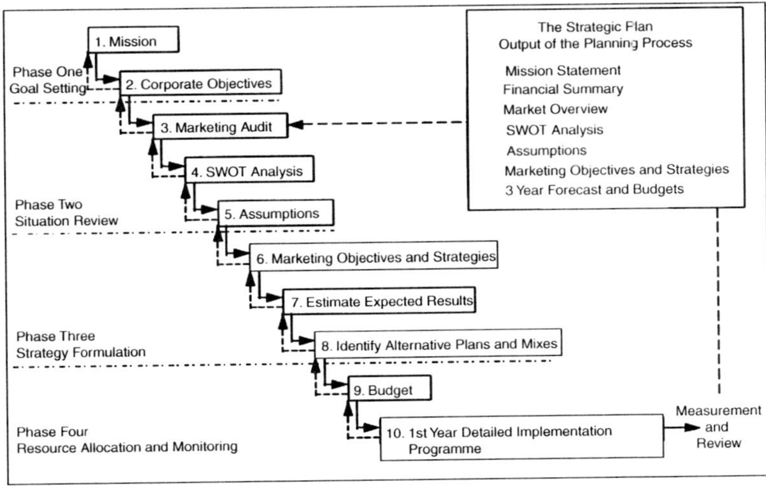

Fig. The Ten Steps of the Strategic Marketing Planning Process

In order to assist companies with the implementation of an effective Strategic Marketing Planning Process many of the techniques were implemented in software programmes. Several prototypes were developed at the Cranfield School of Management, which were widely tested in a variety of commercial environments over a number of years, in order to produce a complete and robust specification of the requirement.

CONSUMER DECISION RULES AND IMPLICATIONS FOR HOTEL CHOICE

Consumers' choices are influenced by the goals they attempt to achieve. Once a person has recognized a need, such as the need for accommodation when traveling for business or pleasure, he or she engages in an information search to identify alternatives from which to choose. Understanding how consumers evaluate competing alternatives in their purchase decision processes enables marketers in the hospitality industry to design better advertising and promotional campaigns leading to a more favourable evaluation of their offerings in travellers' eyes.This is an important step in increasing the likelihood that consumers will choose their offering as opposed to that of competitors.

Given that most travellers' destinations offer several hotels, how do people choose among them? The answer to this question lies, in part, in research on consumers' attitudes and their relation to purchase intentions and subsequent purchase Behaviour. This stage describes several methods consumers may use to make choices based on the evaluation of identified alternatives.

Attitude is the tendency to respond in a consistently favourable or unfavourable manner towards a target. Important to marketers is that, if measured accurately, attitudes are predictive of Behavioural intentions and relatively stable over time.

Simply put, consumers generally form intentions to choose a hotel brand towards which they hold positive attitudes. Behavioural intentions, however, do not always translate into corresponding Behaviour. For example, although some consumers have preferences and therefore form intentions to stay at Fairfield Inn when traveling across the country, they might end up choosing other forms of accommodation from time to time.Why would they act inconsistently with their intentions?

Traveling with friends who have different attitudes and preferences, temporary price reductions of competitors, or the fact that a Fairfield Inn is not readily available in a specific area might be reasons for inconsistencies between Behavioural intentions to stay at a Fairfield Inn and actual choice Behaviour.

Despite situational factors sometimes influencing travellers' choices, attitudes are ultimately useful in predicting actual Behaviour; changing or strengthening the basis of consumer attitudes may therefore increase the likelihood of consumers engaging in desired Behaviours. In order to change attitudes and subsequent related Behaviour, marketers must understand a few basic decision rules associated with consumer attitudes. We introduce decision rules likely to be implemented by different segments of consumers under varying market conditions.

DECISION RULES

Decision rules are strategies consumers use to choose among alternatives. Several factors can influence what decision rule consumers ultimately apply in a specific situation. Typically, the more important and less frequent a purchase decision is, the more time and effort consumers are willing to expend making that decision. Choosing a resort at which to spend a twenty-fifth wedding anniversary, for example, is a decision most consumers face only once and therefore are likely to take a relatively long time to make, and they are likely to be careful and thorough in evaluating alternatives.

On the other hand, a salesperson traveling frequently in a familiar territory likely chooses a hotel using a routine process where far less time and consideration are given to alternatives. Further, brand-loyal customers might choose to stay with the same hotel chain whenever possible, thereby avoiding a situation where they are forced to choose among alternatives. In general, the stronger a consumer is motivated to search and the greater the risk associated with a choice, the greater the complexity of the decision rule he or she implements.

Another important characteristic of modeling decisions is the fact that people often do not attempt to optimize choice. If a person's goal is optimal choice, considerably more time and effort is typically required to identify and evaluate alternatives.

Therefore, consumers often choose a satisfactory alternative in order to save time and effort. The use of decision rules in these instances enables people to take shortcuts in making decisions in the face of the apparently unlimited or overwhelming amounts of information available regarding all possible alternatives. Consumers usually work with a consideration set so they do not have to work as hard cognitively when required to make a decision in a given product category. They then make a final decision from this reduced set of alternatives. Such decision rules are referred to as *heuristics* or rules of thumb. Employing heuristics, people save time and limit complex information processing while still making reasonable or satisfactory choices based on the few brand attributes or characteristics most important to them at the time of choice. In the context of hotel choice, brand attributes are things like location, room rates, and availability of a swimming pool, restaurant, and so forth.

Although the number of consumer decision rules is almost infinite and likely varies by consumer, basic categories and a few specific examples serve as useful tools in modeling and predicting traveller decisions.

Two general categories of decision rules are:

- Compensatory and
- Noncompensatory.

Compensatory Decision Rules

Compensatory decision rules model consumers as deriving an overall brand evaluation such that alternatives performing poorly on one attribute can *compensate* for their respective shortcomings by positive evaluations of other attributes. For example, a high-priced hotel might not be perceived positively on the dimension of room rates by some travellers; however, these same travellers might be willing to spend more money knowing they will receive better service or that the hotel is conveniently located—that is, in this example, service and location compensate for the perceived disadvantage of high room rates. The multi-attribute attitude model described in the next part is perhaps the most popular compensatory decision rule.

MARKETING IMPLICATIONS

Once consumer evaluations of salient attributes are determined and their beliefs regarding a hotel brand's offerings are known, managers can use this information to improve their hotel's competitive positioning in the market. The goal of any marketing strategy is to increase positive attitude towards the offering or to encourage the use of certain decision rules, thereby increasing the likelihood of being chosen by consumers.

When consumers use a compensatory decision rule, the overall attitude towards a hotel is determined by the sum of the products of evaluations multiplied by beliefs regarding salient attributes associated with the offering. Consequently, travellers' overall attitudes towards a hotel can be rendered more positive by strategies targeted at increasing the evaluation of an attribute in consumers' decision making, or by changing consumers' beliefs about a hotel's offerings.

Travellers' attribute evaluations can be influenced by stressing the attribute in advertising. This strategy of influencing attribute evaluations is effective in attitude change and also relatively easy to pursue. It is, however, not a strategy always recommended for changing consumers' attitudes when they are using a compensatory model. The potential problem associated with this approach is that attribute evaluations are constant across brands in a consideration set. Travellers evaluating importance of the availability of an indoor pool is the same for all hotel brands, E, F, G, and H. If Hotel H were successful in a marketing message in increasing the evaluation of an indoor pool with a segment of consumers, say to a rating of _3, it would increase consumers' overall attitude towards its brand. At the same time, however, consumers' overall evaluation of Hotel G would increase by the same amount, as both brands do not differ with respect to consumers' beliefs about their having a great indoor pool. In the end, the attempt to increase consumers' overall attitude towards Hotel H would also benefit some of its competitors.

Thus, sometimes a more effective strategy for improving consumers' overall attitude towards a hotel's offerings is to improve consumers' brand-specific belief ratings. For example, Hotel F could strive to improve consumer belief that it offers a pleasant indoor pool by providing a picture of the pool on its website, or by stressing the availability of the indoor pool in advertisements. While consumer brand-specific beliefs are then likely to increase, Hotel F's competitors will not benefit from its strategy, and Hotel F thereby improves its competitive position.

Assuming that Hotel E cannot do anything to increase consumers' belief that it is not located in proximity of a skiing area, a strategy it may employ to increase consumers' overall attitude towards the property is to add a salient attribute to the set of attributes consumers consider when making hotel choices. For example, Hotel E could provide free accommodation for children staying with their parents. It is likely that parents would consider this option important when choosing a hotel. As long as other competitors do not offer this service, Hotel E enjoys some advantage in the choices made by its target market. It is essential that when adding a new attribute, marketers consider the following: First, the attribute added must be important enough to the hotel's target market to be included in consumers' subsequent decision making. Second, the belief that a particular hotel possesses this attribute must be stronger than the belief that any of its competitors do.

This marketing strategy, often referred to as a *strategy of differentiation,* is likely to be successful when these conditions are met. Differentiation, however, is unlikely to be sustainable— that is, over time, competitors identify what added attributes successfully attract customers and copy them, thereby creating consumer belief regarding their own properties. Thus, the hotel that introduced the new salient attribute often can expect to lose its differential advantage over time unless it maintains a unique characteristic like a special location or a fabulous chef in the kitchen.

Increasing belief strength for a hotel's attributes is not always a successful strategy, assuming a compensatory model is being used. For example, consumers may find it relatively unimportant whether the hotel offers low room rates or not. The importance rating for low room rates is _2—that is, consumers in this particular target segment evaluate low room rates negatively, perhaps because they associate low rates with low quality or with small, underfurnished rooms. In this case, stressing that a particular hotel offers low rates, thereby increasing the strength of consumers' beliefs, may adversely affect consumers' overall evaluation of a property. If you compare Hotels F and H, you will see that the strong belief that Hotel H offers low rates negatively affects its overall evaluation. Hotel F, on the other hand, benefits from consumers not being aware of low rates. It is important to note that importance weights associated with attributes vary across market segments. For example, while business travellers on corporate expense accounts or consumers on a once-in-a-lifetime vacation, such as a honeymoon, may attach less importance to low rates, more price-sensitive market segments usually weigh low rates more heavily in their hotel choice. It is therefore important for marketers to carefully define the targeted market segment prior to conducting their research and applying evaluation weights and beliefs to similarly disposed consumers.

In general, it is crucial to find out what attributes targeted consumers feel are most salient to their decisions and, in response, increase performance regarding these attributes and commensurately inform market segments of this stronger position. The resultant positive attitude towards the offering should then increase the likelihood of the hotel being chosen by travellers using a compensatory decision-making model. Alternatively, as a strategic move, particularly for special niche properties, marketers may want to encourage consumers to abandon the linear compensatory model. Niche market segments may exist or may be created through marketing communications; these target markets might be better served by hotels focusing on one or more of the noncompensatory decision rules presented.

For example, a segment of highly price-sensitive customers predominantly using a lexicographic decision rule with low rates as the most important attribute may constitute the primary target market for a property. In this case, travellers can be targeted by offering low prices and/or frequentstay loyalty programmes. At the same time, services deemed unnecessary or unimportant by this customer segment can be eliminated or minimized. The fact that some customer segments expect a minimal level of performance on several attributes when they use an elimination-by-aspect or conjunctive decision rule, however, implies that focusing performance and/or marketing on a single attribute may be inadequate for some segments of travellers. A hotel would then benefit from creating a level of "at least acceptable" attributes in addition to providing stronger packages of the same attributes offered by competitors targeting the same market segment.

Overall, knowing how consumers make decisions should help hotel managers to design better properties, packages, and services, and help them market those offerings to their respective target segment, thereby improving competitive position.

IMPLEMENTATION OF THE STRATEGIC MARKETING PLANNING PROCESS USING EXMAR

The successful introduction and implementation of the Strategic Marketing Planning Process within an organisation is dependent on management commitment and high quality process consultancy and training, as well as the EXMAR process support tools. This ensures that key members of staff are familiar with, and trained in, all the marketing processes and integrated techniques that have been developed in conjunction with Cranfield School of Management, and that a first class strategy is produced. Experience has shown that the most efficient and beneficial method of implementing the Strategic Marketing Planning Process supported by the EXMAR software is to follow the steps shown below:

MARKET MAPPING AND SEGMENTATION WORKSHOP

The objective of the workshop is to produce a structure for the defined market, which clearly identifies the different requirements that customers look to be satisfied. These different requirements can then be used to develop the alternative strategies that need to be implemented to better access the segments and tune the product offers to suit the customer requirements. It should be noted that most organisations do not have access to the information to produce a definitive segmentation structure that is 100% accurate. However most organisations do have sufficient internal knowledge to produce something that is 'roughly right' and a reasonable starting point. Where this is not the case, the process makes it very clear where the information holes are and the importance of that information. If research is required, the process ensures a rigorous and very targeted brief can be produced.

Market Definition

A market is defined in terms of a need that can be satisfied by the products or services customers' view as alternatives. Once this is clear, the boundaries for the segmentation project can be set.

Market Mapping

A market map defines the distribution and value chain between supplier and final user, which takes into account the various buying mechanisms found in a market, including the part played by 'influencers'.

Market maps help focus attention on key decision makers within a market, and identify key target market segments within a market segmentation project. Market channels and the key players within channels can be easily identified with the help of a graphic presentation of a market. A market map can help deliver key customer and consumer insights, and ensures full awareness of the the total market place.

Market Segmentation

Market segmentation is a concept in economics and marketing. A market segment is a sub-set of a market made up of people or organizations with one or more characteristics that cause them to demand similar product and/or services based on qualities of those products such as price or function. A true market segment meets all of the following criteria: it is distinct from other segments, it is homogeneous within the segment; it responds similarly to a market stimulus, and it can be reached by a market intervention. The term is also used when consumers with identical product and/or service needs are divided up into groups so they can be charged different amounts for the services. The people in a given segment are supposed to be similar in terms of criteria by which they are segmented and different from other segments in terms of these criteria. These can be broadly viewed as 'positive' and 'negative' applications of the same idea, splitting up the market into smaller groups.

Examples:

- Gender
- Price
- Interests
- Location
- Religion
- Income
- Size of Household

While there may be theoretically 'ideal' market segments, in reality every organization engaged in a market will develop different ways of imagining market segments, and create Product differentiation strategies to exploit these segments. The market segmentation and corresponding product differentiation strategy can give a firm a temporary commercial advantage.

Bases for Segmenting Consumer Markets

- Geographic segmentation
- Demographic segmentation
- Psychographic segmentation
- Behavioural segmentation

Geographic Segmentation

The market is segmented just as to geographic criteria- nations, states, regions, counties, cities, neigborhoods, or zip codes. Geo-cluster approach combines demographic data with geographic data to create a more accurate profile of specific

Psychographic Segmentation

Psychographics is the science of using psychology and demographics to better understand consumers.Psychographic segmentation: consumer are divided just as to their lifestyle, personality, values. People within the same demographic group can exhibit very different psychographic profiles.

"Positive" Market Segmentation

Market segmenting is dividing the market into groups of individual markets with similar wants or needs that a company divides into distinct groups which have distinct needs, wants, Behaviour or which might want different products and services. Broadly, markets can be divided just as to a number of general criteria, such as by industry or public versus private. Although industrial market segmentation is quite different from consumer market segmentation, both have similar objectives. All of these methods of segmentation are merely proxies for true segments, which don't always fit into convenient demographic boundaries. Consumer-based market segmentation can be performed on a *product specific* basis, to provide a close match between specific products and individuals. However, a number of generic market segment systems also exist, *e.g.* the system provides a broad segmentation of the population of the United States based on the statistical analysis of household and geodemographic data.

The process of segmentation is distinct from positioning. The overall intent is to identify groups of similar customers and potential customers; to prioritize the groups to address; to understand their Behaviour; and to respond with appropriate marketing strategies that satisfy the different preferences of each chosen segment. Revenues are thus improved.

Improved segmentation can lead to significantly improved marketing effectiveness. Distinct segments can have different industry structures and thus have higher or lower attractiveness Once a market segment has been identified, and targeted, the segment is then subject to positioning. Positioning involves ascertaining how a product or a company is perceived in the minds of consumers. This part of the segmentation process consists of drawing up a perceptual map, which highlights rival goods within one's industry just as to perceived quality and price. After the perceptual map has been devised, a firm would consider the marketing communications mix best suited to the product in question.

Behavioural Segmentation

In Behavioural segmentation, consumers are divided into groups just as to their knowledge of, attitude towards, use of or response to a product.

- *Occasions*: Segmentation just as to occasions.we segment the market just as to the occasions.
- *Benefits*: Segmentations just as to benefits sought by the consumer.
- Users status: nonusers, ex-users, first time users, etc.

Using Segmentation in Customer Retention

The basic approach to retention-based segmentation is that a company tags each of its active customers with 3 values:

- *Tag No.1*: Is this customer at high risk of canceling the company's service? One of the most common indicators of high-risk customers is a drop off in usage of the company's service. For example, in the credit card industry this could be signaled through a customer's decline in spending on his or her card.

- *Tag No.2*: Is this customer worth retaining? This determination boils down to whether the post-retention profit generated from the customer is predicted to be greater than the cost incurred to retain the customer. Managing Customers as Investments.
- *Tag No.3*: What retention tactics should be used to retain this customer? For customers who are deemed "save-worthy", it's essential for the company to know which save tactics are most likely to be successful. Tactics commonly used range from providing "special" customer discounts to sending customers communications that reinforce the value proposition of the given service.

Process for Tagging Customers

The basic approach to tagging customers is to utilize historical retention data to make predictions about active customers regarding:

- Whether they are at high risk of canceling their service
- Whether they are profitable to retain
- What retention tactics are likely to be most effective

The idea is to match up active customers with customers from historic retention data who share similar attributes. Using the theory that "birds of a feather flock together", the approach is based on the assumption that active customers will have similar retention outcomes as those of their comparable predecessor.

Niche Marketing

A niche is a more narrowly defined customer group who seek a distinct set of benefits. Ýdentified by dividing a segment into subsegments,distinct and unique set of needs,requires speciallization, and is not likely to attract too many competitors.

Price Discrimination

Where a monopoly exists, the price of a product is likely to be higher than in a competitive market and the quantity sold less, generating monopoly profits for the seller. These profits can be increased further if the market can be segmented with different prices charged to different segments charging higher prices to those segments willing and able to pay more and charging less to those whose demand is price elastic.

The price discriminator might need to create rate fences that will prevent members of a higher price segment from purchasing at the prices available to members of a lower price segment. This Behaviour is rational on the part of the monopolist, but is often seen by competition authorities as an abuse of a monopoly position, whether or not the monopoly itself is sanctioned. Examples of this exist in the transport industry where business class customers who can afford to pay may be charged prices many times higher than economy class customers for essentially the same service.

Ansoff Matrix

To portray alternative corporate growth strategies, Igor Ansoff presented a matrix that focused on the firm's present and potential products and markets. By considering ways to grow via existing products and new products, and in existing markets and new markets, there are four possible product-market combinations. Ansoff's matrix is shown below:

Table. Ansoff Matrix

	Existing Products	**New Products**
Existing Markets	Market Penetration	Product Development
New Markets	Market Development	Diversification

Ansoff's matrix provides four different growth strategies:

- Market Penetration - the firm seeks to achieve growth with existing products in their current market segments, aiming to increase its market share.
- Market Development - the firm seeks growth by targeting its existing products to new market segments.
- Product Development - the firms develops new products targeted to its existing market segments.
- Diversification - the firm grows by diversifying into new businesses by developing new products for new markets.

Selecting a Product-Market Growth Strategy

The market penetration strategy is the least risky since it leverages many of the firm's existing resources and capabilities. In a growing market, simply maintaining market share will result in growth, and there may exist opportunities to increase market share if competitors reach capacity limits. However, market penetration has limits, and once the market approaches saturation another strategy must be pursued if the firm is to continue to grow.

Market development options include the pursuit of additional market segments or geographical regions. The development of new markets for the product may be a good strategy if the firm's core competencies are related more to the specific product than to its experience with a specific market segment. Because the firm is expanding into a new market, a market development strategy typically has more risk than a market penetration strategy.

A product development strategy may be appropriate if the firm's strengths are related to its specific customers rather than to the specific product itself. In this situation, it can leverage its strengths by developing a new product targeted to its existing customers. Similar to the case of new market development, new product development carries more risk than simply attempting to increase market share. Diversification is the most risky of the four growth strategies since it requires both product and market development and may be outside the core competencies of the firm. In fact, this quadrant of the matrix has been referred to by some as the "suicide cell". However, diversification may be a reasonable choice if the high risk is compensated by the chance of a high rate of return. Other advantages of diversification include the potential to gain a foothold in an attractive industry and the reduction of overall business portfolio risk.

GUIDANCE ON AUDIT PREPARATION

The objective of these two days is to ensure that the data required has been identified in detail and the format of the data is consistent.

DATA COLLECTION AND RESEARCH

The following information needs to be collected and input into EXMAR for each product-market as defined in the Ansoff Matrix. This information is then used to drive the market audit.

For each product-market the following information is required:

- Market size and growth Volume
- Revenue
- Market share

Current figures are requested. Historical data is also useful, as far back as available. If only some of these data items are known, the system will estimate data values where possible. In order for EXMAR to construct the Boston Box and the Directional Policy Matrix, it is necessary to define and gather the following information:

- Market Attractiveness Factors - defined once for the business unit
- MAF scores
- Critical Success Factors
- CSF scores for yourself and important competitors.

SEGMENTATION VERIFICATION

Often our clients sell products and services into horizontal segments. In these cases, the product-offer maps onto how the customers run their business, and segments are often hard to identify in a way that will give maximum leverage in the marketing plan. To help solve this problem, we have developed a set of tools and processes for analysing existing and potential customer data, and generating and sizing segments.

CUSTOMER PROFITABILITY AUDIT

This is an optional audit and will develop a more realistic view of Customer/ Segment Profitability as opposed to Product Profitability. It is often the case that a few segments generate more than 100% of the profit and it is important to identify which segments are actually profitable.

SOFTWARE TRAINING AND DATA INPUT

Two days of hands on training are provided on the EXMAR software including the use of the extensive help system. Data from your company can be entered into EXMAR at this stage.

MARKET AUDIT WORKSHOP

The objective of this workshop is to produce the Market Audit and Trend Analysis, *i.e.* What will happen if we do nothing over the plan period? For each product-market the following information is analysed:

- Financial performance
- Market share
- Relative strengths and weaknesses
- Competitor strategy
- Relative costs
- Market attractiveness trends
- Opportunities and threats
- Assumptions and sensitivity analysis.

Additionally the portfolio of products and services is analysed using various tools including the Directional Policy Matrix and the Boston Box.

DATA VALIDATION

The sensitivity analysis on assumptions, whether they be in terms of relative strength, market growth, or profitability are used to highlight those areas where it is most important to verify the data, as wrong assumptions could lead to inappropriate strategies being developed. This may require highly focused Market Research studies on the particular issues identified.

OBJECTIVES AND STRATEGIES WORKSHOP

The objective of this workshop is to set the overall strategies and those that operate at the product-market level. Objectives are defined as the financial performance and market share required from each product market. Strategies are defined as the set of costed actions required to improve competitive performance in order to reach the objectives. It also includes assigning responsibility for the actions.

The process is iterative and can result for example in the identification of generic problem areas, where one set of actions and investments can affect competitive performance in several productmarkets. These usually provide the best ROI. Additionally the output of the workshop often results in several scenarios, each with its own investment profile, *i.e.* these are the anticipated results of this level of investment as opposed to a larger or smaller sum. These can highlight the implications of the spread of the investment and resources.

REVIEW OBJECTIVES AND STRATEGIES

This phase of the project involves the Client in performing a 'sanity check' on the strategies. This can be both in terms of the viability of implementation, given the internal processes and constraints on the organisation and investment available, as well as a management review.

PLAN REVIEW AND METRICS WORKSHOP

On completion of the project, a day is set aside to review the Strategic Marketing Plan and to identify key metrics for monitoring the implementation and success of the strategies. For example, if 'service levels' are an important Critical Success Factor, then key performance indicators need to be defined that can be measured, such as 'response times to customer requests' or 'adherence to committed delivery schedules'. If required we can offer our Clients further services to help them design and implement appropriate KPIs in their organisation.

DECIDING WHAT TO BE AND WHAT TO OFFER TO WHOM

In an existing hotel, the developer and architect already may have decided many of the things it is—high-rise or resort, in the business center or on the edge of town, large rooms and baths or smallish, one restaurant or several, wood or marble, with ballroom or not, and so on. Even so, the management team must still consciously examine what they intend the hotel to be and offer to whom. The type of customer originally in mind may not be available now in enough numbers to support the hotel.

Perhaps a competitor has come in and taken away a piece of the market. Perhaps the business center has shifted to another part of the city. Perhaps new customers from Korea or California have replaced the original ones from Europe and the East Coast. Even though the owner has provided a basic envelope within which to operate, there still are options—many things the hotel team can control, many choices to be made on what to offer and to emphasize to various market segments. Is the hotel the place to be seen or the place that guards privacy? Is it better to stress family style or crisp, professional business style? Should the hotel add services, like a Japanese breakfast, to meet the needs of one particular group? Should the team put in meetings express and add more small meeting spaces to tap the short-lead-time corporate meetings market? Should it drop some services the market no longer wants to support?

***The answers to what to be and offer are found by studying the marketing situation, which comprises three parts*:**

- Strengths and weaknesses,
- The kinds and numbers of customers available in the marketplace, and
- The other hotels with whom this hotel competes for these customers.

Careful analysis yields a picture of which segments the hotel is best able to attract and serve. These become the *target markets*—the "to whoms"—and their needs and wants become the "what to be's." The key to successfully deciding what to be and offer to whom is a matter of strategic selection of, focus on, and commitment to a well-defined set of markets for whom the hotel is best suited to compete. Trying to be all things to all potential customers is a guarantee of ineffectiveness.

A good example of focus and targeting is Starwood's W. At risk of turning off a sizeable portion of the business and leisure travel market and leaving families well behind, Starwood focuses tightly on a lifestyle segment of professional and business people, with remarkable success.

The talents required to assess the marketing situation, create a data model of the market's segments, calculate a feasible share of each, and select the targets on which to focus are comfort with data, the ability to observe and infer, creativity, patience with detail, comfort with the hypothetical, and an analytic curiosity. Usually, such analyses are uncomfortably foreign to people with backgrounds in sales, and often to operators as well. It is essential that we teach, motivate, and reward curious, careful, insightful analysis of history and market information—skills that are not natural to those typically attracted to hospitality management. the *target markets*—the "to whoms"—and their needs and wants become the "what to be's."The key to successfully deciding what to be and offer to whom is a matter of strategic selection of, focus on, and commitment to a well-defined set of markets for whom the hotel is best suited to compete. Trying to be all things to all potential customers is a guarantee of ineffectiveness.

A good example of focus and targeting is Starwood's W. At risk of turning off a sizeable portion of the business and leisure travel market and leaving families well behind, Starwood focuses tightly on a lifestyle segment of professional and business people, with remarkable success.

The talents required to assess the marketing situation, create a data model of the market's segments, calculate a feasible share of each, and select the targets on which to focus are comfort with data, the ability to observe and infer, creativity, patience with detail, comfort with the hypothetical, and an analytic curiosity. Usually, such analyses are uncomfortably foreign to people with backgrounds in sales, and often to operators as well. It is essential that we teach, motivate, and reward curious, careful, insightful analysis of history and market information—skills that are not natural to those typically attracted to hospitality management.

SETTING PRICES

Having decided what to be and offer and to whom, the next most important decision is price. Pricing is a critical decision because it determines, first, whether or not the intended customers will purchase, and second, whether they will be satisfied with the value offered and, thus, be willing to return. Third, it determines whether the hotel will be financially healthy enough to maintain itself and reward its employees so customers can once again be satisfied when they do return. Three factors must come into consideration in pricing—the Three Cs of pricing, if you will: costs, competition, and customers' comfort zones. In F&B, costs drive pricing of menu items and beverages. Drucker says American industry has too much cost-driven pricing, and that it needs more price-driven costing. Doesn't F&B have the opportunity to build and test menus to discover where price points should be set, and is not the chef challenged to manage ingredients and portion size to deliver the cost and margin structure desired? Yet the cost-driven practice continues. In rooms, competition is most often the dominant factor. Costs play a role, but changes in variable cost of an occupied room are generally small and rooms' contribution margins are large, typically 65 per cent or better. Moreover, hotel accounting does not measure discounts from a standard price, as do almost all other industries. So there is no visible cost in reducing price to meet competitors. Remember: Any damn fool can cut his price, and some damn fool always will. Must everyone follow? No. The key is to get in the head of the customer. The truly controlling factor is customer comfort zones, and all too often hotel management leave money on the table because they don't know what those comfort zones are. At what price does the offer attract and deliver value? That is the key question in setting prices.

Price setting requires talent and skill in data gathering and analysis, accounting and building pro formas, interpreting and drawing inferences, and decision making. Do not let salespeople set prices; do not let controllers set prices. Only one person—the GM—can pull together the inputs of sales, control, operations, reservations, and the rest, and make this crucial judgment call. Also, build at least three price scenarios and have the controller and marketing director agree on occupancy impacts. Then run a GOP pro forma on each.

Out of that exercise will come a sense of the best pricing approach to take. Setting prices is the one task the GM cannot delegate, for he or she must live with and be accountable for all that results from this critical decision.

CREATING AWARENESS AND STIMULATING DEMAND

Herein are the typical roles of the marketing department: using sales, communications, and promotions to attract the target markets. But creating awareness is not only marketing's job. Everything the public sees and hears about the hotel—its name or brand, its signs, its restaurants, the public activities of its managers, its charitable support and festivals—all create a meaning, a picture of what this hotel means and offers.

Starwood's W again offers an example: Every element of their presentation expresses the "to whom" they target. In decor, uniforms tone, and attitude, they focus and send a coherent message. It is critical that every department understands the target markets and agrees on the idea, the meaning the hotel intends to have for each of the target customer groups. This is called *positioning;* it's something done not to the product but to the mind of the prospect.

The team should prepare written positioning statements, including a compatible but individual positioning statement for each market segment they intend to target. These statements are the blueprint against which each ad, promotion, and sales call is tested to assure consistent messages are being sent.

And those statements should be shared with all employees.When all parts of the hotel are sending a coherent and consistent message of what the name or brand means and what underlying promise is being made, the hotel establishes a clear position in the mind of the prospects—ideally, one that is attractively distinctive from competitors.

Marketers can use a variety of tools to create awareness and stimulate demand—for example, sales blitzes, telemarketing, newspaper ads, Internet sites and ads, partnership alliances, radio ads, and price promotions. The marketing mix is the range and balance of tools selected and resources devoted to each to achieve the hotel's marketing goals.

In most hotels, direct selling is still the primary marketing tool used to create awareness and stimulate demand.There are two parts of effective direct selling: sales skills and sales management. Consider one the weapon, the other the shooter.

Sales skills are not natural; enthusiasm may be natural, liking to meet people may be natural, but selling is a process that anyone can learn and that must be practiced. Make sure your salespeople are taught how to research their prospect, to listen for needs and purposes, to acknowledge that they have heard the prospect, to transform relevant features into benefits and to sell the customer's success, to anticipate objections and prepare responses, to negotiate, to ask for the order, and to thank the customer and facilitate delivery.

Sales management is quite another thing; often the top salesperson does not make the best sales manager. The sales manager must be able to select salespeople; reinforce their training; coach, counsel and motivate them; assign them to prospects and market segments; set goals, manage compensation, review performance; and troubleshoot. He or she must also be the gatekeeper on contracts and rates, making sure that inventory Compensation of salespeople need not be complicated. *First principle:* Tie compensation to goals set in terms of what you want them to do—that is, produce contracts and roomnights.

Don't just set room-night goals; add measures of relationship or share of a specific customer's business. Have salespeople suggest their own goals for the coming year; participation builds commitment. *Second:* Provide them near-term reward and reinforcement, not postponed rewards. Pay out bonuses quarterly. *Third:* Build teamwork so that one salesperson supports and encourages another. Add a team bonus multiplier to personal performance measures. *Last:* Separate performance bonuses from overall job appraisal. No one attends to suggestions for performance improvement if he or she has just received a big check for exceeding goal.

Many full-service hotels are overresourced in group sales and underweighted in transient market tools. Sales efforts should be balanced with other parts of the marketing mix—advertising, publicity, and promotions.

The range of communication options increases geometrically with proliferation of new media—cable television, news magazines and national papers, the Internet, and direct mail and telemarketing. But the eyeballs are not growing apace, meaning the audience for any one medium is steadily shrinking, putting increasing demand on measures of productivity, care in allocating resources, and creativity to get through the clutter. As audiences of prospects become increasingly expensive to reach through advertising, the tools of publicity, the Internet, and direct marketing are increasingly the media of choice. The Internet is a demanding medium for communication; use professional help to design, maintain, and market the hotel's website as though it were, itself, a product for which awareness must be created and demand stimulated. To draw audience to the site and manage its visibility in search engines are skills beyond the property team. Set specific goals for the site:They might be to attract qualified prospects, to sell services, to provide customer service. Don't just have a site. And measure the experts against those goals.A passive, unmanaged, and undermarketed site is a waste of money.

Promotions can powerfully stimulate demand, but too often, price promotions are resorted to as a last-minute attempt to prop up a weak demand period. Promotions should be planned, justified on a breakeven basis, and used sparingly. Not all promotions need be price promotions; customers invest energy and time in transactions, too: value-added promotions that offer nonmonetary savings can be used to avoid habituating consumers to buying only on sale or shopping only on price. Well-forged alliances for copromotion can increase both productivity and absolute sales volume.

The skills and talents necessary in a comprehensive effort to create awareness and stimulate demand include:

- *In sales:* Initiative; being goal-directed; listening with empathy and imagination; time management; self-confidence.

- *In sales management:* Coaching and counseling; quantitative skills; priority setting, time management, and sense of urgency; leadership and problem solving; ability to manage incentive programmes.
- *In communications:* Ability to write clearly; ability to select, engage, and manage professional creative talents; ability to evaluate and allocate resources among options; comfort with and appreciation of the Internet and the Web.
- *In promotion:* Ability to analyse breakevens; creativity; anticipation; conceiving and selling partnerships and alliances.

MAKING THE HOTEL AVAILABLE

Once a person in one of your target markets is interested in buying, how does he or she reach you? Your hotel's reservations office, the central reservation system, airline global distribution systems, corporate sales offices, and your property sales office are all parts of a distribution network. Travel agents, corporate travel managers and secretaries, meeting planners, and travellers themselves reach your hotel through this network.

Travel industry distribution channels are in chaos by virtue of the shift of travel agencies from commission to fee-for-service models, the rise of the Internet as a consumer's direct booking channel, and online thirdparty intermediaries like Expedia and Travelocity.

Increasingly, the Internet will become your key distribution channel, but in the meantime, you must manage two parallel systems, the traditional central reservation and travel agency channels and the new electronic channels. Are the rooms you want to offer available in both systems, with helpful and upto-date information? Are your prices sensible in each outlet? Making the hotel available is no longer a passive stance but an active part of your marketing.

In other industries, distribution channel revolutions have brought efficiencies that benefit both consumers and suppliers. In the travel distribution revolution now underway, the consumer has benefited, but costs to hotels—the suppliers—have skyrocketed. Since 1993, full-service hotel costs of distribution more than doubled, to $1,377 per occupied room per year in 2002.

Along with these new channels and thirdparty room merchants has come pressure on prices. In the downturn of 2001–2003, this was devastating. Price comparisons are quick and easy for the consumer. Packagers and auction sites unconsciously cultivate the destructive idea that a hotel room is a commodity, as is an airline seat. But hotels are not commodities; each differs in location, features, and benefits. A hotel team must resist the idea that a room is a room is a room, must emphasize their hotel's distinctive positioning, and must resist the urge to simply match the lowest price offered.

For the foreseeable future, both the traditional and Internet-based distribution systems will coexist and have to be managed. This raises a new question:What channels do you want to encourage, and what ones discourage? Conventional wisdom, in recent years, has been to make the hotel's inventory and rates available via as many channels as possible so as to capture from anywhere in the world the last drop of demand for arrival on a given day. Given their sharply differing costs, however, and the difficulty of managing coordinated presence in these new and overlapping channels, the time may be coming for a new strategy. One possibility is to starve undesirable channels with limited information and access while being fully open and transparent to others. Another approach might be to price differentially among channels to reflect their different costs. A large Hawaiian resort group is already doing that by explaining to consumers what comparative options and costs are. Other chains advertise a guarantee that the lowest price will be found on their own website, which is a low-cost channel for them.

Reservations, revenue, and channel management constitute the fastest-changing part of hotel management today. Channel management requires a comfort with and interest in technology and systems, and a knack for problem solving, anticipating, and risk taking.

CLOSING, CONFIRMING, AND MANAGING REVENUE

How one commits space—a room, meeting space, ballroom, or even a restaurant table— and at what price—determines the revenues and financial health of the hotel and determines the customer's expectation of value.

Revenues must be managed to optimize financial returns and customer satisfaction— that is, the customer's willingness to return. No one department controls the tools of revenue management. They are shared among salespeople, catering and banqueting managers, front desk agents, reservation agents, and so on. To manage properly requires frequent and open conversation between managers, good forecasting, skillful selling by customer contact people, and an appreciation of each week's goals and targets for the hotel. Poor forecasting, inflexible inventory policies, and conflicting approaches by different departments with whom the customer deals can undo all the best advertising, selling, and promotion.

Through the same forecasting disciplines, hotel teams manage their revenues to maximize the productivity of the hotel and assure its financial health. Revenue management tools and increasingly affordable yield systems can have a major and salutory effect on the financial health of the hotel.

Another part of revenue management is incentives for reservations upselling, conversion of callers, and average rate increases, and for front desk agents upselling. In the same way, F&B staff should be viewed as salespeople and given training on suggestive selling. Inventory policies for tier price quotes by forecast levels of occupancy, for stay-through restrictions, for same-rate substitutions and upgrading to clear demand inventory categories— all these are tools through which reservation and revenue managers optimize the RevPAR performance of the hotel.

It is in the area of revenue management that chains, especially multibrand management companies, have achieved significant advantage over independent hotels and franchisees that do not participate in cluster or regional revenue management. Decisions on pricing are still the domain of the property GM, but with a centralized expert staff collecting data and forecasting, the advice and guidance available has brought yield and RevPAR premiums to the chain member properties.

Revenue management requires attention to detail and analytic and forecasting skills; tolerance for ambiguity and comfort with change; and managing, training, leading, and motivating reservations agents. This is one of the most critical and dynamic areas of hotel management, one with which every aspiring general manager or director of sales and marketing should take pains to become familiar.

PREPARING TO DELIVER AND DELIGHT

A marketer of a product can count on the factory quality-control system to deliver a consistent product for sale. When the sale is closed, the customer takes the product away and uses it. In a service business, however, the product is human Behaviour, and the customer uses the product in the hotel. Because we are humans, both customers and employees, our interactions are never the same one time to the next. The job of the marketer is to help employees understand what the customer will want, need, and expect, and to sell employees on doing their job with enthusiasm.

In a full-service hotel, the conference services department embodies this preparing idea as its primary function. Conference service managers are the essential group business brokers between sales and operations. Conference services people can create loyal and repeat meeting planners; the job requires empathy, attention to detail, willingness to work unusual hours, action orientation, internal relationship building, and persuasiveness.

Preparing the hotel to fully satisfy and regularly make customers happy is as much a marketing task as attracting customers in the first place.What makes marketing hospitality services harder than marketing a tangible product is that for every market segment there must be two marketing programmes, one directed externally to customers, the other internally to employees.

RETAINING CUSTOMERS

The key to both financial health and market leadership is retaining a higher proportion of customers than do any of your competitors. Retain more customers than others do, and over time your costs drop—because of efficiency, lower advertising and selling costs, better forecasting—and your occupancy and rates rise. Numerous studies validate the high correlation between profit leadership and customer retention.

Frequent-stay rewards are often mistaken for retention programmes. They are not. Rewards can motivate returns only as long as the customer values the points or airline miles or whatever. But they do not create loyalty.They are valuable only insofar as they give employees the opportunity to come to recognize and satisfy the guest, and insofar as they give the marketing department information on who the customer is and where he or she is coming from.

Retaining customers takes more than just doing the job well. Guests and customers must come to know they are valued. Management must build relationships—the tie that binds regardless of a new hotel opening in the market or a hot promotional offer from across the street. Relationships are built on recognition and familiarity, on trust, and on appreciation.Thus, guest and customer retention must be a planned and creative activity that involves both sides of the relationship— the customers and the employees. It takes more than just smiling and trying hard. Among the talents and skills needed are analytic skills, curiosity, direct marketing planning, and management of data retrieval and direct marketing service providers.

MEASURING SATISFACTION AND EVALUATING PERFORMANCE

If the purpose of the business is, in part, to keep customers, does a financial statement of rate, occupancy, revenue, expense, and profit give enough information? No. Also needed is a scorecard of customer satisfaction, of how likely customers are to return or tell others about your good hotel. That scorecard is the guest satisfaction survey. Accounting statements tell of the hotel's financial health; a guest satisfaction scorecard tells of its reputation's health. The scorecard also helps management spot changes in expectations.

Customers are not the same from one visit to the next. Experience with a new hotel, perhaps even in another city, may raise a customer's standards. To measure satisfaction, one needs quantitative skills for tracking, analysing, and reporting data, and the ability to manage the logistics of repetitive distribution, collection, and processing. The information helps management figure out what the hotel needs to be and to offer next in order to remain competitive and keep customers. Note, now, the return to the first step of the marketing process.

THE CIRCULAR MARKETING PROCESS

In other words, the marketing process isn't the straight-line, step-by-step process, a continuous circle around which management must go again and again as competition improves and as the customer segments in the market change. Only by reviewing and renewing the marketing process will a hotel get ahead and continue to be the leading hotel in its market. This model of the marketing process applies to both the whole hotel and to any revenue or profit center within it. Use it like a checklist when thinking through improving the revenue and competitiveness of any operation.

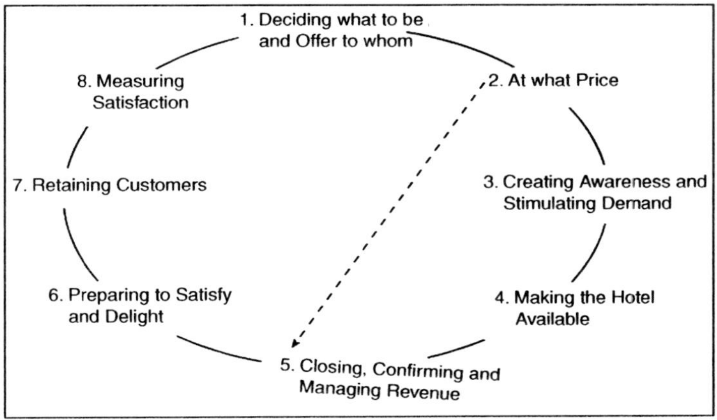

Fig. The Hotel Marketing Process

THE MEASURES OF MARKETING

The health of the marketing process should be measured over a longer time than a month or quarter or fiscal year, and it should be measured by more than just profit and loss data.

A healthy marketing process results in:

- Rising room revenues per available room and rising F&B revenues per available seat and catering space.
- Rising market share to a share index over 100—that is, a larger share of a competitive set's occupied rooms than the hotel's share of the set's available rooms, which is its "fair share."
- Falling costs of acquiring customers, not on a percentage-of-revenue basis but as dollars per unit of sale—for example, dollars per occupied room, dollars per cover, and so on.What is the acquisition cost? The total of the advertising and business promotion budget, plus commissions, reservation costs, franchise fees, and marketing fees. These costs in times of inflation may not actually decline but at least should grow more slowly than do gross operating revenues.
- Rising customer satisfaction ratings. • Increasing retention rates measured by the percentage of business from repeat customers.
- Growing top-of-mind awareness among target customer segments and, if the hotel can afford to measure it, preference by segment rising to number one among your competitive sets.

Management and owners should ask for an annual report card on the health of the marketing process—of the hotel, of a chain, of a franchise group.

MANAGEMENT OF THE PROPERTY'S MARKETING PROCESS

As should by now be clear, the marketing process is larger than any one individual's job. Further, no hotel can afford the myriad talents and skills that must be orchestrated to create and sustain a healthy marketing process; a single hotel is simply not a large enough business to afford having all those talents on staff. Franchise companies and managed chains have the mass to employ a large proportion of those talents at headquarters, but even they must call on outside services in design, database management, advertising, direct marketing, and so on. But the chains' ability to invest in new tools and hire diverse talents has led branded chains, both management companies and franchisers, to collect increasing numbers of hotels under their umbrellas. The trend towards centralizing marketing functions to serve several hotels in a region, often even hotels of different brands, is accelerating, especially with the advent of Internet-driven information sharing. The advantages are the ability to integrate multiple sources of information, to hire experts that a single hotel might not be able to afford, to share the cost of sophisticated systems for forecasting, revenue management and customer relationships, and to reduce the expense of marketing to individual properties.

Independents must counter such attractions with cooperative activities and aggressive local marketing. The Internet has leveled the playing field somewhat, allowing independents to be found and reviewed by consumers and travel agents in a way not possible when GDS systems were the only means of access.

PROPERTY RESPONSIBILITY FOR ITS OWN MARKETING

To optimize performance, a property can neither abdicate its marketing to a chain or franchise group nor passively rely on location and presence to bring customers to the door. Each property, whether flagged or independent, must be responsible for creating and managing a marketing process tailored to its particular marketing situation—that is, its available customers; its inherent strengths, weaknesses, and employees; and its competitors. Each marketing situation is unique, even among cookie-cutter chain properties. Each has its own location, competitor, and customer dynamics.

So, given the wide range of talents and skills that must be orchestrated to create an effective marketing process, who is to lead it? Directors of sales and marketing cannot, for the process is much larger than the marketing department. Only the general manager can lead his or her marketing process; only he or she can integrate chain supports, operating departments, human resources, the controller, and—yes, marketing and sales.

THE GM AS LEADER OF THE MARKETING PROCESS

General managers must come to see themselves as the leader of their marketing process and be comfortable in the role. This does not mean becoming expert in all tools and disciplines; it does mean seeing the whole and appreciating when to bring in what talents, when to apply what tools, and how to judge the effectiveness of the process. It means using the marketing process as an organizing concept for creating the management team and a unified viewpoint of mission and challenge.

When a hotel is led by a general manager who sees herself or himself as leader of the marketing process, when that process is thoughtfully conceived and well executed, when all employees see themselves as joint operators/marketers, that hotel becomes customer-centered, competitive, and a leader in its markets.

Few GMs are trained to do this. Many come to appreciate that location and flag are not enough; many intuitively pick up a smattering of sales, distribution, advertising, and customer retention. But it is the rare GM who weaves these parts into a coherent whole and thinks through the challenge of creating and leading the marketing process. As marketing continues to develop more complex tools and as marketing productivity becomes a more pressing matter, owners, universities, and chains must address this issue of how to develop GM candidates who are comfortable with and capable of leading a comprehensive marketing process.

THE MARKETING PROCESS MODEL AS A PROBLEM-SOLVING TOOL

One last word: The circular model of the marketing process is presented here mainly in terms of rooms marketing. But the model can be applied to every revenue department—to food and beverage outlets, catering, the health club, the business center, and even the laundry. The model can be used for planning, for business reviews, for presentations to lenders and owners, for troubleshooting, and as a checklist when preparing proposals for new services or facilities. Use the model, make it part of your bag of management tools, and get your team to see their role in terms of this holistic and never-ending marketing process. If you achieve that, you will have gone far to create a customer- and competitor-focused organization, one in which employees see themselves as operators/marketers rather than just "in operations" or "in marketing" or "in HR."

The few hotels that achieve and nurture a well-tuned marketing process and whose employees see themselves as integral parts of it become leaders—in market share, in customer and employee loyalty, and in financial returns to owners.

CONCLUSION

For most hotel companies, it was only during the 1980s that the word *marketing* was anything more than a euphemism for sales. Indeed, in the competitive landscape of the not too distant past, an aggressive and knowledgeable sales staff could accomplish most activities that related to putting guests in rooms. In the competitive environment of the present time, this has become impossible. Hotel companies that design and market a sophisticated inventory of hospitality services need a similarly sophisticated scheme for letting potential clientele know about their services.

For most hotel companies in the twentyfirst century, true marketing has evolved to reflect this sophistication. This development also acknowledges increased sophistication on the part of guests and potential clientele.

Business travellers, travel agents, and meeting planners who represent and book group and convention business are educated and informed consumers.To serve this clientele, hotels have had to develop marketing efforts and product segmentation, first to interest the market, and second to allow people representing that market to make intelligent choices among competitors.

Increasingly, individual consumers and small businesses are becoming more sophisticated in arranging their own travel plans over the Internet. This represents yet another challenge to hotel marketers: How do we market most efficiently to all groups? Good question.

Marketing has become an umbrella term that covers a number of strategic and tactical activities designed to tell the clientele the story of the hotel's services and to encourage that clientele to make choices based on how one hotel's marketing message matches their needs better than the available alternatives. In any given hotel or hotel company, marketing includes a range of sales activities, public relations, advertising in all media, design of symbols and images, and the departments of convention services, reservations, revenue management, and, perhaps, catering. It should be noted that research plays a major role in designing marketing strategies and tactics. The monograph presented in this edition by Bianca Grohmann and Eric Spangenberg has a research orientation at its core. It is designed to assist managers in choosing and generating data that are useful to staying successfully competitive. It is important that managers understand the range within which this data may be interpreted and applied. Successful managers and high-quality organizations are always seeking information and data that allow them to make accurate decisions and design effective marketing and managerial efforts.

These data can take a number of forms but, for the most part, deal with the characteristics of the hotel's target market segment that affect their choice of hotels. In this case, the research seeks to understand how consumers make choices among hotels based on the value of their various attributes.

Among other data that hotels find mechanisms to accumulate and interpret are these kinds:

- *Geographic:* What sorts of communities are represented; what parts of the country or world; how far people travel

- *Demographic:* Age, sex, occupation, income, ethnicity, family, education
- *Psychographic:* Client's self-image, social or peer group, lifestyle, personality traits
- *Behavioural:* Whether the hotel choice is a routine or special occasion; what guest seeks in terms of quality, service, economy; user status; usage rate; loyalty.

While many of the specific details or programmes implied under the marketing umbrella may be farmed out to agencies that specialize in advertising or public relations, the genesis of the hotel's strategic marketing plan must be within the hotel organization itself.

The object contributed to this part by Fletch Waller provides a strong argument for broadening the definition of *marketing* to include all operational aspects of the hotel.This object is an excellent overview of the marketing process. Waller shows the relationship between marketing and operations as a "continuing process" without which hotels probably cannot remain competitive.

Yield management, long a practice of the airline industry, has found total acceptance by hotel marketing and reservations systems. Indeed, it has become an industry standard.The object in this part by Paul Chappelle can be read in conjunction with that by Quain and LeBruto for a comprehensive primer on yield management.

Together, these objects explore various aspects of that practice from the viewpoint of Chappelle, current practitioner. Chappelle lives the theory of yield and revenue management on a daily basis and provides insights about how it works in practice. As the revenue manager for over 30 hotels, Chappelle has the experience to back up the theory.

The Sinclair thesis on hotel pricing should be read in the context of the issues and suggestions raised by the contributions on yield management. But it goes beyond that. Drawing on Sinclair's deep experience in hotel operations, particularly sales, this contemporary work on pricing is up to date and useful not only from a conceptual standpoint but a practical one.

Shaw and Morris bring their collaborative talents in academe and industry to the thesis on the organization of the sales function in hotels. Because, as noted elsewhere in this text many times, the potential markets for a hotel's services and the types of hotel are so numerous, sales efforts can be complicated. Shaw and Morris present this complex departmental function in a clear, straightforward fashion that is both theoretically relevant and operationally practical.

Traditionally, the function of public relations for any organization, particularly hotels, was oriented towards the generation of favourable—usually free—publicity and the suppression or management of bad news.

Louis Richmond proposes the different and expanded but not necessarily contrary position that public relations activities can positively enhance the hotel's sales and marketing efforts.

He discusses his experiences in the case of the Seattle Sheraton Hotel and Towers.Using that example, he argues that through creative cooperative efforts with local charity, cultural, and volunteer organizations, hotels can serve the activities of those groups' fundraising efforts and simultaneously position themselves to show the arbiters of potential business how well the hotel can perform.

His examples are instructive. Richmond, who is president of his own very successful public relations firm in Seattle, retains the Sheraton and other hospitality concerns as clients. All in all, the strategies, tactics, activities, personnel, and concepts described in objects and thesiss in this part provide an overview that only hints at everything important to effective management of the marketing function.

Marketing is perhaps the most written-about topic in hospitality literature. Because of the great diversity of opinion, it can be argued that there is no one "right" way to market, nor is any single piece of literature generally considered seminal to hotel marketing. The reader is urged to consider the references cited by contributing authors, the suggested readings, and active perusal of recent hospitality journals to achieve greater understanding of this fascinating process— and, by extension, its management.

6

Advertising Expenditures Influence Hotels

A hotel is an establishment that provides paid lodging, usually on a short-term basis. Hotels often provide a number of additional guest services such as a restaurant, a swimming pool or childcare. Some hotels have conference services and meeting rooms and encourage groups to hold conventions and meetings at their location. Hotels differ from motels in that most motels have drive-up, exterior entrances to the rooms, while hotels tend to have interior entrances to the rooms, which may increase guests' safety and present a more upmarket image. In Australia, a hotel may also be an establishment that serves alcoholic drinks, and usually meals in a casual setting but which does not necessarily provide accommodation. This type of establishment would more usually be called a pub or bar in other countries. In general use in Australia, the terms '"hotel" and pub are usually taken to be synonymous.

In India, the word may also refer to a restaurant since the best restaurants were always situated next to a good hotel. The word hotel derives from the French hotel, which referred to a French version of a townhouse, not a place offering accommodation (in contemporary usage, hotel has the meaning of "hotel", and hotel particular is used for the old meaning). The French spelling (with the circumflex) was once also used in English, but is now rare. The circumflex replaces the 's' once preceding the 't' in the earlier hostel spelling, which over time received a new, but closely related meaning.

SERVICES AND FACILITIES

Basic accommodation of a room with only a bed, a cupboard, a small table and a washstand has largely been replaced by rooms with en-suite bathrooms and climate control. Other features found may be a telephone, an alarm clock, a TV, and broadband Internet connectivity. Food and drink may be supplied by a mini-bar (which often includes a small refrigerator) containing snacks and drinks (to be paid for on departure), and tea and coffee making facilities (cups, spoons, an electric kettle and sachets containing instant coffee, tea bags, sugar, and creamer or milk). In the United Kingdom a hotel is required by law to serve food and drinks to all comers within certain stated hours; to avoid this requirement it is not uncommon to come across "private hotels" which are not subject to this requirement. However, in Japan the capsule hotel supplies minimal facilities and room space. The cost and quality of hotels are usually indicative of the range and type of services available. Due to the enormous increase in tourism worldwide during the last decades of the 20th century, standards, especially those of smaller establishments, have improved considerably. For the sake of greater comparability, rating systems have been introduced, with the one to five stars classification being most common.

TYPES OF HOTELS

Boutique Hotels

Boutique hotel is a term originating in North America to describe intimate, usually luxurious or quirky hotel environments. Boutique hotels differentiate themselves from larger chain/branded hotels and motels by providing personalized level accommodation and services/ facilities. Sometimes known as "design hotels" or "lifestyle hotels," boutique hotels began in the 1980s in major cities like New York, London, and San Francisco. Very often it is the Morgans Hotel in Murray Hill of New York, that is awarded with the title of first boutique hotel in the world. It was opened by Ian Schrager in 1984 according to a design by Andree Putman.

Typically boutique hotels are furnished in a themed, stylish and/or aspirational manner. Although usually considerably smaller than a mainstream hotel (often ranging from 3 to 100 guest rooms), boutique hotels can often have hundreds of rooms in major cities. Guest rooms and suites are fitted with telephony and Wi-Fi Internet, air-conditioning, honesty bars and often cable/ pay TV. Guest services are attended to by 24 hour hotel staff. Many boutique hotels have on-site dining facilities, and the majority offer bars and lounges which may also be open to the general public. Despite this definition, the popularity of the boutique term and concept has lead to some confusion about the term. Boutique hotels have typically been unique properties operated by individials or companies with a small collection. However, their successes have prompted established multi-national hotel companies to establish their own brands. The most notable is Starwood Hotels and Resorts' W Hotels. Currently, there is one publication dedicated to the boutique hotel, boutique DESIGN magazine, which is published quarterly. Boutique hotel resources are more commonly available online. One such site dedicated to boutique hotels is Tablet Hotels. There are also a number of sytlized design and coffee table books highlighting various properties throughout the world.

Apartment Hotel

An Apartment Hotel is a type of accommodation, described as "a serviced apartment complex that uses a hotel style booking system". It is similar to renting an apartment, but with no fixed contracts and occupants can 'check-out' whenever they wish. Apartment hotels are flexible types of accommodation; instead of the rigid format of a hotel room an apartment hotel complex usually offers a complete fully fitted apartment. These complexes are usually custom built, and similar to a hotel complex contain a varied amount of apartments. The length of stay in these apartment hotels are very varied with anywhere from a few days to months or even years. Prices tend to be cheaper than hotels. The people that stay in apartment hotels use them as a home from home therefore they are usually fitted with everything the average home would require.

Apartment hotels were first created in holiday destinations as accommodation for families that needed to 'live' in an apartment rather than 'stay' as they would in a hotel. The apartments would provide a 'holiday home' but generally be serviced. Later on these apartments evolved to be complete homes, allowing occupants to do everything they would at home, such as cleaning, washing and cooking.

Essentially the apartment hotel combines the flexibility of apartment living with the service of a hotel. Many of the apartments take advantage of prime locations with panoramic views of cities seen through wall to ceiling windows. Suites usually include high quality finishes, broadband connection & interactive TV, servicing and integrated kitchen and bathroom. High quality leather sofas in the living area and king size beds bring the hotel experience to a whole new level. Those are the luxuries, they also come with the basics: satellite or cable TV, washer, dryer, dishwasher, cooker, oven, fridge, freezer, sink, shower, bath, wardrobes, all the furnishings to be expected in a luxury home.

Bed and Breakfast

A Bed and Breakfast often referred to as a B&B is a type of boarding house typically operating out of a large single family residence. Guests are accommodated at night in private bedrooms and breakfast is served in the morning - either in the bedroom or, more commonly, in a dining room or the host's kitchen. Bathrooms can be private or shared (with other guests or with the family in smaller establishments) or en-suite (where the ablutions are directly accessed from the guest's bedroom).

B&Bs may be operated either as a primary occupation or as a secondary source of income. Staff often consists of the house's owners and members of their family who live there. Guests are usually expected to pay for their stay upon arrival and leave before noon (or earlier) on the day of departure. A big advantage of this type of hosted accommodation is the local knowledge of the host.

When guests stay more than one night, in some smaller B&Bs they will be expected to be away from the B&B during the main part of the day. This arrangement, however, may not be inconvenient since many popular B&Bs are located in beach and mountain areas, such as Hawaii, New England, and Colorado where daytime recreation and tourism activities are popular. One advantage of staying at a B&B is readier access to popular locations "off the beaten path" which may not be convenient to the city center.

Because most B&Bs are small, rarely with room for more than about 2-12 guests, it is advisable for anyone wanting to stay at a bed and breakfast to make reservations well in advance of their travel date. Consultation with a qualified travel agent knowledgeable in this type of accommodation may be helpful; However, many B&Bs belong to associations and have a web presence. Be aware that prices and tariffs described in various books and travel guides are often obsolete by the time they are published.

The B&B arrangement is actually a very old one; before the 20th century, it was quite normal for country travellers to spend the night at a private house rather than an inn, and the custom persists in many parts of the world. However, prior to the 19th century, this was strictly an informal arrangement constrained by acquaintance and social rank; a doctor might stay with a doctor or pharmacist, while a nobleman would only stay with the local gentry. The abbreviation of 'B&B' on roadside signs first became popular in the British Isles.

In the British Isles, breakfast is usually cooked on demand for the guest and usually features bacon, eggs, sausages, tomatoes, mushrooms, baked beans, etc but increasingly, because of either a desire of owners to economise or guests to minimise their calorie intake, a 'continental breakfast' is becoming more common. In the British Isles where hotel prices are often outrageous, B&B's are a budget option and this tradition continues in many parts of the world.

However, many B&Bs in North America and New Zealand often consciously seek to recall earlier days; they are frequently established in attractive older houses that have been renovated and filled with antique furniture. In some cases in North America an existing inn will relabel itself as a "B&B" to improve business and move itself `up-market'.

In Ireland, most B&Bs serve a traditional Irish breakfast as a point of pride. In Cuba, which opened up to tourism in the 1990s after the financial support of the Soviet Union ended, a form of B&B called casa particular ("private home") became the main form of accommodation outside the tourist resorts. The term "bed and breakfast" is also used to refer to a meal plan where breakfast is the only meal provided, commonly in package holidays, in a major hotel that may provide other meals to only some customers. As they are often run by amateurs, with little lodge management experience, strict laws should govern the operation of B&Bs. However, regulations vary in each jurisdiction both in content and extent and in enforcement. The most common regulations B&Bs must follow pertain to safety. They are required to have fire resistance, a sufficient fire escape plan in place, and smoke detectors in each guest room.

Capsule Hotel

A capsule hotel, is a hotel system of extremely dense occupancy. Guest space is reduced in size to a modular plastic or fibreglass block roughly 2 m by 1 m by 1.25 m, providing room to sleep and little more, although facilities usually include a television and other electronic entertainment. These capsules are then grouped and stacked, two units high. Luggage is usually stored in a locker away from the capsule. Privacy is maintained by a curtain at the open end of the capsule but noise pollution can be high. Washing facilities are communal and there are often restaurants, or at least vending machines, and other entertainment facilities.

This style of hotel accommodation was developed in Japan and has not gained acceptance outside of the country. The Japanese capsule hotels vary widely in size, some having only fifty or so capsules and others over 700. They are often male-only. There are also capsule hotels with separate male and female sleeping quarters. Clothes and shoes are sometimes exchanged for a yukata and slippers on entry. A towel may also be provided. The benefit of these hotels is convenience and price, usually around ¥2000-4000 a night 21-29, $25–34, £15–20). Such hotels are not necessarily regarded as only an option for those with lower incomes—a typical customer would be the business salaryman after a night of drinking who has missed the last train home. Some capsule hotels offer low daytime discounts for those needing an afternoon nap.

The first capsule hotel was the Capsule Inn Osaka, designed by Kisho Kurokawa and located in the Umeda district of Osaka. It opened on February 1, 1979 and the initial room rate was ¥1,600. These rooms can be seen in the movie The Fast and the Furious: Tokyo Drift. They were also used as a basis for sets in the film The Fifth Element. They also appear in the cyberpunk novel Neuromancer under the name of "coffin hotel."

Casa Particular

Casa particular is a phrase meaning private accommodation or private homestays in Cuba, very similar to bed and breakfast although it can also take the form of vacation rental. When the meaning is clear the term is often shortened to simply casa. A casa particular is basically a private family establishment that provides paid lodging, usually on a short-term basis. In general under this term you can find full apartment and houses, rooms inside people homes, mini-apartments or rooms with separate entrance (studio or efficiency type rooms).

It is also considered a type of boarding house typically operated out of a single family residence where guests can be accommodated at night in private bedrooms (which may or may not be equipped with private baths) and where breakfast, sometimes continental and sometimes the full English variety, is served in the morning. The business may be operated either as a primary occupation or as a secondary source of income, and the staff often consists of the house's owner(s) and members of their family who live there.

Because they are usually small, rarely with room for more than about 5-6 guests, it is advisable for anyone wanting to stay at a particular casa particular during high season to make advance reservations. However, outside the season there is no need because there are often many such casas, causing competition and opening opportunities to strike a deal. Prices can then drop to 15 euro or even less for longer stays. During high season they can rise to over 30 euro. Many belong to associations, have a web presence, and are described in various books and travel guides. Casas particulares can be recognised by a small sign on the door, with two blue triangles ('roofs') against a white background, which the owners obtain after paying a fixed per-room annual tax.

In some Cuban cities and tourist resorts, like Varadero, Playa Santa Lucia and Guardalavaca, local authorities determined that casas particulars would represent a threat to the hotel industry, and passed some legislation placing regulations and limits on the industry forbidding the operation of these establishments. "Casa particular" literally means "private house" but it started to be used to mean "private accommodation" in 1997, when the Cuban government finally allowed Cubans to rent out rooms in their houses or apartments to tourists, providing Cuban families with new sources of income. As any other type of accommodation in Cuba such as hotels, camping and motels were owned by the government, the term "casa particular" stated that this kind of paid lodging was privately operated.

Services and Facilities

All rooms are clean, safe and upgraded to tourist standards. It ranges from basic accommodation of a room with a bed, a closet, a small table to full furnished independent apartments upgraded to western standards. Other features found may be a telephone, an alarm clock, and a TV. Food and drink may be supplied by a mini-bar (which often includes a small refrigerator) containing snacks and drinks (to be paid for on departure).

It is possible to have breakfast/dinner in the casa for price. Often breakfasts/dinners sold will decide if case owner will break even or not. So if it becomes clear that one plans to generally eat out, the price may go up because this is an important source of income.

Casas particulares have several advantages over other types of lodgings:

- The guest can quickly develop genuine Cuban relationships and become deeply involved in the culture of the country. Before he/she knows it, the guest will be part of the family. In a big resort one may only meet hotel workers and other tourists.
- The guest will enjoy the free and easy atmosphere, feel completely at home in the casa particular and will be able to invite friends over.

The current regulations for state-run hotels don't allow to have Cuban guests invited to hotel rooms.

- It is almost always cheaper to stay in a private room than in a hotel.
- "Guests" are not usually allowed into the hotels. Usually one can take one local "guest" into his rented casa-particular.
- By renting a casa particular, the guest will be directly contributing to a person or family's standard of living. This is often obvious through the fact that casas particulares are freshly painted.

The cost and quality of casas particulars are usually indicative of the accommodation type and type of services available. Most of the casas particulars are rented for short term to travellers. Long term accommodation is also provided by some casas, especially for foreign students. In Havana, the casas particulares are usually family apartments and a smaller number of them are houses. In other cities, private accommodation is provided mainly in family houses.

Types of Casas Particulares rentals:

- Private Room: a room is rented out most of the times with private bathroom and a key to the apartment/house is usually given to the guest.
- Private Room with independent entrance. Sometimes the house/ apartment is split in order to allow this.
- Apartment: the guest can enjoy the privacy and independency of a full furnished apartment for his/her vacations. Sometimes this apartment is part of house being split by a wall usually with a connecting door.
- Studio-type or mini-apartment: it is not an apartment with several rooms but just the bedroom, a kitchen-living-dining room and a bathroom.

Condo-hotel

A condo-hotel or a hotel-condo is a building used as both a condominium and a hotel. This type of residential building meets several needs that make it attractive. As development costs increase, the cost of hotel development can make developing new hotels difficult, especially in major cities. By selling the units as condos, the developer moves much of the development cost to the condo owners. By owning units that can be rented as hotel rooms, the owners are able to get a return on their investment allowing them the ability to own a residence in a resort or major city.

It should be noted that the U.S. Government is very strict about the type of advertising that can be done vis a vis Condo Hotel projects. Some condo projects have advertised themselves as "Real Estate Investments" - since the value of these condos as a real estate investment is not entirely clear - the U.S. Government currently disallows use of this reference when advertising condo hotels.

Condo hotels have been criticized in California for allowing developers to skirt laws designed to protect public access to beaches. Because such a facility has hotel rooms, it can be classified as a public accommodation, even though the majority of the units are privately held, and the facility does little to accommodate the public.

Destination Hotel

A destination hotel is a place of lodging whose inherent location and amenities attract visitors regardless of the route needed to arrive or the areawide features of interest. The destination hotel concept has existed at least since the 19th century and occupies a significant market share of all lodging in the world as of 2006. From the late 1980s to the present the extent of amenities and conference facilities has greatly expanded for many destination hotels. Destination hotels are also called destination lodgings and destination resorts. Considerable academic and business analysis has been conducted in the field of destination hotels. In the Arnold Encyclopedia of Real Estate a destination hotel is characterized as a place of lodging not chosen for convenience and not chosen for people in transit to other areas.

The following typically are characteristics of a destination hotel:

- Amenities which are quite complete and self-contained
- Upscale nature of the lodging operation
- Distinctive characteristics of the building, gardens or adjacent natural feature
- Activity set which makes leaving the property unnecessary

Since the 1800s, the traditional concept of a destination hotel has been based upon a venue which is typically remote and has a natural feature as its attraction. For example, the Kviknes Hotel in Norway is a difficult to reach remote location which provides visitors access to the scenic fjord at Balestrand. Historically there were certain built-in amenities such as gourmet cuisine, music recitals and shoreline trails; however, the amenities of modern destination hotels dwarf the scale of these earlier models. Many of the Las Vegas and Carribbean resort hotels have complete shopping malls, conference centers and large entertainment halls on site; thus, the contemporary version of a destination often features large on-site capital investment in activities, although the access to a local natural feature is still retained by many newer destination hotels.

Luxury Resorts

A luxury resort, sometimes referred to as an exclusive resort, is a very expensive vacation facility which is fully staffed and has been rated with five stars. Luxury resorts often boast many visitor activities and attractions such as golf, watersports, spa and beauty facilities, skiing, natural ecology and tranquility. Because of the extent of amenities offered, a luxury resort is also considered a destination resort. A luxury resort is an elite luxury property which exhibits an exceptionally high degree of customer service and hospitality. A flawless execution of guest services will be the resort staff's and managements main concern. A luxury resort will commonly also feature a superb architectural interior and exterior design as well as an interesting physical location.

The interior design will normally be elegant with stylish bedroom decor, exceptional dining facilities, and manicured landscaping and meticulous grounds. Luxury resorts will often also be in based in exceptionally desirable and strategic worldwide locations, from beautiful tropical islands, to snow caked mountains, to scenic lakes and rivers, to exhilarating cities. The locations will often be famous for featured activities from skiing to golf, water spots, diving, fishing, sailing and nature walks to glamorous shopping and nightlife entertainment.

A luxury resort may vary greatly in character, style and theme from resort to resort. A luxury resort will, however, normally be characterized by a high level of luxury, sophistication and off course price. Accommodations are first class, whether they follow a classic and traditional nature or a more minimalist and modern styling. An unmatched level of comfort will be available at a luxury resort, as well as many personalized services and amenities.

Extended Stay Hotel

Extended stay hotels are a type of lodging with features unavailable at standard hotels. These features are intended to provide more home-like amenities. There are currently 27 extended stay chains in North America with at least 7 hotels, representing over 2,000 properties. There is substantial variation among extended stay hotels with respect to quality and the amenities that are available. Some of the economy chains attract clientele who use the hotels as semi-permanent lodging. Occasionally, these budget establishments can be the scene of criminal activity.

Extended-stay hotels typically have self-serve laundry facilities and offer discounts for extended stays, beginning at 5 or 7 days. They also have guestrooms (or "suites") with kitchens. The kitchens include at a minimum usually: a sink, a refrigerator (usually full size), a microwave oven, and a stovetop. Some kitchens also have dishwashers and conventional ovens.

Extended stay hotels are popular with business travelers on extended assignments, families in the midst of a relocation, and anyone else in need of temporary housing. Extended stay hotels are also used by travelers who appreciate the larger space a typical suite provides. Residence Inn is credited with popularizing the "extended stay" concept. The chain was launched in 1975 in Wichita, Kansas by Jack DeBoer, and acquired by Marriott Corporation in

1987. As of April 2005, there were over 450 Residence Inn hotels in the United States, Canada and Mexico. Some extended stay hotels are coming up in United Kingdom and Ireland as well.

One of today's most popular long term lodging brands came from the merger of Extended Stay America and Homestead Hotels. Both these chains were already well established when they combined in 2004 to become Extended Stay Hotels with over 670 owned and operated properties nationwide. Another worldwide hotel chain, Choice Hotels International, franchisor for name brands such as Comfort Inn, Comfort Suites, Sleep Inn and Quality Inn, entered the extended stay market with their MainStay Suites brand. They proceeded to acquire the Suburban Extended Stay hotel chain in 2005, making them a sizeable extended stay system with over 150 hotels open and under development.

Flophouse

A flophouse or dosshouse is a place that offers very cheap lodging, generally by providing only minimal services. Occupants of flophouses generally share bathroom facilities and reside in very cramped quarters. The people who make use of these places are often transients, although some people will stay in flophouses for long periods of time—years or decades. Some people who live in flophouses may be just a step above homelessness. In the late 20th century, typical cost might be about US$6 per night. A typical flophouse might advertise its services with a sign such as "Hotel for Men; Transients Welcome".

Quarters in flophouses are very small, and may resemble office cubicles more than a regular room in a hotel or apartment building. A cubicle might only have wire mesh for a ceiling. In the past, flophouses were sometimes called "workingmen's hotels" and catered to hobos and transient workers such as seasonal railroad and agriculture workers, or migrant lumberjacks who would travel west during the summer to work and then return to an eastern or midwestern city such as Chicago to stay in a flophouse during the winter. This is described in the 1930 novel The Rambling Kid by Charles Ashleigh and the 1976 book The Human Cougar by Lloyd Morain. Another theme in Morain's book is the gentrification which was then beginning and which has led cities to pressure flophouses to close.

George Orwell also discussed flophouses in the UK in his book Down and Out in Paris and London. He described them as having rather poor cleanliness standards, often issuing unwashed and badly stained blankets, and sometimes renting beds in a large common room resembling barracks more than private rooms. He noted that at the time he wrote the book (1933) the term "dosshouse" was already falling out of use.

Some city districts that currently have or once had flophouses in abundance became well-known in their own right, such as the Bowery in New York, New York. The movies The Blues Brothers (1980) and Staying Alive (1983) both feature their lead characters living in flophouses. Another slang term for flophouses was mentioned in the movie Kids. This variation of the definition is a house or apartment (usually apartment) where substance abusers stay to party and abuse drugs and/or alcohol. Such people, whether employed or unemployed, lead a hedonist self-destructive lifestyle. If they are employed, their money usually goes to drugs and/or alcohol. Other bums and partygoers can also temporarily stay for parties.

Some low-end flophouses have graffiti sprayed on the walls and lack beds, instead just have matresses on the floor. Some of the characters in the film Trainspotting lived in these conditions. Michael Dominic's documentary film Sunshine Hotel (2001) follows the lives of the denizens of one of the few remaining Bowery flophouses.

ORGANIZATION WITHIN HOTELS

Hotel Manager

The Hotel manager oversees all of a hotel's daily operations, from staffing to coordinating fresh-cut flowers for the lobby. Many, over time, are given long-term responsibility for negotiating contracts with vendors (such as maintenance supplies), negotiating leases with on-site shops, and physically upgrading the hotel. Hotel managers usually relish "the ability to put your own distinctive style on the [hotel] experience." While managing a hotel and giving it your unique flair are wonderful, they come with full responsibility for failure. "The better you are at what you do, the more responsibilities you are given, the more chances you have to fail," mentioned one hotel manager. When things fall apart, "no one is a hotel manager's friend."

Hotel managers can feel great about their positions, create strong relationships with regular customers, and maintain an amicable working environment. But should the bottom line waver and financial woes occur, the first neck on the chopping block is the hotel manager's. Those in the hotel management industry say that sometimes it seems that you need "to be born on the planet Krypton" to be a good hotel manager because only Superman could juggle the administrative, aesthetic, and financial decisions which constitute daily life on the job. Over 70 percent of the respondents said that tired was an understatement about how they felt at the end of the day or night.

A hotel manager's position as a liaison between the ownership and the staff can be difficult and isolating. But those who can put up with the long hours, the high degree of responsibility, and the variety of tasks emerge with a solid degree of satisfaction and a desire to continue in the profession. The average tenure of a hotel manager is 6.7 years, though this figure doesn't represent the number of managers who work for two years and those who work for decades. Many work at a variety of hotels, build up their resumes, and then find positions that allow them the freedom to operate their own establishments.

Aspiring hotel managers used to begin at the reception desk, as part of the wait staff, or as members of the cleaning staff, then work their way up the ladder. As hotels have become more commercial properties and the duties of hotel managers have expanded, this avenue of advancement has closed off. Now hotel manager hopefuls go to hotel management school, and those who don't should garner as much practical hotel experience as possible. Each chain or specific hotel puts new employees through their own training programmes, so those applying for jobs should learn all they can about the scope and functioning of the specific hotels where they wish to work. Part of life as a hotel manager can be similar to the life of a doctor, as managers can be called to duty at any time of the day or night. Hotel managers must handle any and all emergencies, and those who wish to remain in the profession and maintain respect must be quick-thinking and decisive. Candidates should have a good organizational and financial background, excellent communication and interpersonal skills, and strong self-discipline. They should also be extremely detail-oriented; when running a hotel, there is no such thing as an unimportant detail. The good manager drives himself to improve and upgrade the hotel at every available opportunity.

A hotel manager is responsible for the day-to-day management of a hotel and its staff and has commercial accountability for planning, organising and directing all hotel services, including front-of-house (reception, concierge, reservation), banqueting and housekeeping. In larger hotels, managers often have a specific remit (guest services, accounting, marketing) and make up a general management team.

Financial management - preparing budgets and marketing strategies and achieving targets for the business - plays a major role. The manager must strike a balance between customer satisfaction and effective business management, ensuring financial viability, and facilitate a smooth-running customer service, whilst ensuring staff work together as a team.

Typical Work Activities

Typical work activities vary depending on the size and type of hotel, but may include:

- Planning and organising accommodation, catering and other hotel services;
- Promoting and marketing the business;
- Managing budgets and financial plans;
- Maintaining statistical and financial records;
- Achieving profit targets;
- Recruiting, training and monitoring staff;
- Planning work schedules;
- Meeting and greeting customers;

- Dealing with customer complaints and comments;
- Addressing problems and troubleshooting;
- Ensuring events and conferences run smoothly;
- Supervising maintenance, supplies and furnishings;
- Dealing with contractors and suppliers;
- Ensuring security is effective;
- Carrying out inspections of property and services;
- Ensuring compliance with licensing laws, health and safety and other statutory regulations.

The manager of a large hotel may have less contact with guests but will spend time meeting heads of department and planning and monitoring the progress of business strategies. In a smaller establishment, the manager is much more involved in the hands-on day-to-day running of the hotel, which may include carrying out reception duties or serving meals if the need arises.

A significant number of hotel managers are self-employed and this can lead to a more general management experience, from greeting guests to managing finances.

How to Become a Hotel Manager

- Ask yourself if you have excellent interpersonal, communication and organizational skills. They are necessary for a successful hotel management career.
- Obtain a college degree in hotel management or restaurant management. Remember that a food services department contributes greatly to the profits of a hotel; a successful restaurant manager can see his or her career advance quickly.
- Take advantage of work-study programmes offered by many colleges so that you will gain solid experience working in hotels.
- Expect to go through a hotel's training programme once you are hired after college. During the first couple of years you will be handling only relatively mundane duties, instead of providing your input on issues such as staffing, hotel decor or conventions.
- Understand that you might be offered a position as a front office manager, a food and beverage manager, a convention services manager, or any of a number of administrative positions after your training period. If you are successful at different managerial positions, your career will benefit in the long run.
- Be aware that a promotion might require you to relocate for a few years if you work for a hotel chain that has properties throughout the country.
- You will need to quickly become proficient with computers because of their widespread use in hotel reservations, billing and overall management operations.

- Consider working for hotels in warm tourist destinations or snowy mountains, depending on your preferred lifestyle.
- Be prepared for long hours, night and weekend work, and the occasional unhappy guest.

Different managerial personnel working as hotel managers —

Catering managers plan, organise and manage the food and beverage services of organisations and businesses, both inside and outside the hospitality industry, with the aim of achieving good quality at low cost and maintaining high standards of hygiene and customer satisfaction.

There is a range of jobs in catering management, along with a number of different routes into the industry. Roles include: managing restaurants, bars and other outlets in hotels, resorts or liners; providing catering services at events; and running catering operations at hospitals, schools and other organisations. With ongoing growth in the service industry, opportunities in this demanding but rewarding area continue to grow.

The role varies according to the size and nature of the establishment: in a small operation, the catering manager has more of a 'hands on' role and will be involved in the day-to-day running of the operation; in contract catering, the catering manager will spend time negotiating with the client organisation, assessing its requirements and ensuring that it is satisfied with the service delivered.

Typical tasks will include:

- Recruiting and training permanent and casual staff;
- Organising, leading and motivating the catering team;
- Planning menus in consultation with chefs;
- Ensuring health and safety regulations are strictly observed;
- Budgeting and establishing financial targets;
- Monitoring the quality of the product and service provided;
- Keeping financial and administrative records;
- Managing the payroll and monitoring spending levels;
- Maintaining stock levels and ordering new supplies as required;
- Interacting with customers if involved with 'front of house' work;
- Liaising with suppliers and clients;
- Negotiating contracts with customers (in contract catering).

In more senior posts, principal tasks will involve:

- Setting and agreeing budgets;
- Monitoring quality standards;
- Overseeing the management of the facilities, for example checking events bookings and the allocation of resources and staff;
- Planning new promotions and initiatives, and contributing to business development;
- Dealing with staffing and client issues, as they arise.

Food and Restaurant Manager

Fast food restaurant managers are responsible for the provision of standardised food and customer service in outlets based in the high street, motor service areas, stations, airports or multiplexes.

Drawing on all the operational functions of a business, the work involves applying financial, marketing and operational know-how, and supervising and training staff.

Managers plan, organise, and co-ordinate all resources and activities in a store. The work involves: setting targets, planning budgets, and controlling stock; recruiting, training and inspiring restaurant teams; creating and driving marketing campaigns; and building bridges with the local community.

Ultimately, it is the manager's ideas, initiative and personality that shape the restaurant.

Tasks typically involve:

- Organising the store in terms of products, equipment and people;
- Planning and checking work schedules;
- Carrying out audits to check health safety, food safety and quality of service in the restaurant;
- Making sure the fast-track audit is completed daily to check the safety of equipment and that food is properly cooked, only in-date stock is used, and all other products are discarded;
- Carrying out work outside the restaurant, including 'mystery shopping' at other restaurants within the chain;
- Attending weekly meetings with senior managers;
- Dealing with problems, queries, complaints, staff and customers in the store;
- Monitoring and maintaining high standards of food, service and hygiene;
- Ensuring the company's required standards of customer care are met;
- Administering payrolls;
- Checking and securing cash receipts;
- Budgeting to ensure maximum profitability;
- Achieving set profit and loss targets;
- Maintaining and securing equipment and buildings and all company assets contained within the unit;
- Publicising and marketing restaurants in the locality;
- Motivating restaurant teams;
- Recruiting, selecting and training new staff and fully inducting the restaurant team in accordance with company policy;
- Developing all team members to their fullest potential using the performance management/review system and identifying individual training needs;

- Ensuring the implementation and maintenance of legislation, company standards and procedures;
- Recognising new trends and implementing action plans accordingly;
- Acting as a communication link between senior teams and the restaurant team;
- Leading by example, acting as a role model for the restaurant team.

A successful manager will strike the right balance between creating both a good service for restaurant customers and a fun work environment for members of staff.

Human Resources

Human resources has at least two meanings depending on context. The original usage derives from political economy and economics, where it was traditionally called labour, one of three factors of production. The more common usage within corporations and businesses refers to the individuals within the firm, and to the portion of the firm's organization that deals with hiring, firing, training, and other personnel issues.

Modern analysis emphasizes that human beings are not predictable commodity "resources" with definitions totally controlled by contract, but are creative and social beings that make contributions beyond "labour" to a society and to civilization. The broad term human capital has evolved to contain the complexity of this term, and in macro-economics the term "firm-specific human capital" has evolved to represent the original meaning of term "human resources".

Advocating the central role of "human resources" or human capital in enterprises and societies has been a traditional role of socialist parties, who claim that value is primarily created by their activity, and accordingly justify a larger claim of profits or relief from these enterprises or societies. Critics say this is just a bargaining tactic which grew out of various practices of medieval European guilds into the modern trade union and collective bargaining unit. A contrary view, common to capitalist parties, is that it is the infrastructural capital and (what they call) intellectual capital owned and fused by "management" that provides most value in financial capital terms. This likewise justifies a bargaining position and a general view that "human resources" are interchangeable.

A significant sign of consensus on this latter point is the ISO 9000 series of standards which requires a "job description" of every participant in a productive enterprise. In general, heavily unionized nations such as France and Germany have adopted and encouraged such descriptions especially within trade unions. One view of this trend is that a strong social consensus on political economy and a good social welfare system facilitates labour mobility and tends to make the entire economy more productive, as labour can move from one enterprise to another with little controversy or difficulty in adapting.

An important controversy regarding labour mobility illustrates the broader philosophical issue with usage of the phrase "human resources": governments of developing nations often regard developed nations that encourage immigration or "guest workers" as appropriating human capital that is rightfully part of the developing nation and required to further its growth as a civilization. They argue that this appropriation is similar to colonial commodity fiat wherein a colonizing European power would define an arbitrary price for natural resources, extracting which diminished national natural capital.

The debate regarding "human resources" versus human capital thus in many ways echoes the debate regarding natural resources versus natural capital. Over time the United Nations have come to more generally support the developing nations' point of view, and have requested significant offsetting "foreign aid" contributions so that a developing nation losing human capital does not lose the capacity to continue to train new people in trades, professions, and the arts.

An extreme version of this view is that historical inequities such as African slavery must be compensated by current developed nations, which benefitted from stolen "human resources" as they were developing. This is an extremely controversial view, but it echoes the general theme of converting human capital to "human resources" and thus greatly diminishing its value to the host society, i.e. "Africa", as it is put to narrow imitative use as "labour" in the using society.

In the very narrow context of corporate "human resources", there is a contrasting pull to reflect and require workplace diversity that echoes the diversity of a global customer base. Foreign language and culture skills, ingenuity, humor, and careful listening, are examples of traits that such programmes typically require. It would appear that these evidence a general shift to the human capital point of view, and an acknowledgement that human beings do contribute much more to a productive enterprise than "work": they bring their character, their ethics, their creativity, their social connections, and in some cases even their pets and children, and alter the character of a workplace. The term corporate culture is used to characterize such processes.

The traditional but extremely narrow context of hiring, firing, and job description is considered a 20th century anachronism. Most corporate organizations that compete in the modern global economy have adopted a view of human capital that mirrors the modern consensus as above. Some of these, in turn, deprecate the term "human resources" as useless.

As the term refers to predictable exploitations of human capital in one context or another, it can still be said to apply to manual labour, mass agriculture, low skill "McJobs" in service industries, military and other work that has clear job descriptions, and which generally do not encourage creative or social contributions. In general the abstractions of macro-economics treat it this way - as it characterizes no mechanisms to represent choice or ingenuity. So one interpretation is that "firm-specific human capital" as defined in macro-economics is the modern and correct definition of "human resources" - and that this is inadequate to represent the contributions of "human resources" in any modern theory of political economy. In terms of recruitment and selection it is important to consider carrying out a thorough job analysis to determine the level of skills/technical abilities, competencies, flexibility of the employee required etc. At this point it is important to consider both the internal and external factors that can have an impact on the recruitment of employees. The external factors are those out-with the powers of the organization and include issues such as current and future trends of the labour market e.g. skills, education level, government investment into industries etc. On the other hand internal influences are easier to control, predict and monitor, for example management styles or even the organizational culture.

In order to know the business environment in which any organization operates, three major trends should be considered:

- Demographics – the characteristics of a population/workforce, for example, age, gender or social class. This type of trend may have an effect in relation to pension offerings, insurance packages etc.
- Diversity – the variation within the population/workplace. Changes in society now mean that a larger proportion of organizations are made up of female employees in comparison to thirty years ago. Also over recent years organizations have become more culturally diverse and have increased the number of working patterns (part-time, casual, seasonal positions) to cope with the changes in both society and the global market. It is important to note here that an organisation must consider the ethic and legal implications of their decisions in relation to the HRM policies they enact to protect employees. Employers have to be acutely aware of the rise in discrimination, unfair dismissal and sexual/racial harassment cases in recent years and the detrimental effects this can have on the employees and the organisation. Anti-discrimination legislation over the past 30 years has provided a foundation for an increasing interest in diversity at work which is "about creating a working culture that seeks respects and values difference."
- Skills and qualifications – as industries move from manual to a more managerial professions so does the need for more highly skilled graduates. If the market is 'tight' i.e. not enough staff for the jobs, employers will have to compete for employees by offering financial rewards, community investment etc.also the political issues

In regards to how individuals respond to the changes in a labour market the following should be understood:

- Geographical spread – how far is the job from the individual? The distance to travel to work should be in line with the pay offered by the organization and the transportation and infrastructure of the area will also be an influencing factor in deciding who will apply for a post.

- Occupational structure – the norms and values of the different careers within an organization. Mahoney 1989 developed 3 different types of occupational structure namely craft (loyalty to the profession), organization career (promotion through the firm) and unstructured (lower/unskilled workers who work when needed).
- Generational difference –different age categories of employees have certain characteristics, for example their behaviour and their expectations of the organisation.

Recruitment methods are wide and varied, it is important that the job is described correctly and any personal specifications stated. Job recruitment methods can be through job centres, employment agencies/consultants, headhunting, and local/national newspapers. It is important that the correct media is chosen to ensure an appropriate response to the advertised post.

Human Resources within Firms

Though human resources have been part of business and organizations since the first days of agriculture, the modern concept of human resources began in reaction to the efficiency focus of Taylorism in the early 1900s. By 1920, psychologists and employment experts in the United States started the human relations movement, which viewed workers in terms of their psychology and fit with companies, rather than as interchangeable parts. This movement grew throughout the middle of the 20th century, placing emphasis on how leadership, cohesion, and loyalty played important roles in organizational success. Although this view was increasingly challenged by more quantitatively rigorous and less "soft" management techniques in the 1960s and beyond, human resources had gained a permanent role within the firm.

Facing mankind's problems it is opportune to mobilize as many intellectual resources as possible in order to resolve the emerging troubles. The students have to be trained to construct pertinent knowledge together (for example using the method Learning by teaching). Students can be trained in constructing knowledge outside the classroom too. They have to adopt following attitudes:

- Be aware that they are bearing resources
- Be aware that they have to increase their own resources in order to be more attractive inside the community
- Be aware that they can increase their own resources if they communicate
- Be aware that they can increase their own resources if they share their knowledge with other people
- Ability to identify resource from other community members and to make this resource available for all the group

- Ability to search for pertinent resources outside the group
- Ability to connect people looking for proposing resources
- Ability to organize collective thinking in networks

Employee Engagement

Employee engagement is a concept that is generally viewed in terms of employees feeling a strong emotional bond to the organization that employs them. (Robinson) This is associated with people demonstrating a willingness to recommend the organization to others and commit time and effort to help the organization succeed. (Harter) It suggests that people are motivated by intrinsic factors (e.g. personal growth, working to a common purpose, being part of a larger process) rather than simply focusing on extrinsic factors (e.g. pay/ reward). (Ryan) The concept has gained popularity as various studies have demonstrated links with productivity.

In 1999, The Gallup Organization published research that showed that engaged employees are more productive, more profitable, more customer-focused, safer, and less likely to leave their employer. The review stated that "engagement with employees within a firm has shown to motivate the employee to work beyond personal factors and work more for the success of the firm." (Harter) Watson Wyatt found that high-commitment organizations (one with loyal and dedicated employees) out-performed those with low commitment by 47% in the 2000 study and by 200% in the 2002 study. (Wyatt) In a study of professional service firms, the Hay Group found that offices with engaged employees were up to 43% more productive, based on a comparison of revenue generation.

Recent research has focused on developing a better understanding of how variables such as quality of work relationships and values of the organization interact and their link to important work outcomes. From the perspective of the employee, "outcomes" range from strong commitment to the isolation of oneself from the organization. The study done by the Gallup Management Journal has shown that only 29 percent of employees are actively engaged in their jobs. Those "engaged" employees work with passion and feel a strong connection to their company. Moreover, 54 percent of employees are not engaged meaning that they go through each workday putting time but no passion into their work. Also, Seventeen percent of employees are actively disengaged, meaning that they are busy acting out of their own personal unhappiness, which undermines what their engaged co-workers are trying to accomplish.

Access to a reliable model enables organizations to conduct validation studies to establish the relationship of employee engagement to productivity/ performance and other measures linked to effectiveness.

It is an important principle of occupational psychology (i.e. the application of psychological theories, research methods, and intervention strategies involving workplace issues) that validation studies should be anchored in reliable scales (i.e. organized and related groups of items) and not simply focus on individual elements in isolation.

To understand how high levels of employee engagement affect organizational performance/productivity it is important to have an a priori model that demonstrates how the scales interact. (Konrad) There is also overlap between this concept and those relating to well-being at work and the psychological contract.

As employee productivity is clearly connected with employee engagement, creating an environment that encourages employee engagement is considered to be essential in the effective management of human capital.

Employee engagement will be influenced by:

- Employee perceptions of job importance. This study has found that "...an employees attitude toward the job['s importance] and the company had the greatest impact on loyalty and customer service then all other employee factors combined."
- Employee clarity of job expectations. "If expectations are not clear and basic materials and equipment not provided, negative emotions such as boredom or resentment may result, and the employee may then become focused on surviving more then thinking about how he can help the organization succeed."
- Career advancement/improvement opportunities. "Plant supervisors and managers indicated that many plant improvements were being made outside the suggestion system, where employees initiated changes in order to reap the bonuses generated by the subsequent cost savings."
- Regular feedback and dialogue with superiors. "Feedback is the key to giving employees a sense of where they're going, but many organizations are remarkably bad at giving it." (Hay Group) "'What I really wanted to hear was 'Thanks. You did a good job.' But all my boss did was hand me a check."
- Quality of working relationships with peers, superiors, and subordinates. "...if employee's relationship with their managers is fractured, then no amount of perks will persuade the employees to perform at top levels. Employee engagement is a direct reflection of how employees feel about their relationship with the boss."
- Perceptions of the ethos and values of the organization. "'Inspiration and values' is the most important of the six drivers in our Engaged Performance model. Inspirational leadership is the ultimate perk. In its absence, [it] is unlikely to engage employees."

As additional research becomes available, the significance of the various factors will become more evident.

Human Interaction Management

Human Interaction Management (HIM) is the set of principles and patterns for structuring, supporting and controlling human work practices proposed by Keith Harrison-Broninski in his 2005 book "Human Interactions".

Current mainstream techniques and tools for work support, whether categorized as Workflow or as Business Process Management (BPM), deal only with "mechanistic" business processes. In such business processes, human involvement is limited to key data entry and decision points. Workflow/BPM techniques and tools deal with only the externally-observable aspects of work - tasks, that are visible from outside.

HIM extends this to include support for "human-driven" processes focused on human creativity and collaboration. To achieve this, HIM deals not only with tasks, but also with those aspects of work visible from inside - information, interaction and innovation.

In HIM, a business process requiring human knowledge, judgement and experience is divided into Roles, which are then assigned to the appropriate members of an organization via a Human Interaction Management System (HIMS). A HIMS is also used to manage the work and integrate it with organizational strategy/tactics, via separation into "levels of control".

The main focus of HIM is currently on the integration of organizational objectives with human work practices, in order to implement strategy/tactics and fulfil requirements for compliance. However, HIM has application beyond the improvement of organizational efficiency, since it provides a rich set of patterns for structuring and managing collaborative work that are also finding application in spheres such as social/political negotiation, law enforcement and healthcare.

Accounting Management (Business) is the practical application of management techniques to control and report on the financial health of the organization. This involves the analysis, planning, implementation, and control of programmes designed to provide financial data reporting for managerial decision making. This includes the maintenance of bank accounts, developing financial statements, cash flow and financial performance analysis. Accounting management is a mandatory knowledge module of any MBA programme. Cost management is the process whereby companies use cost accounting to report or control the various costs of doing business. The term CM is widely used in business today. Unfortunately there is no uniform definition. We use CM to describe the approaches and activities of managers in short run and long run planning and control decisions that increase value for customers and lower costs of products and services. For example, managers make decisions regarding the amount and kind of material being used, changes of plant processes, and changes in product designs. Information from accounting systems helps managers make such decisions, but the information and the accounting systems themselves are not cost management. Cost management has a broad focus. It includes – but is not confined to – the continuous reduction of costs. The planning and control of costs is usually inextricably linked with revenue and profit planning. For instance, to enhance revenues and profits, managers often deliberately incur additional costs for advertising and product modifications. Cost management is not practiced in isolation. It's an integral part of general management strategies and their implementation. Examples include programme that enhance customer satisfaction and quality as well as programmes that promote blockbuster new product development.

Customer Relationship

Customer relationship management (CRM) covers methods and technologies used by companies to manage their relationships with clients. Information stored on existing customers (and potential customers) is analyzed and used to this end. Automated CRM processes are often used to generate automatic personalized marketing based on the customer information stored in the system. Customer relationship management is a corporate level strategy, focusing on creating and maintaining relationships with customers. Several commercial CRM software packages are available which vary in their approach to CRM. However, CRM is not a technology itself, but rather a holistic approach to an organisation's philosophy, placing the emphasis firmly on the customer.

CRM governs an organization's philosophy at all levels, including policies and processes, front-of-house customer service, employee training, marketing, systems and information management. CRM systems are integrated end-to-end across marketing, sales, and customer service.

A CRM system should:

- Identify factors important to clients.
- Promote a customer-oriented philosophy
- Adopt customer-based measures
- Develop end-to-end processes to serve customers
- Provide successful customer support
- Handle customer complaints
- Track all aspects of sales
- Create a holistic view of customers' sales and services information

There are three fundamental components in CRM:

- Operational - automation of basic business processes (marketing, sales, service)
- Analytical - analysis of customer data and behaviour using business intelligence
- Collaborative - communicating with clients

Operational CRM provides automated support to "front office" business processes (sales, marketing and service). Each interaction with a customer is generally added to a customer's history, and staff can retrieve information on customers from the database as necessary.

Sales force automation (SFA): SFA automates some of a company's critical sales and sales force management tasks, such as forecasting, sales administration, tracking customer preferences and demographics, performance management, lead management, account management, contact management and quote management.

Customer service and support (CSS): CSS automates certain service requests, complaints, product returns and enquiries.

Enterprise marketing automation (EMA) : EMA provides information about the business environment, including information on competitors, industry trends, and macroenvironmental variables. EMA applications are used to improve marketing efficiency.

Integrated CRM software is often known as a "front office solution", as it deals directly with customers. Many call centers use CRM software to store customer information. When a call is received, the system displays the associated customer information (determined from the number of the caller). During and following the call, the call center agent dealing with the customer can add further information. Some customer services can be fully automated, such as allowing customers to access their bank account details online or via a WAP phone.

Analytical CRM

Analytical CRM analyses data (gathered as part of operational CRM, or from other sources) in an attempt to identify means to enhance a company's relationship with its clients. The results of an analysis can be used to design targeted marketing campaigns, for example:

- Acquisition: Cross-selling, up-selling
- Retention: Retaining existing customers (antonym: customer attrition)
- Information: Providing timely and regular information to customers

Other examples of the applications of analyses include:

- Contact optimization
- Evaluating and improving customer satisfaction
- Optimizing sales coverage
- Fraud detection
- Financial forecasts
- Price optimization
- Product development
- Programme evaluation
- Risk assessment and management
- Strategic Marketing
- Operational marketing

Data collection and analysis is viewed as a continuing and iterative process. Ideally, business decisions are refined over time, based on feedback from earlier analyses and decisions. Most analytical CRM projects use a data warehouse to manage data.

Collaborative CRM

Collaborative CRM focuses on the interaction with customers (personal interaction, letter, fax, phone, Internet, e-mail etc.)

Collaborative CRM includes:

- Providing efficient communication with customers across a variety of communications channels
- Providing online services to reduce customer service costs
- Providing access to customer information while interacting with customers

Driven by authors from the Harvard Business School (Kracklauer/Mills/ Seifert), Collaborative CRM also seems to be the new paradigma to succeed the leading Efficient Consumer Response and Category Management concept in the industry/ trade relationship.

In its broadest sense, CRM covers all interaction and business with customers. A good CRM programme allows a business to acquire customers, provide customer services and retain valued customers.

Customer services can be improved by:

- Providing online access to product information and technical assistance around the clock
- Identifying what customers value and devising appropriate service strategies for each customer
- Providing mechanisms for managing and scheduling follow-up sales calls
- Tracking all contacts with a customer
- Identifying potential problems before they occur
- Providing a user-friendly mechanism for registering customer complaints
- Providing a mechanism for handling problems and complaints
- Providing a mechanism for correcting service deficiencies
- Storing customer interests in order to target customers selectively
- Providing mechanisms for managing and scheduling maintenance, repair, and on-going support
- Scalability: the system should be highly scalable, as the volume of data stored in the system grows over time
- Communication channels: CRM can interface with a variety of different channels (phone, WAP, Internet etc.)
- Workflow - a company's business processes need to be represented

by the system with the ability to track the individual stages and transfer information between steps
- Assignment - the ability to assign requests, such as service requests, to a person or group.
- Database - the means of storing customer data and histories (in a data warehouse)
- Customer privacy considerations, such as data encryption and legislation.

Improving Customer Relationships

CRM applications often track customer interests and requirements, as well as their buying habits. This information can be used to target customers selectively. Furthermore, the products a customer has purchased can be tracked throughout the product's life cycle, allowing customers to receive information concerning a product or to target customers with information on alternative products once a product begins to be phased out.

Repeat purchases rely on customer satisfaction, which in turn comes from a deeper understanding of each customer and their individual needs. CRM is an alternative to the "one size fits all" approach. In industrial markets, the technology can be used to coordinate the conflicting and changing purchase criteria of the sector.

The data gathered as part of CRM raises concerns over customer privacy and enables persuasive sales techniques. However, CRM does not necessarily involve gathering new data, but also includes making better use of customer information gathered as a result of routine customer interaction.

The privacy debate generally focuses on the customer information stored in the centralized database itself, and fears over a company's handling of this information. For example, there is virtually no way a consumer can determine if the company shares private (personally identifiable) data with third parties. Furthermore, companies may not always accurately declare to the consumer the types of information collected by CRM systems and the specific purposes for which the information is used.

CRM is also important to non-profit organizations, which sometimes use the terms "constituent relationship management", "contact relationship management" or "community relationship management" to describe their information systems for managing donors, volunteers and other supporters. salesforce.com, a popular CRM service that is on demand, offers its products for free to nonprofit organizations

Financial Management

New business leaders and managers have to develop at least basic skills in financial management. Expecting others in the organization to manage finances is clearly asking for trouble. Basic skills in financial management start in the critical areas of cash management and bookkeeping, which should be done according to certain financial controls to ensure integrity in the bookkeeping process. New leaders and managers should soon go on to learn how to generate financial statements (from bookkeeping journals) and analyze those statements to really understand the financial condition of the business. Financial analysis shows the "reality" of the situation of a business — seen as such, financial management is one of the most important practices in management. This topic will help you understand basic practices in financial management, and build the basic systems and practices needed in a healthy business.

If your small business is a corporation, you would do well to find someone experienced in financial management and encourage them to be your board treasurer (your board chair has this responsibility to find someone suitable, as well). Therefore, it's important to understand the role of the board treasurer.

New, more "organic" forms or organizations (self-organizing organizations, self-managed teams, network organizations, etc.) allow organizations to be more responsive and adaptable in today's rapidly changing world. These forms also cultivate empowerment among employees, much more than the hierarchical, rigidly structured organizations of the past.

Many people assert that as the nature of organizations has changed, so must the nature of management control. Some people go so far as to claim that management shouldn't exercise any form of control whatsoever. They claim that management should exist to support employee's efforts to be fully productive members of organizations and communities — therefore, any form of control is completely counterproductive to management and employees.

Some people even react strongly against the phrase "management control". The word itself can have a negative connotation, e.g., it can sound dominating, coercive and heavy-handed. It seems that writers of management literature now prefer use of the term "coordinating" rather than "controlling".

Regardless of the negative connotation of the word "control", it must exist or there is no organization at all. In its most basic form, an organization is two or more people working together to reach a goal. Whether an organization is highly bureaucratic or changing and self-organizing, the organization must exist for some reason, some purpose, some mission (implicit or explicit) — or it isn't an organization at all. The organization must have some goal. Identifying this goal requires some form of planning, informal or formal. Reaching the goal means identifying some strategies, formal or informal. These strategies are agreed upon by members of the organization through some form of communication, formal or informal. Then members set about to act in accordance with what they agreed to do. They may change their minds, fine. But they need to recognize and acknowledge that they're changing their minds.

This form of ongoing communication to reach a goal, tracking activities toward the goal and then subsequent decisions about what to do is the essence of management coordination. It needs to exist in some manner — formal or informal. The following are rather typical methods of coordination in organizations. They are used as means to communicate direction and guide behaviours in that direction. The function of the following methods is not to "control", but rather to guide. If, from ongoing communications among management and employees, the direction changes, then fine. The following methods are changed accordingly.

Note that many of the following methods are so common that we often don't think of them as having anything to do with coordination at all. No matter what one calls the following methods — coordination or control — they're important to the success of any organization.

Administrative Controls

Organizations often use standardized documents to ensure complete and consistent information is gathered. Documents include titles and dates to detect different versions of the document. Computers have revolutionized administrative controls through use of integrated management information systems, project management software, human resource information systems, office automation software, etc. Organizations typically require a wide range of reports, e.g., financial reports, status reports, project reports, etc. to monitor what's being done, by when and how. Delegation is an approach to get things done, in conjunction with other employees. Delegation is often viewed as a major means of influence and therefore is categorized as an activity in leading (rather than controlling/coordinating). Delegation generally includes assigning responsibility to an employee to complete a task, granting the employee sufficient authority to gain the resources to do the task and letting the employee decide how that task will be carried out. Typically, the person assigning the task shares accountability with the employee for ensuring the task is completed. Evaluation is carefully collecting and analyzing information in order to make decisions. There are many types of evaluations in organizations, for example, evaluation of marketing efforts, evaluation of employee performance, programme evaluations, etc. Evaluations can focus on many aspects of an organization and its processes, for example, its goals and processes, outcomes.

Financial Statements

Once the organization has establish goals and associated strategies (or ways to reach the goals), funds are set aside for the resources and labour to the accomplish goals and tasks. As the money is spent, statements are changed to reflect what was spent, how it was spent and what it obtained. Review of financial statements is one of the more common methods to monitor the progress of programmes and plans. The most common financial statements include the balance sheet, income statement and cash flow statement. Financial audits are regularly conducted to ensure that financial management practices follow generally accepted standards, as well.

Performance management focuses on the performance of the total organization, including its processes, critical subsystems (departments, programmes, projects, etc.) and employees. Most of us have some basic impression of employee performance management, including the role of performance reviews. Performance reviews provide an opportunity for supervisors and their employees to regularly communicate about goals, how well those goals should be met, how well the goals are being met and what must be done to continue to meet (or change) those goals. The employee is rewarded in some form for meeting performance standards, or embarks on a development plan with the supervisor in order to improve performance.

Policies help ensure that behaviours in the workplace conform to federal and state laws, and also to expectations of the organization. Often, policies are applied to specified situations in the form of procedures. Personnel policies and procedures help ensure that employee laws are followed (e.g., laws such as the Americans with Disabilities Act, Occupational Health and Safety Act, etc.) and minimize the likelihood of costly litigation. A procedure is a step-by-step list of activities required to conduct a certain task. Procedures ensure that routine tasks are carried out in an effective and efficient fashion.

Quality Control and Operations Management

The concept of quality control has received a great deal of attention over the past twenty years. Many people recognize phrases such as "do it right the first time, "zero defects", "Total Quality Management", etc. Very broadly, quality includes specifying a performance standard (often by benchmarking, or comparing to a well-accepted standard), monitoring and measuring results, comparing the results to the standard and then making adjusts as necessary. Recently, the concept of quality management has expanded to include organization-wide programmes, such as Total Quality Management, ISO9000, Balanced Scorecard, etc. Operations management includes the overall activities involved in developing, producing and distributing products and services.

Risk, Safety and Liabilities

For a variety of reasons (including the increasing number of lawsuits), organizations are focusing a great deal of attention to activities that minimize risk, avoid liabilities and ensure safety of employees. Several decades ago, it was rare to hear of an organization undertaking contingency planning, disaster recovery planning or critical incident analysis. Now those activities are becoming commonplace.

Evaluation Activities

Evaluation, in the context of management activities, is carefully collecting information about something in order to make necessary decisions about it. There are a large number and wide variety of evaluations that can occur in businesses, whether for-profit or nonprofit. Evaluation is closely related to performance management (whether about organizations, groups, processes or individuals), which includes identifying measures to indicate results. Evaluation often includes collecting information around these measures to conclude the extent of performance.

Advertising and Promotions

Before you learn more about advertising, you should get a basic impression of what advertising is. Advertising is a major "phase" of overall product or service development and management. Advertising is specifically part of the "outbound" marketing activities, or activities geared to communicate to the market, eg, advertising, promotions, public relations, etc. Inbound" marketing activities are geared to communicate from the market, and include, eg, market research about the market. Although your use of the latest hot marketing and sales strategies may improve the bottom line of your business, you may get into hot "legal waters" if you do not exercise the proper restraints. This article discusses the boundaries beyond which you do not want to stray lest you run afoul of the laws governing false advertising.

Two conflicting principles are involved in advertising law. On the one hand, the First Amendment, which is part of the U.S. Constitution and grants us the right of free speech, protects all forms of communication, including advertising (referred to by lawyers as "commercial speech"). On the other hand, the U.S. Constitution gives the federal government the power to regulate interstate commerce. Most state constitutions similarly give state governments the power to regulate commerce conducted solely within that state.

In exercising its power over interstate commerce, the Congress has enacted two statutes that have the greatest effect on advertising. These are the Federal Trade Commission (FTC) Act and the Lanham Act.

Employees

Your employees of usually the people who interact the most with your customers. Ask them about products and services that customers are asking for. Ask employees about what the customers complain about.

Comment Cards

Provide brief, half-page comment cards on which they can answer basic questions such as: Were you satisfied with our services? How could we provide the perfect services? Are there any services you'd like to see that don't exist yet?

Competition

What is your competition selling? Ask people who shop there. Many people don't notice sales or major items in stores. Start coaching those around you to notice what's going on with your competition.

Customers

One of the best ways to find out what customers want is to ask them. Talk to them when they visit your facility or you visit theirs.

Documentation and Records

Notice what customers are buying and not buying from you. If you already know what customers are buying, etc., then is this written down somewhere? It should be so that you don't forget, particularly during times of stress or when trying to train personnel to help you out.

Focus Groups

Focus groups are usually 8-10 people that you gather to get their impressions of a product or service or an idea.

Surveys by Mail

You might hate answering these things, but plenty of people don't — and will fill our surveys especially if they get something in return. Promise them a discount if they return the completed form to your facility.

Competitive Analysis

Marketing should include competitor analysis. Who are your competitors? What customer needs and preferences are you competing to meet? What are the similarities and differences between their products/services and yours? What are the strengths and weaknesses of each of their products and services? How do their prices compare to yours? How are they doing overall? How do you plan to compete? Offer better quality services? Lower prices? More support? Easier access to services? How are you uniquely suited to compete with them?

Competitive Intelligence for Business Success

Some businesses think it is best to get on with their own plans and ignore the competition. Others become obsessed with tracking the actions of competitors (often using underhand or illegal methods). Many businesses are happy simply to track the competition, copying their moves and reacting to changes.

Competitor analysis has several important roles in strategic planning:

- To help management understand their competitive advantages/ disadvantages relative to competitors

- To generate understanding of competitors' past, present (and most importantly) future strategies
- To provide an informed basis to develop strategies to achieve competitive advantage in the future
- To help forecast the returns that may be made from future investments (e.g. how will competitors respond to a new product or pricing strategy?

Questions to Ask

What questions should be asked when undertaking competitor analysis? The following is a useful list to bear in mind:

- Who are our competitors?
- What threats do they pose?
- What is the profile of our competitors?
- What are the objectives of our competitors?
- What strategies are our competitors pursuing and how successful are these strategies?
- What are the strengths and weaknesses of our competitors?
- How are our competitors likely to respond to any changes to the way we do business?

Sources of Information for Competitor Analysis

Davidson describes how the sources of competitor information can be neatly grouped into three categories:

- Recorded data: this is easily available in published form either internally or externally. Good examples include competitor annual reports and product brochures;
- Observable data: this has to be actively sought and often assembled from several sources. A good example is competitor pricing;
- Opportunistic data: to get hold of this kind of data requires a lot of planning and organisation. Much of it is "anecdotal", coming from discussions with suppliers, customers and, perhaps, previous management of competitors.

The table below lists possible sources of competitor data using Davidson's categorisation:

Recorded Data	Observable Data	Opportunistic Data
Annual report and accounts	Pricing/ price lists	Meetings with suppliers
Press releases	Advertising campaigns	Trade shows
Newspaper articles	Promotions	Sales force meetings
Analysts reports	Tenders	Seminars/ conferences
Regulatory reports	Patent applications	Recruiting ex-employees
Government reports		Discussion with shared distributors
Presentations/ speeches		Social contacts with competitors

In his excellent book Even More Offensive Marketing, Davidson likens the process of gathering competitive data to a jigsaw puzzle. Each individual piece of data does not have much value. The important skill is to collect as many of the pieces as possible and to assemble them into an overall picture of the competitor. This enables you to identify any missing pieces and to take the necessary steps to collect them.

What Businesses Need to Know about their Competitors

The tables below lists the kinds of competitor information that would help businesses complete some good quality competitor analysis.

You can probably think of many more pieces of information about a competitor that would be useful. However, an important challenge in competitor analysis is working out how to obtain competitor information that is reliable, up-to-date and available legally.

What businesses probably already know their competitors
Overall sales and profits
Sales and profits by market
Sales by main brand
Cost structure
Market shares (revenues and volumes)
Organisation structure
Distribution system
Identity/ profile of senior management
Advertising strategy and spending
Customer/ consumer profile and attitudes
Customer retention levels
What businesses would really like to know about competitors
Sales and profits by product
Relative costs
Customer satisfaction and service levels
Customer retention levels
Distribution costs
New product strategies
Size and quality of customer databases
Advertising effectiveness
Future investment strategy
Contractual terms with key suppliers
Terms of strategic partnerships
Competitor array

One common and useful technique is constructing a competitor array. The steps include:

- Define your industry - scope and nature of the industry
- Determine who your competitors are
- Determine who your customers are and what benefits they expect
- Determine what the key success factors are in your industry

- Rank the key success factors by giving each one a weighting - The sum of all the weightings must add up to one.
- Rate each competitor on each of the key success factors - this can best be displayed on a two dimensional matrix - competitors along the top and key success factors down the side.
- Multiply each cell in the matrix by the factor weighting.
- Sum columns for a weighted assessment of the overall strength of each competitor relative to each other.

Based on material presented in "Beat the Competition: How to Use Competitive Intelligence to Develop Winning Business Strategies", Ian Gordon, Basil Blackwell Publishers, Oxford, UK, 1989.

Competitor Profiling

Another common technique is to create detailed profiles on each of your major competitors. These profiles give an in-depth description of the competitor's background, finances, products, markets, facilities, personnel, and strategies. This involves:

- Background
  - Location of offices, plants, and online presences
  - History - key personalities, dates, events, and trends
  - Ownership, corporate governance, and organizational structure
- Financials
  - P-E ratios, dividend policy, and profitability** various financial ratios, liquidity, and cash flow
  - Profit growth profile; method of growth (organic or acquisitive)
- Products
  - Products offered, depth and breadth of product line, and product portfolio balance
  - New products developed, new product success rate, and R&D strengths
  - Brands, strength of brand portfolio, brand loyalty and brand awareness
  - Patents and licenses
  - Quality control conformance
  - Reverse engineering
- Marketing
  - Segments served, market shares, customer base, growth rate, and customer loyalty
  - Promotional mix, promotional budgets, advertising themes, ad agency used, sales force success rate, online promotional strategy
  - Distribution channels used (direct and indirect), exclusivity agreements, alliances, and geographical coverage
  - Pricing, discounts,and allowances

- Facilities
  - Plant capacity, capacity utilization rate, age of plant, plant efficiency, capital investment
  - Location, shipping logistics, and product mix by plant
- Personnel
  - Number of employees, key employees, and skill sets
  - Strength of management, and management style
  - Compensation, benefits, and employee morale and retention rates
- Corporate and marketing strategies
  - Objectives, mission statement, growth plans, acquisitions, and divestitures
  - Marketing strategies

Media Scanning

We can learn a lot about the competitive environment by scanning our competitors' ads. Changes in a competitor's advertising message can reveal new product offerings, new production processes, a new branding strategy, a new positioning strategy, a new segmentation strategy, line extensions and contractions, problems with previous positions, insights from recent marketing or product research, a new strategic direction, a new source of sustainable competitive advantage, or value migrations within the industry. It might also indicate a new pricing strategy such as penetration, price discrimination, price skimming, product bundling, joint product pricing, discounts, or loss leaders. It may also indicate a new promotion strategy such as push, pull, balanced, short term sales generation, long term image creation, informational, comparative, affective, reminder, new creative objectives, new unique selling proposition, new creative concepts, appeals, tone, and themes, or a new advertising agency. It might also indicate a new distribution strategy, new distribution partners, more extensive distribution, more intensive distribution, a change in geographical focus, or exclusive distribution. Little of this intelligence is definitive : additional information is needed before conclusions should be drawn.

A competitor's media strategy reveals budget allocation, segmentation and targeting strategy, and selectivity and focus. From a tactical perspective, it can also be used to help a manager implement his/her own media plan. By knowing the competitor's media buy, media selection, frequency, reach, continuity, schedules, and flights, the manager can arrange his/her own media plan so that they do not coincide.

Other sources of corporate intelligence include trade shows, patent filings, mutual customers, annual reports, and trade associations.

Some firms hire competitor intelligence professionals to obtain this information.

New Competitors

In addition to analysing current competitors, it is necessary to estimate future competitive threats. The most common sources of new competitors are:

- Companies competing in a related product/market
- Companies using related technologies
- Companies already targeting your prime market segment but with unrelated products
- Companies from other geographical areas and with similar products
- New start-up companies organised by former employees and/or managers of existing companies

The entrance of new competitors is likely when:

- There are high profit margins in the industry
- There is unmet demand (insufficient supply) in the industry
- There are no major barriers to entry
- There is future growth potential
- Competitive rivalry is not intense
- Gaining a competitive advantage over existing firms is feasible

Marketing through advertising

Marketing is a social and managerial function that attempts to create, expand and maintain a collection of customers. It attempts to deliver demand satisfying output through profitable exchanges.

- Marketing, as suggested by the American Marketing Association, is "an organizational function and a set of processes for creating, communicating and delivering value to customers and for managing customer relationships in ways that benefit the organization and its stakeholders".
- Philip Kotler, in his earlier books, defines marketing as: "human activity directed at satisfying needs and wants through exchange processes". Still another marketing definition, coined by Brian Norris: "The process of repeatedly moving people closer to making a decision to purchase, use, follow, refer, upload, download, obey, reject, conform, become complacent to another person's, society's or organization's value. Simply, if it doesn't facilitate a "sale" then it's not marketing."
- Identifying needs/wants and finding and implimenting solutions that satisfy those needs and wants.
- Add to Kotler's and Norris' definitions, a response from the Chartered Institute of Marketing (CIM). The association's definition claims marketing to be the "management process of anticipating, identifying and satisfying customer requirements profitably". Thus, operative marketing involves the processes of market research, market segmentation, new product development, product life cycle management, pricing, channel management as well as promotion.

- Marketing-"taking actions to define, create, grow, develop, maintain, defend and own markets".
- An approach to business that seeks to identify, anticipate and satisfy customers needs.
- Al Ries and Jack Trout defined marketing as simply "war" between competitors.
- Any activity that connects producers with consumers.
- At a macro level, marketing is the process of raising the standards of living, by identifying the existing problems and unsatisfied needs of people and then satisfying that need with a product/service that delivers value to the customer.

The practice of marketing is almost as old as humanity itself. Whenever a person has an item or is capable of performing a service, and he or she seeks another person who might want that item or service, that person is involved in marketing. A Market was originally simply a gathering place where people with a supply of items or capacity to perform a service could meet with those who might desire the items or services, perhaps at a pre-arranged time.

Such meetings embodied all the aspects of today's marketing methods, although in an informal way. Sellers and buyers sought to understand each other's needs, capacities, and psychology, all with the goal of getting the exchange of items or services to take place. Open air markets throughout the world, with buyers and sellers freely mingling, are today's example of this basic activity. Today's New York Stock Exchange had its humble beginnings as an open air market located at Wall Street in New York City.

The rise of Agriculture undoubtedly influenced markets as the earliest means of 'mass production' of an item, namely foodstuffs. As agriculture allowed one to grow more food than could be eaten by the grower alone, and most food is perishable, there was likely motivation to seek out others who could use the excess food, before it spoiled, in exchange for other items.

Prior to the advent of market research, most companies were product-focused, employing teams of salespeople to push their products into or onto the market, regardless of market desire. A market-focused, or customer-focused, organization instead first determines what its potential customers desire, and then builds the product or service. Marketing theory and practice is justified on the belief that customers use a product/service because they have a need, or because a product/service has a perceived benefit. Two major factors of marketing are the recruitment of new customers (acquisition) and the retention and expansion of relationships with existing customers (base management).

Once a marketer has converted the prospective buyer, base management marketing takes over. The process for base management shifts the marketer to building a relationship, nurturing the links, enhancing the benefits that sold the buyer in the first place, and improving the product/service continuously to protect her business from competitive encroachments. Marketing methods are informed by many of the social sciences, particularly psychology, sociology, and economics. Anthropology is also a small, but growing, influence. Market research underpins these activities. Through advertising, it is also related to many of the creative arts.

For a marketing plan to be successful, the mix of the four "Ps" must reflect the wants and desires of the consumers in the target market. Trying to convince a market segment to buy something they don't want is extremely expensive and seldom successful. Marketers depend on marketing research, both formal and informal, to determine what consumers want and what they are willing to pay for. Marketers hope that this process will give them a sustainable competitive advantage. Marketing management is the practical application of this process. The offer is also an important addition to the 4P's theory. Within most organizations the activities encompassed by the marketing function are led by a Chief Marketing Officer, or an equivalent executive. Most often the CMO position reports to the Chief Executive Officer.

The big debate in the marketing discipline is whether marketing is an art or a science. Marketing is a technology or set of technologies. Marketing can be neither an art nor a science because arts and sciences only seek to explain natural phenomena. The objective of marketing is to manipulate and influence natural phenomena to create practical unnatural outcomes, specifically to manufacture, grow, sustain and defend markets. Marketers use their knowledge of economics, psychology, sociology, anthropology and strategy to arrange and control the external environment to their advantage and lock in profit. To understand what marketing is one must understand that marketing operates on three different levels.

Corporate Level Marketing

Marketing at the corporate levels asks this question as 'What business should we be in and what opportunities should we pursue?' This is marketing before we even have a business, idea or product. This is what is known as entreprenuership. This level of marketing strategy is where the Ted Turners, Bill Gates' and Michael Dells of the world make market changing decisions. This level is also where corporate management of existing companies decide to branch off into new uncharted territories and opportunities.

Business Level Marketing

Marketing at the business level asks this question as 'How are we going to compete against the competition?' When Jack Trout says that marketing is 'the war between competitors' and 'the conflict between companies' what he is really doing is defining marketing at the business level. Business level marketing deals with high level strategic marketing concerns. This level deals with long term sustainable advantages and business models.

Functional Level Marketing

Marketing at the functional level (also known as the operating level) ask this question as 'How do we create and keep customers?' This level deals with marketing tactics and the '4ps' of the marketing mix. This level of marketing defines and develops products, prices them, promotes them and then distributes them in a way that helps a company create and sustain demand for their products.

In popular usage, "marketing" is the promotion of products, especially advertising and branding. However, in professional usage the term has a wider meaning which recognizes that marketing is customer centered. Products are often developed to meet the desires of groups of customers or even, in some cases, for specific customers. E. Jerome McCarthy divided marketing into four general sets of activities. His typology has become so universally recognized that his four activity sets, the Four Ps, have passed into the language.

The four Ps are:

- Product: The Product management and Product marketing aspects of marketing deal with the specifications of the actual good or service, and how it relates to the end-user's needs and wants.
- Pricing: This refers to the process of setting a price for a product, including discounts.
- Promotion: This includes advertising, sales promotion, publicity, and personal selling, and refers to the various methods of promoting the product, brand, or company.
- Placement or distribution refers to how the product gets to the customer; for example, point of sale placement or retailing. This fourth P has also sometimes been called Place, referring to the channel by which a product or service is sold (e.g. online vs. retail), which geographic region or industry, to which segment (young adults, families, business people), etc.

These four elements are often referred to as the marketing mix. A marketer can use these variables to craft a marketing plan. The four Ps model is most useful when marketing low value consumer products. Industrial products, services, high value consumer products require adjustments to this model. Services marketing must account for the unique nature of services. Industrial or B2B marketing must account for the long term contractual agreements that are typical in supply chain transactions. Relationship marketing attempts to do this by looking at marketing from a long term relationship perspective rather than individual transactions. As a counter to this, Morgan, in Riding the Waves of Change (Jossey-Bass, 1988), adds "Perhaps the most significant criticism of the 4 Ps approach, which you should be aware of, is that it unconsciously emphasizes the inside–out view (looking from the company outwards), whereas the essence of marketing should be the outside–in approach". Even so, having made this important caveat, the 4 Ps offer a memorable and quite workable guide to the major categories of marketing activity, as well as a framework within which these can be used.

As well as the standard four Ps (Product, Pricing, Promotion and Place), services marketing calls upon an extra three, totalling seven and known together as the extended marketing mix. These are:

- People: Any person coming into contact with customers can have an impact on overall satisfaction. Whether as part of a supporting service to a product or involved in a total service, people are particularly important because, in the customer's eyes, they are generally inseparable from the total service. As a result of this, they must be appropriately trained, well motivated and the right type of person. Fellow customers are also sometimes referred to under 'people', as they too can affect the customer's service experience, (e.g., at a sporting event).
- Process: This is the process(es) involved in providing a service and the behaviour of people, which can be crucial to customer satisfaction.
- Physical evidence: Unlike a product, a service cannot be experienced before it is delivered, which makes it intangible. This, therefore, means that potential customers could perceive greater risk when deciding whether or not to use a service. To reduce the feeling of risk, thus improving the chance for success, it is often vital to offer potential customers the chance to see what a service would be like. This is done by providing physical evidence, such as case studies, or testimonials.

As well as the other 7 Packaging has been added to this list by some people. The rationale is that it is very important how the product is presented to the customer, and the packaging is often the first contact that a customer has with a product. Although some disagree because packaging is seen as a subfield of promotion. "Philosophy" is the potential 8th P of marketing. Products (or services) should reflect the underlying philosophy or ethos of the organization. It should also be clear what the philosophy behind the introduction of the particular product is, as well. In his book, "Meeting Need", Ian Bruce explains this concept as it relates to marketing for charities. It also applies to other products and services

Business Models

Marketing in the past focused mainly on basic concepts like the 4 Ps, and primarily on the psychological and sociological aspects of marketing.

Competitive advantage was created by directly appealing to the needs, wants and behaviours of customers, better than the competition. Successful marketing was based on who could create the better brand or the lowest price or the most hype. Marketing in the future will be based on a more strategic approach to competitive marketing success. Marketers will consciously build and allocate resources, relationships, offerings and business models that other companies find hard to match.

Companies with a greater amount of resources than their competitors will have an easier time competing in the marketplace. Resources include: financial (cash and cash reserves), physical (plant and equipment), human (knowledge and skill), legal (trademarks and patents), organizational (structure, competencies, policies), and informational (knowledge of consumers and competitors). Small companies usually have a harder time competing with larger corporations because of their disadvantage in resource allocation.

Success in business, as in life, is based on the relationships you have with people. Marketers must aggressively build relationships with consumers, customers, distributors, partners and even competitors if they want to have success in today's competitive marketplace.

Most companies sell a mix of products and/or services. Today's marketplace is often too competitive for "one-trick ponies". Companies that sell the right mix products and services can have a competitive advantage over companies that sell just one product or service.

The concept of product vs. product in competitive marketing is dying. It's slowly becoming business model vs. business model. Business model innovation can make the competition's product superiority irrelevant. Business model innovation allows a marketer to change the game instead of competing on a level playing field.

Customer Focus

Most companies today have a customer orientation (also called customer focus). This implies that the company focuses its activities and products on ever changing consumer demands. Generally there are tthree ways of doing this: the customer-driven approach, the sense of identifying market changes and the product innovation approach.

In the consumer-driven approach, consumer wants are the drivers of all strategic marketing decisions. No strategy is pursued until it passes the test of consumer research. Every aspect of a market offering, including the nature of the product itself, is driven by the needs of potential consumers. The starting point is always the consumer. The rationale for this approach is that there is no point spending R&D funds developing products that people will not buy. History attests to many products that were commercial failures in spite of being technological breakthroughs.

The next big thing is a concept in marketing that refers to a product or idea that will allow for a high amount of sales for that product and related products. Marketers believe that by finding or creating the next big thing they will spark a cultural revolution that results in this sales increase.

Product Focus

In a product innovation approach, the company pursues product innovation, then tries to develop a market for the product. Product innovation drives the process and marketing research is conducted primarily to ensure that a profitable market segment(s) exists for the innovation. The rationale is that customers may not know what options will be available to them in the future so we should not expect them to tell us what they will buy in the future. However, marketers can aggressively over pursue product innovation and try to overcapitalize on a niche. When pursuing a product innovation approach, marketers must ensure that they have a varied and multi-tiered approach to product innovation. It is claimed that if Thomas Edison depended on marketing research he would have produced larger candles rather than inventing light bulbs. Many firms, such as research and development focused companies, successfully focus on product innovation. Many purists doubt whether this is really a form of marketing orientation at all, because of the ex post status of consumer research. Some even question whether it is marketing.

Other Aspects

- An emerging area of study and practice concerns internal marketing, or how employees are trained and managed to deliver the brand in a way that positively impacts the acquisition and retention of customers (employer branding).
- Diffusion of innovations research explores how and why people adopt new products, services and ideas.
- A relatively new form of marketing uses the Internet and is called internet marketing or more generally e-marketing, affiliate marketing or online marketing. It typically tries to perfect the segmentation strategy used in traditional marketing. It targets its audience more precisely, and is sometimes called personalized marketing or one-to-one marketing.
- With consumers' eroding attention span and willingness to give time to advertising messages, marketers are turning to forms of Permission marketing such as Branded content and Reality marketing.
- The use of herd behaviour in marketing.

Some aspects of marketing, especially promotion, are treated as the subject of criticism. It is especially problematic in classical economic theory, which is based on the assumption that supply and demand are independent. However, product promotion is an attempt coming from the supply side to influence demand. In this way producer market power is attained as measured by profits that would not be realized under a free market. Then the argument follows that non-free markets are imperfect and lead to production and consumption of suboptimal amounts of the product.

Critics acknowledge that marketing has legitimate uses in connecting goods and services to the consumers who want them. Critics also point out that marketing techniques have been used to achieve morally dubious ends by businesses, governments and criminals. Critics see a systemic social evil inherent in marketing. Marketing is accused of creating ruthless exploitation of both consumers and workers by treating people as commodities whose purpose is to consume.

Most marketers believe that marketing, like any other technology, is amoral. It can be used for good or evil purposes, but the technique itself is ethically neutral.

The Observer's survey among 1'206 UK adult consumers in 2001 highlighted some of the stark changes our society has gone through in the last two decades. This raises a question on the effectiveness of the CIM's definition of marketing (anticipating, identifying and satisfying customer needs profitably), mainly in consumer marketing. There are similar concerns in industrial markets, also known as business-to-business or B2B.

Core marketing elements such as segmentation, targeting and positioning are still relevant in the modern (or post-modern) world. However, they are complex topics that need a high level of effort, intelligent thinking as well as resources to be implemented successfully. A definitive statement cannot be made whether the conventional marketing concept is applicable in today's environment. Its relevance is very much situational and depends on many factors such as the product, the segment, time, location, political and economic conditions and the inner workings of a company.

However, some scholars such as Stephen Brown challenge the marketing concept in an extreme language. Their statements, though self-contradicting and sometimes unfair, are relevant, which is why Post Modern Marketing 2 was chosen as a key reference point for this chapter.

On the one hand Brown makes positive statements about marketing, e.g. marketing is endowed with considerable personal charm and has enjoyed more than its fair share of conquests; and indeed, the increasing academic attention that is being devoted to marketing and consumption-related phenomena by non-business disciplines such as sociology, anthropology and history; far from being the second-hand rose of the scholarship, marketing is now something of a fashion leader.

On the other hand, he condemns marketing by saying "marketing has to decide whether to expose its intellectual nakedness or press itself against the searing heat of postmodernism"; and using quotes such as "mid-life crisis"; "in decline; failing; anachronistic; being abandoned; no longer appropriate; in an unprecedented state of crisis; delivered nothing of value; failure; confusion; misunderstanding; occasional inexplicable hitting of the jackpot".

This apparent love-hate relationship is proof in itself that even a sceptic Mr. Brown cannot deny the contribution that marketing has made and can make to customer satisfaction and economic value. It has contributed to both customers' and suppliers' quality of life by selecting profitable customer satisfaction as its sole objective. The marketing concept, together with other business disciplines, helped the UK to make the transition from a 19th-century manufacturing economy to a modern model of success in the service industry, creating an economic growth period never seen in UK history before.

It is marketing that has helped create value through customised products, no-questions-asked refund policies, comfortable cars, environmental attention, shopkeepers' smile, and guaranteed delivery dates. Even some government departments address the public not as 'the Queen's subjects' or 'the applicants' any more but as 'customers'. Of course all of the above is done for economic or political gain, for better or worse. Despite all this achievement, to dismiss marketing as a failure is unfair.

Marketing also helps companies avoid unnecessary R&D, operational and sales costs by helping to develop products because customers want them, not for the sake of innovation. Another success is the now commonly implemented value-pricing principle, whereby a product or service is sold for the price the customer is willing to pay, not on a cost-plus basis. This way, both suppliers and customers get a fair deal.

In the context of segmentation, Brown suggests that "the traditional, linear, step-by-step marketing model of analysis, planning, implementation and control no longer seems applicable, appropriate or even pertinent to what is actually happening on the ground". If Mr. Brown had studied "the ground" before making his statement, he would have realised that companies are successful the world over precisely because they implement this model.

They segment their markets, relate their products and services to them, define their value proposition and serve their customers accordingly. Examples are GE, HSBC, PriceWaterhouseCoopers, Smiths Aerospace, BAE Systems, BOC Edwards, Weir Group and BT to name but a few. A brief visit to their websites can make this point clear.

Brown also has a constructive suggestion: "I reckon we need more passion in marketing, not less; it is time we banished banishing passion from works of marketing scholarship" (p. 256). This refers mainly to promotion, which is only one element within the marketing concept. The truth is that marketing today leads the way in segmentation, innovation, pricing, product management, distribution, and last but not least, promotion. After all the contribution as well as further potential, to deny its successes and try to reduce it to only promotion is a great injustice to the marketing profession as well as to academic insight. Contrary to Brown's suggestion in his final paragraph, we need objectivity, rigour, quantification, models, relationships, paradigm shifts and (some application of) science.

Marketing is not full of holes, but a management process that has helped generate wealth and satisfied millions of customers for the most part of the 20th century. It can do even better in the 21st provided practitioners and scholars do not loose faith and focus. Kotler is not dead, but very much alive, and still kicking.

expanding business through Advertising

The need for advertising of the several prospect of the hotel is utmost important for the development of the business in long term. It will create awareness of the people. Advertising is typically paid communication through a non-personal medium in which the sponsor is identified and the message is controlled. However, it can also include variations, such as publicity, public relations, personal selling, product placement, sponsorship, underwriting, and sales promotion. Major advertisers are typically corporations, but may also include schools, the military, political candidates, advocacy groups, churches, and other organizations that pay to have their message delivered to an audience. The media through which the message is delivered are varied: they include network and cable TV, radio, magazines, newspapers, the internet, billboards, handmade signs, sky writing, and bumper stickers; the list is almost endless.

Strictly speaking, word-of-mouth is not advertising because it is not paid, the message is not controlled, and it is delivered by a personal rather than non-personal medium. Ironically, word-of-mouth communications are often far more effective than advertising campaigns that may have cost many millions of dollars. "Buzz advertising" is a recent term used to describe an attempt by advertisers to simulate word-of-mouth communications.

In ancient times, commercial messages and political campaign displays have been found in the ruins of Pompeii. Egyptians used papyrus to create sales messages and wall posters, while lost-and-found advertising on papyrus was common in Greece and Rome. Wall or rock painting for commercial advertising is another manifestation of an ancient media advertising form, which is present to this day in many parts of Asia, Africa, and South America. For instance, the tradition of wall painting can be traced back to Indian rock-art paintings that goes back to 4000 BC. As printing developed in the 15th and 16th century, advertising expanded to include handbills. In the 17th century advertisements started to appear in weekly newspapers in England.

These early print ads were used mainly to promote books,and newspapers which became increasingly affordable thanks to the printing press, and medicines, which were increasingly sought after as disease ravaged Europe.

However, false advertising and so-called "quack" ads became a problem, which ushered in regulation of advertising content.

As the economy was expanding during the 19th century, the need for advertising grew at the same pace. In the United States, classified ads became popular, filling pages of newspapers with small print messages promoting all kinds of goods. The success of this advertising format led to the growth of mail-order advertising such as the Sears Catalog, at one time referred to as the "Farmer's Bible". In 1843 the first advertising agency was established by Volney Palmer in Philadelphia. At first the agencies were just brokers for ad space in newspapers, but it wasn't until N.W. Ayer & Son came along, advertising agencies started to take over responsibility for the content as well. N.W. Ayer and Son was the first full service Ad Agency. They were also the first agency to start to charge commission on ads.

When commercial radio stations began broadcasting in the early 1920's, the programmes were aired without advertising. Many radio stations were established by radio equipment manufacturers and retailers. Programming was provided to sell radio transmitters and receivers. The radio station owners soon realized they could earn more money by selling sponsorship rights to other businesses. In those days, each show was usually sponsored by a single business, in exchange for a brief mention of the sponsor at the beginning and end of the show. This practice was carried over to televsion in the late 1940's and early 1950's.

In the early 1950's, the Dumont television network began the modern trend of selling advertisement time to multiple sponsors. Dumont had trouble finding sponsors for many of their programmes and compensated by selling smaller blocks of advertising time to several businesses. This eventually became the norm for the commercial television industry in the United States. The 1960s saw advertising transform into a modern, more scientific approach in which creativity was allowed to shine, producing unexpected messages that made advertisements more tempting to consumers' eyes. The Volkswagen ad campaign featuring such headlines as "Think Small" and "Lemon" ushered in the era of modern advertising by promoting a "position" or "unique selling proposition" designed to associate each brand with a specific idea in the reader or viewer's mind.

The late 1980s and early 1990s saw the introduction of cable television and particularly MTV. Pioneering the concept of the music video, MTV ushered in a new type of advertising: the consumer tunes in for the advertisement, rather than it being a byproduct or afterthought. As cable (and later satellite) television became increasingly prevalent, "specialty" channels began to emerge, and eventually entire channels, such as QVC and Home Shopping Network and ShopTV, devoted to advertising merchandise, where again the consumer tuned in for the ads.

Marketing through the Internet opened new frontiers for advertisers and led to the "dot-com" boom of the 1990s. Entire corporations operated solely on advertising revenue, offering everything from coupons to free Internet access. At the turn of the 21st century, the search engine Google revolutionized online advertising by emphasizing contextually relevant, unobtrusive ads intended to help, rather than inundate, users. This has led to a plethora of similar efforts and an increasing trend of interactive advertising.

The share of advertising spending relative to total economic output (GDP) has changed little across large changes in media. For example, in the U.S. in 1925, the main advertising media were newspapers, magazines, signs on streetcars, and outdoor posters. Advertising spending as a share of U.S. GDP was about 2.6% in 1925. By 1998, television and radio had become major advertising media. Nonetheless, advertising spending as a share of GDP was slightly lower — about 2.4%.

A recent advertising innovation is "guerrilla promotions", which involve unusual approaches such as staged encounters in public places, giveaways of products such as cars that are covered with brand messages, and interactive advertising where the viewer can respond to become part of the advertising message. This reflects an increasing trend of interactive and "embedded" ads, such as via product placement, having consumers vote through text messages, and various innovations utilizing social networking sites (e.g. Myspace).

Product Advertising

Certain products use a specific form of advertising known as "Custom publishing". This form of advertising is usually targeted at a specific segment of society, but may also "draw" the attention of others.

The same advertising techniques used to promote commercial goods and services can be used to inform, educate and motivate the public about non-commercial issues, such as AIDS, political ideology, energy conservation, religious recruitment, and deforestation.

Advertising, in its non-commercial guise, is a powerful educational tool capable of reaching and motivating large audiences. "Advertising justifies its existence when used in the public interest - it is much too powerful a tool to use solely for commercial purposes." - Attributed to Howard Gossage by David Ogilvy

Public service advertising, non-commercial advertising, public interest advertising, cause marketing, and social marketing are different terms for (or aspects of) the use of sophisticated advertising and marketing communications techniques (generally associated with commercial enterprise) on behalf of non-commercial, public interest issues and initiatives.

In the United States, the granting of television and radio licenses by the FCC is contingent upon the station broadcasting a certain amount of public service advertising. To meet these requirements, many broadcast stations in America air the bulk of their required Public Service Announcements during the late night or early morning when the smallest percentage of viewers are watching, leaving more day and prime time commercial slots available for high-paying advertisers.

Public service advertising reached its height during World Wars I and II under the direction of several governments. Commercial advertising media can include wall paintings, billboards, street furniture components, printed flyers, radio, cinema and television ads, web banners, web popups, skywriting, bus stop benches, magazines, newspapers, town criers, sides of buses, taxicab doors and roof mounts, musical stage shows, subway platforms and trains, elastic bands on disposable diapers, stickers on apples in supermarkets, the opening section of streaming audio and video, posters, chicken niblets, and the backs of event tickets and supermarket receipts. Any place an "identified" sponsor pays to deliver their message through a medium is advertising.

Covert advertising embedded in other entertainment media is known as product placement. A more recent version of this is advertising in film, by having a main character use an item or other of a definite brand - an example is in the movie Minority Report, where Tom Cruise's character Tom Anderton owns a computer with the Nokia logo clearly written in the top corner, or his watch engraved with the Bulgari logo. Another example of advertising in film is in I, Robot, where main character played by Will Smith mentions his Converse shoes several times, calling them "classics," because the film is set far in the future. Cadillac chose to advertise in the movie The Matrix Reloaded, which as a result contained many scenes in which Cadillac cars were used. Similarly, product placement for Omega Watches, BMW and Aston-Martin cars are featured in recent James Bond films, most notably, Casino Royale.

The TV commercial is generally considered the most effective mass-market advertising format and this is reflected by the high prices TV networks charge for commercial airtime during popular TV events. The annual Super Bowl football game in the United States is known as much for its commercial advertisements as for the game itself, and the average cost of a single thirty-second TV spot during this game has reached $2.5 million (as of 2006).

Virtual advertisements may be inserted into regular television programming through computer graphics. It is typically inserted into otherwise blank backdrops or used to replace local billboards that are not relevant to the remote broadcast audience. More controversially, virtual billboards may be inserted into the background where none existing in real-life. Virtual product placement is also possible. Increasingly, other mediums such as those discussed below are overtaking television due to a shift towards consumer's usage of the Internet as well as devices such as TiVo. Advertising on the World Wide Web is a recent phenomenon. Prices of Web-based advertising space are dependent on the "relevance" of the surrounding web content and the traffic that the website receives. E-mail advertising is another recent phenomenon. Unsolicited bulk E-mail advertising is known as "spam". Some companies have proposed to place messages or corporate logos on the side of booster rockets and the International Space Station. Controversy exists on the effectiveness of subliminal advertising, and the pervasiveness of mass messages.

Unpaid advertising (also called word of mouth advertising), can provide good exposure at minimal cost. Personal recommendations ("bring a friend", "sell it"), spreading buzz, or achieving the feat of equating a brand with a common noun ("Xerox" = "photocopier", "Kleenex" = tissue, and "Vaseline" = petroleum jelly) — these are the pinnacles of any advertising campaign. However, some companies oppose the use of their brand name to label an object.

The most common method for measuring the impact of mass media advertising is the use of the rating point (rp) or the more accurate target rating point (trp). These two measures refer to the percentage of the universe of the existing base of audience members that can be reached by the use of each media outlet in a particular moment in time. The difference between the two is that the rating point refers to the percentage to the entire universe while the target rating point refers to the percentage to a particular segment or target. This becomes very useful when focusing advertising efforts on a particular group of people.

- For example, think of an advertising campaign targeting a female audience aged 25 to 45. While the overall rating of a TV show might be well over 10 rating points it might very well happen that the same show in the same moment of time is generating only 2.5 trps (being the target: women 25-45). This would mean that while the show has a large universe of viewers it is not necessarily reaching a large universe of women in the ages of 25 to 45 making it a less desirable location to place an ad for an advertiser looking for this particular demographic. Conversely, a TV show with a low overall rating point may be more successful at selling ads when its target rating points are high. In the United States, networks like the WB and FOX have had success with shows based on this premise; the shows had low overall ratings points, but delivered strong target rating points in the desired demographic.

Advertisement Impact

The impact of advertising has been a matter of considerable debate and many different claims have been made in different contexts. During debates about the banning of cigarette advertising, a common claim from cigarette manufacturers was that cigarette advertising does not encourage people to smoke who would not otherwise. The (eventually successful) opponents of advertising, on the other hand, claim that advertising does in fact increase consumption. According to many media sources, the past experience and state of mind of the person subjected to advertising may determine the impact that advertising has. Children under the age of four may be unable to distinguish advertising from other television programmes, whilst the ability to determine the truthfulness of the message may not be developed until the age of 8.

As advertising and marketing efforts become increasingly ubiquitous in modern Western societies, the industry has come under criticism of groups such as AdBusters via culture jamming which criticizes the media and consumerism using advertising's own techniques. The industry is accused of being one of the engines powering a convoluted economic mass production system which promotes consumption. Recognizing the social impact of advertising, Mediawatch-uk, a British special interest group, works to educate consumers about how they can register their concerns with advertisers and regulators. It has developed educational materials for use in schools. The award-winning book, Made You Look How Advertising Works and Why You Should Know, by former Mediawatch (a feminist organisation founded by Ann Simonton not linked to mediawatch-uk) president Shari Graydon, provides context for these issues for young readers.

Public interest groups are increasingly suggesting that access to the mental space targeted by advertisers should be taxed, in that at the present moment that space is being freely taken advantage of by advertisers with no compensation paid to the members of the public who are thus being intruded upon. This kind of tax would be a Pigovian tax in that it would act to reduce what is now increasingly seen as a public nuisance. Efforts to that end are gathering momentum, with Arkansas and Maine considering bills to implement such taxation. Florida enacted such a tax in 1987 but was forced to repeal it after six months, as a result of a concerted effort by national commercial interests, which withdrew planned conventions, causing major losses to the tourism industry, and cancelled advertising, causing a loss of 12 million dollars to the broadcast industry alone.

An extensively documented effect is the control and vetoing of free information by the advertisers. Any negative information on a company or its products or operations often results in pressures from the company to withdraw such information lines, threatening to cut their ads. This behaviour makes the editors of the media self-censor content that might upset their ad payers. The bigger both companies are, the bigger their relation gets, maximizing control over a single information. Advertisers may try to minimize information about or from consumer groups, or consumer controlled purchasing initiatives (as joint purchase systems), or consumer controlled quality information systems.

Another indirect effect of advertising is to modify the very nature of the communication media where it is shown. Media that get most of their revenues from publicity try to make their medium a good place for communicating ads before anything else. The most clear example is television, where this means trying to make the public stay for a long time and in a mental state that encourages spectators not to switch the channel through the ads. Programmes that are low in mental stimulus and require light concentration and are varied are best for long sitting times. These make for much easier emotional jumps to ads, which can become more entertaining than regular shows. A simple way to understand the objectives in television programming is to compare contents from channels paid and chosen by the viewer with channels that get their income mainly from advertisements.

There have been increasing efforts to protect the public interest by regulating the content and the reach of advertising. Some examples are the ban on television tobacco advertising imposed in many countries, and the total ban on advertising to children under twelve imposed by the Swedish government in 1991. Though that regulation continues in effect for broadcasts originating within the country, it has been weakened by the European Court of Justice, which has found that Sweden was obliged to accept whatever programming was targeted at it from neighbouring countries or via satellite.

In Europe and elsewhere there is a vigorous debate on whether and how much advertising to children should be regulated. This debate was exacerbated by a report released by the Kaiser Family Foundation in February 2004 which suggested that food advertising targeting children was an important factor in the epidemic of childhood obesity in the United States. In many countries - namely New Zealand, South Africa, Canada, and many European countries - the advertising industry operates a system of self-regulation. Advertisers, advertising agencies and the media agree on a code of advertising standards that they attempt to uphold. The general aim of such codes is to ensure that any advertising is 'legal, decent, honest and truthful'. Some self-regulatory organizations are funded by the industry, but remain independent, with the intent of upholding the standards or codes (like the Advertising Standards Authority in the UK).

Naturally, many advertisers view governmental regulation or even self-regulation as intrusion of their freedom of speech or a necessary evil. Therefore, they employ a wide-variety of linguistic devices to bypass regulatory laws (e.g. giving English words in bold and French translations in fine print to deal with the Article 12 of the 1994 Toubon Law limiting the use of English in French advertising); The advertising of controversial products such as cigarettes and condoms is subject to government regulation in many countries. For instance, the tobacco industry is required by law in India and Pakistan to display warnings cautioning consumers about the health hazards of their products. Linguistic variation is often used by advertising as a creative device to reduce the impact of such requirement.

With the dawn of the Internet have come many new advertising opportunities. Popup, Flash, banner, advergaming, and email advertisements (the last often being a form of spam) abound. Each year, greater sums are paid to obtain a commercial spot during the Super Bowl, which is by most measures considered to be the most important football game of the year. Companies attempt to make these commercials sufficiently entertaining that members of the public will actually want to watch them.

Another problem is people recording shows on DVRs (ex. TiVo). These devices allow users to record the programmes for later viewing enabling them to fast forward through commercials. Additionally, as more seasons or "Boxed Sets" come out of Television shows; fewer people are watching their shows on TV. However, the fact that these sets are sold, means that the company will additionally receive profits from the sales of these sets. To counter this effect, many advertisers have opted for product placement on TV shows like Survivor.

Particularly since the rise of "entertaining" advertising, some people may like an advert enough that they wish to watch it later or show a friend. In general, the advertising community has not yet made this easy, although some have used the Internet to widely distribute their adverts to anyone wishing to see or hear them.

Another significant trend to note for the future of advertising is the growing importance of niche or targeted ads. Also brought about by the Internet and the theory of The Long Tail, advertisers will have an increasing ability to reach narrow audiences. In the past, the most efficient way to deliver a message was to blanket the largest mass market audience possible. However, usage tracking, customer profiles and the growing popularity of niche content brought about by everything from blogs to social networking sites, provides advertisers with audiences that are smaller but much better defined, leading to ads that are more relevant to viewers and more effective for companies marketing products. Among others, Comcast Spotlight is one such advertiser employing this method in their video on demand menus. These advertisements are targeted to a specific group and can be viewed by anyone wishing to find out more about a particular business or practice at any time, right from their home. This causes the viewer to become proactive and actually choose what advertisements they want to view.

Advertising Campaign

An advertising campaign is a series of advertisement messages that share a single idea and theme which make up an integrated marketing communication (IMC). Advertising campaigns appear in different media across a specific time frame.

The critical part of making an advertising campaign is determining a campaign theme, as it sets the tone for the individual advertisements and other forms of marketing communications that will be used. The campaign theme is the central message that will be communicated in the promotional activities. The campaign themes are usually developed with the intention of being used for a substantial period but many of them are short lived due to factors such as being ineffective or market conditions and/or competition in the marketplace.

Communication Design

Communication design is a sub-discipline of design which is concerned with how media intermission such as printed, crafted, electronic media or presentations communicate with people. A communication design approach is more concerned with messages communicated than aesthetics in media. The distinction between communication design and other applied arts is in the motivation: while the communication design process does involve a certain amount of self-expression and creativity, the goals are often those of the commissioning body rather than the artist's, and the parameters set by the commissioning body are often more constraining.

The term communication design is often used interchangeably with visual communication and more specifically graphic design, but has an alternate broader meaning that includes auditory communications as well as visual. Examples of Communication Design include information architecture, editing, typography, illustration and professional writing skills applied to creative industries.

Environmental Scanning

For a company to gain or maintain a sustainable competitive advantage, it must be ever vigilant, watching for changes in the business environment. It must also be agile enough to alter its strategies and plans when the need arises.

There are three ways of scanning the business environment:

- Ad-hoc scanning - Short term, infrequent examinations usually initiated by a crisis
- Regular scanning - Studies done on a regular schedule (say, once a year)
- Continuous scanning - (also called continuous learning) - continuous structured data collection and processing on a broad range of environmental factors

Most commentators feel that in today's turbulent business environment the best scanning method available is continuous scanning. This allows the firm to act quickly, take advantage of opportunities before competitors do, and respond to environmental threats before significant damage is done. Environmental scanning usually refers just to the macroenvironment, but it can also include industry and competitor analysis, consumer analysis, product innovations, and the company's internal environment.

Macroenvironmental scanning involves analysing:

- The Economy
  - GNP or GDP per capital
  - GNP or GDP growth
  - Unemployment rate
  - Inflation rate
  - Consumer and investor confidence
  - Inventory levels
  - Currency exchange rates
  - Merchandise trade balance
  - Financial and political health of trading partners
  - Balance of payments
  - Future trends
- Government
  - Political climate - amount of government activity
  - Political stability and risk
  - Government debt
  - Budget deficit or surplus
  - Corporate and personal tax rates
  - Payroll taxes
  - Import tariffs and quotas
  - Export restrictions
  - Restrictions on international financial flows
- Legal
  - Minimum wage laws
  - Environmental protection laws
  - Worker safety laws
  - Union laws
  - Copyright and patent laws
  - Anti- monopoly laws
  - Sunday closing laws
  - Municipal licences
  - Laws that favour business investment
- Technology
  - Efficiency of infrastructure, including: roads, ports, airports, rolling stock, hospitals, education, healthcare, communication, etc.
  - Industrial productivity
  - New manufacturing processes
  - New products and services of competitors
  - New products and services of supply chain partners
  - Any new technology that could impact the company
  - Cost and accessibility of electrical power

- Ecology
  - Ecological concerns that affect the firms production processes
  - Ecological concerns that affect customers' buying habits
  - Ecological concerns that affect customers' perception of the company or product
- Socio-Cultural
  - Demographic factors such as:
    i. Population size and distribution
    ii. Age distribution
    iii. Education levels
    iv. Income levels
    v. Ethnic origins
    vi. Religious affiliations
  - Attitudes towards:
    i. Materialism, capitalism, free enterprise
    ii. Individualism, role of family, role of government, collectivism
    iii. Role of church and religion
    iv. Consumerism
    v. Environmentalism
    vi. Importance of work, pride of accomplishment
  - Cultural structures including:
    i. Diet and nutrition
    ii. Housing conditions
- Potential Suppliers
  - Labour supply
    i. Quantity of labour available
    ii. Quality of labour available
    iii. Stability of labour supply
    iv. Wage expectations
    v. Employee turn-over rate
    vi. Strikes and labour relations
    vii. Educational facilities
  - Material suppliers
    i. Quality, quantity, price, and stability of material inputs
    ii. Delivery delays
    iii. Proximity of bulky or heavy material inputs
    iv. Level of competition among suppliers
  - Service Providers
    i. Quantity, quality, price, and stability of service facilitators
    ii. Special requirements

Scanning these macroenvironmental variables for threats and opportunities requires that each issue be rated on two dimensions. It must be rated on its potential impact on the company, and rated on its likeliness of occurrence. Multiplying the potential impact parameter by the likeliness of occurrence parameter gives us a good indication of its importance to the firm.

Sustainable Competitive Advantage

Competitive advantage (CA) is a position that a firm occupies in its competitive landscape. Michael Porter posits that a competitive advantage, sustainable or not, exists when a company makes economic rents, that is, their earnings exceed their costs, especially including cost of capital. That means that normal competitive pressures are not able to drive down the firm's earnings to the point where they cover all costs and just provide minimum sufficient additional return to keep capital invested. Most forms of competitive advantage cannot be sustained for any length of time because the promise of economic rents drives competitiors to duplicate the competitive advantage held by any one firm.

A firm possesses a Sustainable Competitive Advantage when it has value-creating processes and positions that cannot be duplicated or imitated by other firms that lead to the production of above normal rents. An SCA is different from a competitive advantage (CA) in that it provides a long-term advantage that is not easily replicated. But these above-normal rents can attract new entrants who drive down economic rents. A CA is a position a firm attains that lead to above-normal rents or a superior financial performance. The processes and positions that engender such a position is not necessarily non-duplicable or inimitable. It is possible for some companies to make profits for a time above the cost of capital without sustainable competitive advantage.

A key difference between CA and SCA is that the processes and positions a firm may hold are non-duplicable and inimitable when a firm possesses a SCA. Hence a sustainable competitive advantage is one that can be maintained for a significant amount of time even in the presence of competition. This brings us to the question what is a "significant amount of time". A CA becomes SCA when all duplication and imitation efforts have ceased and the rival firms have not been able to create the same value that the said firm is creating.

Analysis of the factors of profitability is the subject of numerous theories of strategy including the five forces model pioneered by Michael Porter of the Harvard Business School.

In marketing and strategic management, sustainable competitive advantage is an advantage that one firm has relative to competing firms. The source of the advantage can be something the company does that is distinctive and difficult to replicate, also known as a core competency — for example Procter & Gamble's ability to derive superior consumer insights and implement them in managing its brand portfolio. It can also be an asset such as a brand (e.g. Coca Cola) or a patent, such as Viagra. It can also simply be a result of the industry's cost structure — for example, the large fixed costs that tend to create natural monopolies in utility industries. To be sustainable, the advantage must be:

- Distinctive, and
- Proprietary

Building Sustainable Competitive Advantage

There are basically three types of assets that help build an SCA. These categories are exhaustive and include all of the company's SCAs:

- Organization and managerial process
  - Coordination and integration: Coordination among teams in organization is key to organizational success. Interdepartmental coordination and resource sharing to reach a common goal is fundamental to creating "value". Integrating resources is key to the success of firms. Firms that are able to integrate resources see synergistic effects of resources coming together.
  - Learning: Organizational learning is key to the success of a firm. It determines how a firm collects, distributes, interprets and responds to market based information collection and changes in the environment. These changes in the environment could be customer based changes, technological developments, legal and government restrictions. Firms have to develop robust market sensing and spanning capabilities to effectively collect information. Once they collect info they have embed this knowledge in the products they produce.
  - Reconfiguring and transformation: The environment for firms is constantly changing and constant reconfiguring and transformation is key to forming SCA. A double loop learning and transformation is key to producing innovative products. Innovative capacity of a firm determines how it reacts and learns from market information.
- Positions: market positions are the assets of a company. Most of them are self-explanatory:
  - Technological assets
  - Financial assets
  - Reputational assets
  - Structural assets: The structure of a company can determine how it performs. The hierarchy of a company can influence its culture, procedure and routines.
- Paths:
  - Path dependencies: At the birth of a company usually accompanied with certain orientations. The progenitor brings certain orientations and attributes that stay with the company for a long time. The path the company takes then determines the development of its competencies.

- Technological opportunities: technology development at a time can determine how a firm can exploit opportunities to form SCA. Very often we see the advent of several technological factors converging into a capability that forms a SCA. An example would be the rise of companies such as Genentech at the turn of the previous century with the advent of gene mapping, significant developments in target selection and databases of previous studies and gene pools.

Strategic Management of hotel

Strategic management is that set of managerial decisions and actions that determines the long-run performance of a corporation. It includes environmental scanning, strategy formulation, strategy implementation and evaluation and control.

An organization's strategy must be appropriate for its resources, environmental circumstances, and core objectives. The process involves matching the company's [internal resources (eg IT) and capabilities (eg quality management)] to the external business environment the organization faces. Strategy formulation involves:

- Doing a situation analysis: both internal and external; both micro-environmental and macro-environmental.
- Concurrent with this assessment, objectives are set. This involves crafting vision statements (long term view of a possible future), mission statements (the role that the organization gives itself in society), overall corporate objectives (both financial and strategic), strategic business unit objectives (both financial and strategic), and tactical objectives.
- These objectives should, in the light of the situation analysis, sugsgest a strategic plan. The plan provides the details of how to achieve these objectives.

This three-step strategy formulation process is sometimes referred to as determining where you are now, determining where you want to go, and then determining how to get there. These three questions are the essence of strategic planning. SWOT Analysis: I/O Economics for the external factors and RBV for the internal factors.

Strategy Implementation involves:

- Allocation of sufficient resources (financial, personnel, time, technology support)
- Establishing a chain of command or some alternative structure (such as cross functional teams)
- Assigning responsibility of specific tasks or processes to specific individuals or groups

- It also involves managing the process. This includes monitoring results, comparing to benchmarks and best practices, evaluating the efficacy and efficiency of the process, controlling for variances, and making adjustments to the process as necessary.
- When implementing specific programmes, this involves acquiring the requisite resources, developing the process, training, process testing, documentation, and integration with (and/or conversion from) legacy processes.

Strategy formulation and implementation is an on-going, never-ending, integrated process requiring continuous reassessment and reformation. Strategic management is dynamic; It involves a complex pattern of actions and reactions. It is partially planned and partially unplanned. Strategy is both planned and emergent, dynamic, and interactive. Some people (such as Andy Grove at Intel) feel that there are critical points at which a strategy must take a new direction in order to be in step with a changing business environment. These critical points of change are called strategic inflection points.

Time Scales

Strategic management operates on several time scales. Short term strategies involve planning and managing for the present. Long term strategies involve preparing for and preempting the future. Marketing strategist Derek Abell (1993), has suggested that understanding this dual nature of strategic management is the least understood part of the process. He claims that balancing the temporal aspects of strategic planning requires the use of dual strategies simultaneously. Strategic Management is actually a solid foundation or a framework within which all the functionning managerial operations are bundled together. This is the highest level corporate activity that sets the terms and goals for a company that it should follow for prosperity.

In general terms, there are two main approaches to strategic management which are opposite but complement each other in some ways:

- 'The Industrial Organization Approach'
  - Based on economic theory — deals with issues like competitive rivalry, resource allocation, economies of scale
  - Assumptions — rationality, self discipline behaviour, profit maximization
- The Sociological Approach
  - Deals primarily with human interactions
  - Assumptions — bounded rationality, satisficing behaviour, profit sub-optimality. An example of a company that currently operates this way is Google

Strategic management techniques can be viewed as bottom-up, top-down, or collaborative processes. In the bottom-up approach, employees submit proposals to their managers who, in turn, funnel the best ideas further up the organization. This is often accomplished by a capital budgeting process. Proposals are assessed using financial criteria such as return on investment or cost-benefit analysis. The proposals that are approved form the substance of a new strategy, all of which is done without a grand strategic design or a strategic architect. The top-down approach is the most common by far. In it, the CEO, possibly with the assistance of a strategic planning team, decides on the overall direction the company should take. Some organizations are starting to experiment with collaborative strategic planning techniques that recognize the emergent nature of strategic decisions.

In most (large) corporations there are several levels of strategy. Strategic management is the highest in the sense that it is the broadest, applying to all parts of the firm. It gives direction to corporate values, corporate culture, corporate goals, and corporate missions. Under this broad corporate strategy there are often functional or business unit strategies.

Functional strategies include marketing strategies, new product development strategies, human resource strategies, financial strategies, legal strategies, and information technology management strategies. The emphasis is on short and medium term plans and is limited to the domain of each department's functional responsibility. Each functional department attempts to do its part in meeting overall corporate objectives, and hence to some extent their strategies are derived from broader corporate strategies.

Many companies feel that a functional organizational structure is not an efficient way to organize activities so they have reengineered according to processes or strategic business units (called SBUs). A strategic business unit is a semi-autonomous unit within an organization. It is usually responsible for its own budgeting, new product decisions, hiring decisions, and price setting. An SBU is treated as an internal profit centre by corporate headquarters. Each SBU is responsible for developing its business strategies, strategies that must be in tune with broader corporate strategies.

The "lowest" level of strategy is operational strategy. It is very narrow in focus and deals with day-to-day operational activities such as scheduling criteria. It must operate within a budget but is not at liberty to adjust or create that budget. Operational level strategy was encouraged by Peter Drucker in his theory of management by objectives (MBO). Operational level strategies are informed by business level strategies which, in turn, are informed by corporate level strategies. Business strategy, which refers to the aggregated operational strategies of single business firm or that of an SBU in a diversified corporation refers to the way in which a firm competes in its chosen arenas.

Corporate strategy, then, refers to the overarching strategy of the diversified firm. Such corporate strategy answers the questions of "in which businesses should we compete?" and "how does being in one business add to the competitive advantage of another portfolio firm, as well as the competitive advantage of the corporation as a whole?"

Since the turn of the millennium, there has been a tendency in some firms to revert to a simpler strategic structure. This is being driven by information technology. It is felt that knowledge management systems should be used to share information and create common goals. Strategic divisions are thought to hamper this process. Most recently, this notion of strategy has been captured under the rubric of dynamic strategy, popularized by the strategic management textbook authored by Carpenter and Sanders. This work builds on that of Brown and Eisenhart as well as Christensen and portrays firm strategy, both business and corporate, as necessarily embracing ongoing strategic change, and the seamless integration of strategy formulation and implementation. Such change and implementation are usually built into the strategy through the staging and pacing facets.

Why Strategic Plans Fails

There are many reasons why strategic plans fail, especially:

- Failure to understand the customer
  - Why do they buy
  - Is there a real need for the product
  - Inadequate or incorrect marketing research
- Inability to predict environmental reaction
  - What will competitors do
    1. Fighting brands
    2. Price wars
  - Will government intervene
- Over-estimation of resource competence
  - Can the staff, equipment, and processes handle the new strategy
  - Failure to develop new employee and management skills
- Failure to coordinate
  - Reporting and control relationships not adequate
  - Organizational structure not flexible enough
- Failure to obtain senior management commitment
  - Failure to get management involved right from the start
  - Failure to obtain sufficient company resources to accomplish task
- Failure to obtain employee commitment
  - New strategy not well explained to employees
  - No incentives given to workers to embrace the new strategy
- Under-estimation of time requirements
  - No critical path analysis done
- Failure to follow the plan
  - No follow through after initial planning

  - No tracking of progress against plan
  - No consequences for above
- Failure to manage change
  - Inadequate understanding of the internal resistance to change
  - Lack of vision on the relationships between processes, technology and organization
- Poor communications
  - Insufficient information sharing among stakeholders
  - Exclusion of stakeholders and delegates
- Failure to focus
  - Inability or unwillingness to make choices which are true to the strategic mission (i.e. to do fewer things, better), leads to mediocrity, inability to compete

Although a sense of direction is important, it can also stifle creativity, especially if it is rigidly enforced. In an uncertain and ambiguous world, fluidity can be more important than a finely tuned strategic compass. When a strategy becomes internalized into a corporate culture, it can lead to group think. It can also cause an organization to define itself too narrowly. An example of this is marketing myopia.

Most theories of strategic management seem to have a lifespan less than that of the popularity of the latest teen music idol. Many critics claim that this is because most of them generally do not work. Keep in mind that this article describes only the 50 or so most successful theories, thus exhibiting survivorship bias (ironically, itself an area of research in strategic management). For every theory that gets incorporated into strategic management textbooks there are many that are quickly forgotten. Many theories tend either to be too narrow in focus to build a complete corporate strategy on, or too general and abstract to be applicable to specific situations. The low success rate is further fueled by the management lecture circuit in which hundreds of self-appointed gurus, many without serious academic credentials or substantial expertise, attempt to sell books and explain their "revolutionary" and "groundbreaking" theories to audiences of business executives for a sizable fee. While there are undoubtedly inspirational ideas contained in these seminars, the theories expounded therein have not, for the most part, been subjected to serious study.

Some critics take the opposite approach claiming effectively that there are not enough theories, and when they arrive they are too late to help managers make any important decisions. These commentators remind us that the basic, everyday purpose of strategic management is to match a company's strategy with the business environment that the organization is in. Because the environment is constantly changing, effective strategic management requires a continuous flow of new theories suitable for the new circumstances. The problem with most theories is that they solve yesterday's problems, similar to a business Maginot Line. Various approaches to solve this problem have emerged, however, including Mintzberg's ideas of 'emergent strategies' and use of ideas from complexity theory in what is often called complexity strategy.

Gary Hamel coined the term strategic convergence to explain the limited scope of the strategies being used by rivals in greatly differing circumstances. He lamented that strategies converge more than they should, because the more successful ones get imitated by firms that do not understand that the strategic process involves designing a custom strategy for the specifics of each situation.

Bibliography

A.K. Sarkar: *Action Plan and Priorities in Tourism Development*, Kanishka Publication, Delhi, 2010.

A.S. Dileep and T. Rajesh: *Ayurvedic Tourism*, Sonali Publications, Delhi, 2012.

Amit Gaur: *Adventure Tourism*, Sonali Publication, Delhi, 2011.

Anupama Srivastava and Keya Pandey: *Anthropology and Tourism*, Serials Publications, Delhi, 2012.

Anurag Kothari: *A Textbook of Tourism Marketing*, Wisdom Press, Delhi, 2011.

B S Badan and Harish Bhatt: *Adventure Tourism*, Commonwealth Publication, Delhi, 2007.

Babu P. George and Sampad Kumar Swain: *Advancements in Tourism Theory and Practice : Perspectives from India*, Abhijeet Publication, Delhi, 2005.

Cynthia vanden Driesen and Satendra Nandan: *Austral-Asian Encounters : From Literature and Women's Studies to Politics and Tourism*, Prestige Books, 2003.

David Carr: *Community Tourism and Natural Resource Conservation*, Discovery Publication, Delhi, 2011.

Dileep Makan: *Conceptualization of Tourism*, Adhyayan Publication, Delhi, 2006.

Gagandeep Singh: *Civil Aviation and Tourism Administration*, Aadi Publication, Delhi, 2011.

Geetanjali: *Career in Tourism*, Centrum Press, Delhi, 2010.

Jack Randall: *Agriculture Tourism*, Discovery Publishing House, Delhi, 2011.

Krishan K. Kamra and Mohinder Chand: *Basics of Tourism: Theory, Operation and Practice*, Kanishka Publication, Delhi, 2002.

Lalita Sharma: *An Introduction to Ecotourism*, Centrum Press, Delhi, 2003.

Mahadev Kertwal: *Advertising in Leisure and Tourism*, Cyber Tech Publication, Delhi, 2012.

N. Jayapalan: *An Introduction to Tourism*, Atlantic Publication, Delhi, 2001.

Prateek A. Aggarwal: *Aspects of Crosscultural Interaction and Tourism*, Mohit Publication, Delhi, 2005.

Ramesh Raj Kunwar: *Anthropology of Tourism : A Case Study of Chitwan-Sauraha, Nepal*, Adroit Publication, Delhi, 2002.

Rattandeep Singh: *Commonwealth Games and Sports Tourism : Global and National Perspectives*, Kanishka Publishers, Delhi, 2010.

Ravee Chauhan: *Advanced Book on Marketing of Tourism*, Vista International Publishing House, Delhi, 2011.

Ravee Chauhan: *Advanced Hotel Industry and Tourism*, Vista International Publishing House, Delhi, 2011.

Romila Chawla: *Accommodation Management and Tourism*, Sonali Publication, Delhi, 2006.

Romila Chawla: *Agri-Tourism*, Sonali Publication, Delhi, 2006.

Romila Chawla: *Coastal Tourism and Development*, Sonali Publication, Delhi, 2004.

Saurab Kumar Dixit: *Aspects of Tourism Development*, Mohit Publication, Delhi, 2005.

Suddhendu Narayan Misra and Sapan Kumar Sadual: *Basics of Tourism Management*, Excel Books, Delhi, 2005.

Thomas Walsh: *Adventure Tourism*, Discovery Publishing House, Delhi, 2011.

U.P. Sinha: *Bihar Tourism : Retrospect and Prospect*, Concept Publication, Delhi, 2012.

Varinder Singh Rana: *Catering Hospitality and Tourism*, Centrum Press, Delhi, 2012.

Vikash Choudhary: *Business of Tourism*, Centrum Press, Delhi, 2010.

Index

I

M

O

P

R

S

T

U